Global Issues in Freedom of Speech and Religion

By

Alan Brownstein
Boochever and Bird Professor of Law
University of California, Davis, School of Law

Leslie Gielow Jacobs
Professor of Law
University of the Pacific, McGeorge School of Law

AMERICAN CASEBOOK SERIES®

A Thomson Reuters business

Mat #40642603

American Casebook Series and West Group are trademarks registered in the U.S. Patent and Trademark Office.

© 2009 Thomson/Reuters
      610 Opperman Drive
      St. Paul, MN 55123
      1–800–313–9378

Printed in the United States of America

ISBN: 978–0–314–18454–2

TEXT IS PRINTED ON 10% POST CONSUMER RECYCLED PAPER

Preface

Law schools have begun to recognize the need to provide global perspectives in courses that have focused almost exclusively on domestic law. *See, e.g.*, Mathias Reimann, *From the Law of Nations to Transnational Law*, 22 Penn. St.Intl. L.R. 397 (2004); *Making Transnational Law Mandatory: Requirements, Costs, Benefits*, 23 Penn. St. Intl. L.R. 787 (2005); Franklin A. Gevurtz, et al., *Report Regarding the Pacific McGeorge Workshop on Globalizing the Law School Curriculum*, 19 Pac. McGeorge Global Bus. & Dev. L.J. 267 (2006). This recognition extends to Constitutional Law. *See, e.g.*, Neil S. Siegel, *Some Modest Uses of Transnational Legal Perspectives in First-Year Constitutional Law*, 56 J. Legal Ed. 201 (2006); Mark Tushnet, *How (And How Not) to Use Comparative Constitutional Law in Basic Constitutional Law Courses*, 49 St. Louis U.L.J. 671 (2005). Nonetheless, the case books commonly used in law schools to teach Constitutional Law, as well as more specialized courses on the First Amendment, and issues of speech and religion in society, contain almost no comparative or international materials. *But see*, Donald Kommers, *American Constitutional Law: Cases, Essays and Comparative Notes* (2d ed. 2004). The most obvious reason is that the case books already have more pages than a conscientious professor can cover in the time allotted. Faculty must almost always make hard choices as to which material to cover.

Including global issues adds to the coverage dilemma. We nevertheless believe that some threshold level of exposure to comparative and international law is essential for today's students to understand the meaning, interpretation and practical impact of the individual rights guarantees contained within the U.S. Constitution. In addition, of course, international law is a direct source of constitutional law. Moreover, exposure to foreign law helps prepare students for practice in a globalized society. Limited exposure will not, of course, lead to a deep understanding of other constitutions or legal systems. It is, however, an important start, which will alert students to the potential applicability of global issues to legal questions as they enter practice. Courses devoted to International Law and Comparative Constitutional Law offer more complete coverage. (For very fine case books, *see, e.g.*, Norman Dorsen, Michel Rosenfeld, András Sajó, and Susanne Baer, *Comparative Constitutionalism: Cases and Materials* (2003) and Vicki C. Jackson and Mark Tushnet, *Comparative Constitutional Law* (2d ed. 2006)). Finally, exposure to foreign constitutional cases can help students understand the debate over the use of foreign law as persuasive authority in American constitutional cases.

This book is designed to help professors who want to provide some exposure to global perspectives in their First Amendment or related courses, but are concerned about detracting unduly from core coverage. The amount of comparative and international law material available even as to this subset of Constitutional Law is overwhelming. Our object was not to write a comprehensive book but to give faculty a modest menu of comparative and international materials from which to choose. We have kept it short, in an effort to minimize the need to cut domestic coverage in order to add comparative and international coverage. The materials are keyed to the major themes of most First Amendment courses, and a teacher's manual helps explain how and where material can be used. Some professors may want to assign the entire book, while others will want to pick and choose.

We want to thank Professors Vikram D. Amar, Michel Rosenfeld, Mark V. Tushnet, and Lorraine Weinreb, who participated with us in the Constitutional Law break-out section of the August 2005 Pacific McGeorge Workshop on Globalizing the Law School Curriculum.

We are also grateful to Kim Clarke, Director of the Pacific McGeorge library; UC Davis School of Law librarians Peg Durkin and Elisabeth McKechnie, and UC Davis School of Law research assistants John Ryan, Amanda Sherwood, and Kelli Smith, for invaluable assistance in gathering materials and cite-checking. Finally, thanks to Pacific McGeorge Professor Franklin Gevurtz, who spearheaded the Globalizing the Curriculum book project, which now includes over 15 volumes, to Louis Higgins and Laura Holle at Thomson West, and to Dean Elizabeth Rindskopf Parker and Pacific McGeorge, for their support of the project.

Acknowledgments

We gratefully acknowledge receiving permission to reprint the following materials:

Eric Barendt, Freedom of Speech (2005). Reprinted with permission of the author.

Laura Barnett, PRB 04–14Z: Freedom of Religion and Religious Symbols in the Public Square, 14 March 2006, Law and Government Division, Parliamentary Information and Research Service, Library of Parliament. Reprinted with permission of the Library of Parliament, 2008.

Church of the New Faith v. Commissioner of Pay-Roll Tax (Victoria) (1983) 154 CLR 120; Adelaide Co. of Jehovah's Witnesses v. Commonwealth (1943) 67 CLR 116; Attorney-General (Vic); Ex Rel Black v. Commonwealth (1981) 146 CLR 559. Reprinted with permission of the High Court of Australia.

Peter G. Danchin, Of Prophets and Proselytes: Freedom of Religion and the Conflict of Rights in International Law, 49 Harv. Int. L. J. 249 (2008). Reprinted with permission of The President and Fellows of Harvard College and the Harvard International Law Journal Copyright © 2008.

Peter Danchin & Lisa Foreman, The Evolving Jurisprudence of the European Court of Human Rights and the Protection of Religious Minorities in Protecting the Human Rights of Religious Minorities in Eastern Europe (Peter Danchin & Elizabeth A. Cole, eds. 2002). Reprinted with permission of the Columbia University Press.

W. Cole Durham, Jr., Perspectives on Religious Liberty: A Comparative Framework, in Religious Human Rights in Global Perspective: Legal Perspectives (Johan D. van der Vyver and John Witte, Jr. eds. 1996). Reprinted with permission of the publisher, Martinus Nijhoff Publishers.

Carolyn Evans & Christopher A. Thomas, Church-State Relations in the European Court of Human Rights, 2006 BYU L. Rev. 699. Reprinted with permission of the BYU Law Review.

Leszek Lech Garlicki, Perspectives on Freedom of Conscience and Religion in the Jurisprudence of Constitutional Courts, 2001

BYU L. Rev. 467. Reprinted with permission of the BYU Law Review.

Leszek Lech Garlicki, Collective Aspects of the Religious Freedoms: Recent Developments in the Case Law of the European Court of Human Rights in Issues in Constitutional Law 4. Censorial Sensitivities: Free Speech and Religion in a Fundamentalist World (András Sajó ed., 2007). Reprinted with permission of Eleven Publishing.

Jeremy Gunn, The Complexity of Religion and the Definition of "Religion" in International Law, 16 Harv. Hum. Rts. J. 189 (2003). Reprinted with permission of The President and Fellows of Harvard College and the Harvard Human Rights Journal Copyright © 2003.

Donald Kommers, The Constitutional Jurisprudence of the Federal Republic of Germany (2nd ed. 1997). Reprinted with permission of the author and Duke University Press.

Governments Target Internet-Phenomenon YouTube, March 11, 2008. Reprinted with permission of BBC Monitoring World Media, © British Broadcasting Corporation 2008.

Israeli Website Posts Bomb-Making Instructions for "Terrorism" Against Arabs, Sept. 2, 2007, Source: The Financial Times Limited. Reprinted with permission of BBC Monitoring Service.

Napalli Peter Williams v. Institute of Technical Education, [1999] 2 S.L.R. 569. Reprinted with permission of LexisNexis.

Samuel Issacharoff, Fragile Democracies, 120 Harv. L. Rev. 1405 (2007). Reprinted with permission of the author and of The President and Fellows of Harvard College and the Harvard Law Review Copyright © 2007.

Ronald J. Krotoszynski, The First Amendment in Cross-Cultural Perspective: A Comparative Legal Analysis of the Freedom of Speech (2006). Reprinted with permission of the author.

Javier Martínez-Torrón, Freedom of Religion in the Case Law of the Spanish Constitutional Court, 2001 BYU L. Rev. 711. Reprinted with permission of the BYU Law Review.

Javier Martínez-Torrón, Freedom of Expression versus Freedom of Religion in the European Court of Human Rights, in Issues in Constitutional Law 4. Censorial Sensitivities: Free Speech and Religion in a Fundamentalist World (András Sajó ed., 2007). Reprinted with permission of Eleven Publishing.

Monroe E. Price, Religious Communication and Its Relation to the State: Comparative Perspectives in Issues in Constitutional Law 4. Censorial Sensitivities: Free Speech and Religion in a Fundamentalist World (András Sajó ed., 2007). Reprinted with permission of Eleven Publishing.

Arch Puddington, Freedom of Expression after the "Cartoon Wars," in Freedom House, Freedom of the Press 2006. Reprinted with permission of Freedom House.

Reporters Without Borders, Press Freedom Round-up 2007. Reprinted with permission of Reporters Without Borders.

Isabelle Rorive, Strategies to Tackle Racism and Xenophobia on the Internet—Where are We in Europe?, Int'l J. Comm. L. & Policy 1 (2002/2003). Reprinted with permission of the author and of the International Journal of Comparative Law & Policy.

Joan Wallach Scott, The Politics of the Veil (2007). Reprinted with permission of Princeton University Press.

Ruti Teitel, Militating Constitutional Democracy: Comparative Perspectives in Issues in Constitutional Law 4. Censorial Sensitivities: Free Speech and Religion in a Fundamentalist World (András Sajó ed., 2007). Reprinted with permission of Eleven Publishing.

Daria Vaisman, Turkey's restriction, Europe's problem (Sept. 28, 2006). Reprinted with permission of openDemocracy.

James Q. Whitman, The Two Western Cultures of Privacy: Dignity Versus Liberty, 113 Yale L.J. 1151 (2004). Reprinted with permission of the author and the Yale Law Journal.

*

Global Issues Series

Series Editor, Franklin A. Gevurtz

Titles Available Now

Global Issues in Civil Procedure by Thomas Main, University of the Pacific, McGeorge School of Law
ISBN 978–0–314–15978–6

Global Issues in Constitutional Law by Brian K. Landsberg, University of the Pacific, McGeorge School of Law and Leslie Gielow Jacobs, University of the Pacific, McGeorge School of Law
ISBN 978–0–314–17608–0

Global Issues in Contract Law by John A. Spanogle, Jr., George Washington University, Michael P. Malloy, University of the Pacific, McGeorge School of Law, Louis F. Del Duca, Pennsylvania State University, Keith A. Rowley, University of Nevada, Las Vegas, and Andrea K. Bjorklund, University of California, Davis
ISBN 978–0–314–16755–2

Global Issues in Corporate Law by Franklin A. Gevurtz, University of the Pacific, McGeorge School of Law
ISBN 978–0–314–15977–9

Global Issues in Criminal Law by Linda Carter, University of the Pacific, McGeorge School of Law, Christopher L. Blakesley, University of Nevada, Las Vegas and Peter Henning, Wayne State University
ISBN 978–0–314–15997–7

Global Issues in Employment Discrimination Law by Samuel Estreicher, New York University School of Law and Brian K. Landsberg, University of the Pacific, McGeorge School of Law
ISBN 978–0–314–17607–3

Global Issues in Employment Law by Samuel Estreicher, New York University School of Law and Miriam A. Cherry, University of the Pacific, McGeorge School of Law
ISBN 978–0–314–17952–4

Global Issues in Environmental Law by Stephen McCaffrey, University of the Pacific, McGeorge School of Law and Rachael Salcido, University of the Pacific, McGeorge School of Law
ISBN 978–0–314–18479–5

Global Issues in Family Law by Ann Laquer Estin, University of Iowa College of Law and Barbara Stark, Hofstra University School of Law
ISBN 978–0–314–17954–8

Global Issues in Income Taxation by Daniel Lathrope, University of California, Hastings College of Law
ISBN 978–0–314–18806–9

Global Issues in Labor Law by Samuel Estreicher, New York University School of Law
ISBN 978–0–314–17163–4

Global Issues in Legal Ethics by James E. Moliterno, College of William & Mary, Marshall-Wythe School of Law and George Harris, University of the Pacific, McGeorge School of Law
ISBN 978–0–314–16935–8

Global Issues in Property Law by John G. Sprankling, University of the Pacific, McGeorge School of Law, Raymond R. Coletta, University of the Pacific, McGeorge School of Law, and M.C. Mirow, Florida International University College of Law
ISBN 978–0–314–16729–3

Global Issues in Tort Law by Julie A. Davies, University of the Pacific, McGeorge School of Law and Paul T. Hayden, Loyola Law School, Los Angeles
ISBN 978–0–314–16759–0

Summary of Contents

Table of Contents

*

Table of Cases

The principal cases are in bold type. Cases cited or discussed in the text are roman type. References are to pages. Cases cited in principal cases and within other quoted materials are not included.

*

Global Issues in Freedom of Speech and Religion

*

PART I

FREEDOM OF SPEECH

———

Chapter One

FREE SPEECH—A GLOBAL OVERVIEW

The United States was the first to protect free speech in a written constitution. Now, almost all nations of the world do so. This chapter first compares the text, history and enforcement of free speech guarantees in selected national constitutions. Next, this chapter briefly reviews the impact of international, supranational, and comparative law on the interpretation by national high courts of their domestic free speech guarantees.

I. CONSTITUTIONAL TEXT, HISTORY AND ENFORCEMENT

A. UNITED STATES

The First Amendment to the United States Constitution provides:

Congress shall make no law ... abridging the freedom of speech, or of the press.

Although the free speech guarantee became a part of the Constitution in 1791, and the Supreme Court articulated its power to interpret the meaning of constitutional provisions and declare acts of Congress unconstitutional in 1803, the Court did not begin to interpret the First Amendment as a limit on government action until the cases challenging enforcement of the Espionage Act of 1917. Still, like the text, the U.S. Supreme Court free speech jurisprudence, approaching 100 years in age is the oldest in the world.

B. GERMANY

Germany adopted its Basic Law in 1949, after its World War II defeat. Article 5 provides:

(1) Everyone has the right freely to express and to disseminate his opinion by speech, writing and pictures and freely to inform himself from generally accessible sources. Freedom of the press and freedom of reporting by radio and motion pictures are guaranteed. There shall be no censorship.

(2) These rights are limited by the provisions of the general laws, the provisions of law for the protection of youth and by the right to inviolability of personal honor.

(3) Art and science, research and teaching are free. Freedom of teaching does not absolve from loyalty to the constitution.

Grundgesetz für die Bundesrepublik Deutschland [GG] [Basic Law], art. 5 (F.R.G.) (Basic Law).

The Basic Law establishes a Federal Constitutional Court as the supreme authority on constitutional meaning and application (art. 93). The Federal Constitutional Court hears only constitutional cases, and is separate from the Federal Court of Justice, which is the final national judicial authority on non-constitutional cases. The Federal Constitutional Court has held that the Basic Law establishes "an objective order of values," which must influence its interpretation of the meaning and scope of the Basic Law's individual rights guarantees. Listed as the priority in Article 1 of the Basic Law, and termed "inviolable" in the individual rights hierarchy, is "human dignity."

C. ENGLAND

England has never had a written constitution, and no court has the power to invalidate acts of Parliament as outside the scope of its constitutional powers or in violation of constitutional individual rights guarantees. Parliament is supreme. Still, even without a single written document, English government operates under a system of "conventions," which are traditional structures and limits, found in a range of writings and unwritten understandings, which players in the legal system routinely observe. In this spirit, English courts developed a common law jurisprudence of free speech protections, which they invoked to limit application of other common law rules and in construing Acts of Parliament. The Human Rights Act 1998, c. 42 (Eng.) (HRA 1998), which came into force in 2000, provides a statutory supplement to the common law free speech protections, incorporating provisions of the European Convention on Human Rights and Fundamental Freedoms (ECHR), including its free speech protections, into English law. In the same words as the ECHR, Section 10 of the HRA 1998 states:

1. Everyone has the right to freedom of expression. This right shall include freedom to hold opinions and to receive and impart information and ideas without interference by public authority and regardless of frontiers. This Article shall not prevent States from requiring the licensing of broadcasting, television or cinema enterprises.

2. The exercise of these freedoms, since it carries with it duties and responsibilities, may be subject to formalities, conditions, restrictions or penalties as are prescribed by law and are necessary in a democratic society, in the interests of national security, territorial integrity or public safety, for the prevention of disorder or crime, for the protection of health or morals, for the protection of the reputation or rights of others, for preventing the disclosure of information received in confidence, or for maintaining the authority and impartiality of the judiciary.

The HRA 1998 directs courts to interpret statutes and regulations, so far as possible, as consistent with its rights guarantees (§ 3). If a saving construction is not possible, the HRA 1998 instructs courts to issue a "declaration of incompatibility" (§ 4). The legislative or regulatory authority may revise its law to correct the incompatibility, but is under no legal obligation to do so. The final appellate authority with respect to incompatibility as well as other matters involving the consistency of domestic laws with the HRA 1998 individual rights guarantees, consistent with the system of parliamentary supremacy, remains the designated panel within the House of Lords, a unit of the legislative branch.

D. CANADA

Canada implemented a constitutional free speech guarantee in 1982. The Canadian Charter of Rights and Freedoms states:

Everyone has the following fundamental freedoms:

(a) freedom of conscience and religion;

(b) freedom of thought, belief, opinion and expression, including freedom of the press and other media of communication;

(c) freedom of peaceful assembly; and

(d) freedom of association.

Constitution Act, 1982, § 2, enacted by Canada Act, 1982, c. 11, Schedule B (U.K.) (Charter).

Other sections of the Charter qualify the rights guarantee. Section 1 provides:

The Canadian Charter of Rights and Freedoms guarantees the rights and freedoms set out in it subject only to such reasonable limits prescribed by law as can be demonstrably justified in a free and democratic society.

Additionally, Section 33 allows Parliament or the legislature of a province to "expressly declare" that an enactment "shall operate notwithstanding a provision included in section," for a period of five years or indefinitely, if the legislative body reenacts it. The Supreme Court of Canada reviews government actions for conformity with the provisions of its Constitution, including the free speech guarantee of the Charter, and has the power to declare government acts unconstitutional.

E. AUSTRALIA

Australia has no written constitutional or statutory free speech guarantee. Courts have protected free speech interests through common law interpretation. Additionally, in 1992, the Australian High Court, building on common law precedent, held that its constitution contains an implied right to political speech in its guarantee of representative democracy. *Australian Capital Television v. Commonwealth* (1992) 177 C.L.R. 106 (Austl.). The Australian Constitution grants the High Court the power to invalidate government actions that transgress constitutional boundaries and it has struck down acts of Parliament as contrary to the implied constitutional free speech right.

F. FRANCE

Inspired by the U.S. Declaration of Independence, and predating the U.S. constitutional free speech guarantee, Article 11 of the Declaration of the Rights of Man and of the Citizen of 1789 states:

> The free communication of ideas and of opinions is one of the most precious rights of man. Any citizen may therefore speak, write and publish freely, except what is tantamount to the abuse of this liberty in the cases determined by Law.

The 1789 Declaration has always existed, alone and by reference in the Preamble to the Constitution of 1958, as an admonition to Parliament. Since 1971, the compatibility of law with the free speech right articulated in the 1789 Declaration has been subject to constitutional, although not judicial, review. Under the French system, a nine-member non-judicial appointed Constitutional Council reviews acts of Parliament after they are adopted but before they become law. Some review is automatic. Other review occurs upon referral by certain government officials, most often minority members of Parliament seeking a ruling that a law enacted by the majority violates a constitutional guarantee. Although courts may construe statutes and regulations in light of constitutional, including free speech, provisions, individuals do not have a legal right to challenge the constitutionality of implemented law.

G. CHINA

The Constitution of the People's Republic of China, adopted in 1982, provides:

Article 35. Freedom of speech, press, assembly.

Citizens of the People's Republic of China enjoy freedom of speech, of the press, of assembly, of association, of procession and of demonstration.

Article 51. Non-infringement of rights.

Citizens of the People's Republic of China, in exercising their freedoms and rights, may not infringe upon the interests of the state, of society or of the collective, or upon the lawful freedoms and rights of other citizens.

The National People's Congress (NPC), which is the national legislature, is the supreme state organ, situated above both the State Council (the national executive) and the People's Court (the national judiciary). The NPC has the exclusive power to write, amend, and interpret the Constitution. Because there is no judicial review of the conformity of government action with constitutional rights guarantees, no case law interpreting the free speech guarantee exists.

Notes and Questions

1. *Text.* How is the text of the U.S. Constitution different from the more recently adopted texts of the German, English/European Convention, and Canadian free speech guarantees? What substantive differences in the scope of the right and in the methodology of interpretation would you expect to see? What effect on interpretation would you expect given that free speech is guaranteed in the U.S. Constitution's First Amendment and in Germany's Basic Law, in Article 5, after human dignity? How would you expect interpretation to differ in Australia, which lacks an explicit constitutional provision but where the High Court has implied the guarantee from the provision ensuring representative democracy?

2. *History.* The U.S. free speech guarantee became part of the Constitution after the American experience of repressive colonialism. Germans crafted their Basic Law after the experience of the abuses of a government at least initially supported by a democratic majority. England implemented a free speech provision only after a treaty required it. Canada and Australia, also British colonies, did not adopt or imply free speech guarantees until recently. France adopted its free speech language in the wake of violent revolution, but, until the 1970's,

provided no method of enforcement against a parliamentary majority. China adopted its free speech provision in 1982 with no apparent intention of limiting the government repression of individual speech. How are these different histories reflected in the texts of the free speech guarantees? How would you expect the different histories to affect interpretation and enforcement of the free speech guarantee? How would you expect the timing of the implementation of the free speech rights to affect their texts, scope and interpretative methodology?

3. *Interpretation as a Limit on the Actions of Political Majorities. Enforcement.* Identify how the method and scope of constitutional review differs among the nations. Why would Germany choose a specialized constitutional court, instead of an all-purpose U.S.-style Supreme Court? Does the statutory free speech right in England impose a real limit on the actions of democratic majorities if there is no judicial review? What about the constitutional free speech right in China? Are there limits to interpretation of the free speech right as a limit on democratic majority action in Australia because the right is implied? How would you expect France's pre-enactment review to differ from post-enactment interpretation? In which countries would you expect to see the most developed constitutional jurisprudence? In which would you expect the least?

II.   FREE SPEECH IN INTERNATIONAL, SUPRANATIONAL AND COMPARATIVE LAW

As national borders become ever more porous, interpretation and application of national constitution provisions, including free speech guarantees, become less discrete. International law consists of the rules and customs explicitly or implicitly accepted by nations as governing relations among them. Supranational law is law agreed to by a group of nations, which is promulgated or interpreted by a collective entity, and which has binding force among the member nations. Both international and supranational law may influence the text and interpretation of domestic constitutional, including free speech, guarantees. Comparative law occurs when national courts look outside their jurisdictional boundaries for information or guidance in drafting or interpreting domestic law. As constitutions and constitutional interpretations proliferate, comparative law increasingly influences the text and interpretation of nations' free speech guarantees.

A.   INTERNATIONAL LAW

The Universal Declaration of Human Rights, G.A. Res. 217A (III), U.N. Doc. A/810 (Dec. 12, 1948) (UDHR), issued by the United Nations General Assembly provides, in Article 19:

Everyone has the right to freedom of opinion and expression; this right includes freedom to hold opinions without interference and to seek, receive and impart information and ideas through any media and regardless of frontiers.

The International Covenant on Civil and Political Rights, opened for signature Dec. 16, 1966, 6 I.L.M. 368, 999 U.N.T.S. 171 (ICCPR), is a global treaty, modeled on the UDHR, which contains a similar free speech guarantee. As a treaty, the ICCPR is termed "binding" on its approximately 160 signatories. An 18–member Human Rights Committee monitors compliance by reviewing annual reports submitted by member countries. The free speech provisions of the UDHR and ICCPR have served as models for numerous regional conventions and treaties.

The effect of treaty obligations, such as a free speech guarantee, on domestic law and constitutional provisions varies by country. The U.S. Constitution provides that treaties are part of the "supreme law of the land" and that Congress has the power to make all laws "necessary and proper for carrying into execution" all powers vested in the government of the United States. The Supreme Court has interpreted this to mean that Congress has the power to enact legislation implementing treaty obligations beyond the scope of its enumerated powers, that treaty provisions prevail over conflicting prior legislation only if they are "self-executing," and that treaty provisions, whether or not self-executing, cannot contradict or modify U.S. constitutional individual rights guarantees. So, for example, in ratifying the ICCPR, the U.S. Senate declared that the treaty was not self-executing, which means it does not create individual rights enforceable in U.S. courts. The United States has made such declarations, or reservations, in signing or ratifying other human rights treaties, which means that the terms do not directly modify domestic law and are not enforceable by individuals in U.S. courts. The United States also seeks treaty modifications to address concerns about conflict of terms with U.S. individual rights guarantees. In negotiations leading up to the adoption of the Framework Convention for Tobacco Control, a global treaty regulating tobacco use, the United States repeatedly objected that proposed advertising restrictions would violate the U.S. Constitution's free speech guarantee, and ultimately succeeded in obtaining language that requires each state party to implement the advertising provisions *in accordance with its constitution and constitutional principles*. The United States signed the treaty in 2003, but the Senate has not ratified it.

In most other constitutional democracies, treaty provisions guaranteeing human rights influence domestic law, including constitutional meaning and interpretation more directly, as the following excerpt summarizes:

[N]ational constitutional systems afford a variety of accommodations to the international human rights regime. Some constitutions elevate human rights treaty norms to the level of constitutional rights; others expressly make international human rights norms a source of guidance in constitutional interpretation. Even without such instructions, constitutional courts may voluntarily take international interpretations of human rights into consideration in construing constitutional rights. Some constitutional courts adopt this method as part of a deliberate strategy of institutional coordination with the international regime, for the mutual strengthening of both. For constitutional courts in none of the preceding categories, a minimal form of accommodation remains: to treat international interpretations as a relevant source of insight on the human rights issues they address.

Gerald L. Neuman, *Human Rights and Constitutional Rights: Harmony and Dissonance*, 55 Stan. L. Rev. 1863, 1890 (2003). The South African Constitution provides one example of an express constitutional directive:

When interpreting the Bill of Rights, a court, tribunal or forum—

> (a) must promote the values that underlie an open and democratic society based on human dignity, equality and freedom;
>
> (b) must consider international law; and
>
> (c) may consider foreign law.

S. Afr. Const. 1996, art. 39.

B. SUPRANATIONAL LAW

Supranational law differs from treaty and other international law in that the states party agree not only to initial terms, but to an ongoing structure under which the provisions that bind the member states may grow or change. The most fully developed instance of supranational law directly impacting domestic human rights, including free speech rights, is the structure for implementing the European Convention on Human Rights (ECHR). The text of Article 10 of the Convention, which pertains to free speech, is reproduced in Part I, C, *supra*, as enacted into English law by the Human Rights Act 1998. All signatory nations must comply with Convention provisions, including Article 10's free speech guarantee. Individuals from signatory nations who believe that any of their Convention rights have been violated may file petitions with the European Court of Human Rights, located in Strasbourg, which adjudicates disputes and issues decisions that form a body of case law interpreting the Convention's free speech guarantee. The Court's case law accords nations a degree of deference, termed "a margin of appreciation," when assessing whether, under Article 10, a challenged speech restriction is "necessary in a democratic society." Nevertheless, if subject to an adverse ruling, signatory nations are bound to implement the Strasbourg Court's judgment. Implementation may include paying reparations to individuals, changing domestic court judgments, or, ultimately, altering national law to comply with the Strasbourg Court's interpretation of the free speech guarantee.

The European Union (EU) has a separate, but overlapping, membership to the group of ECHR signatories. As of January 2008, the EU consisted of 27 countries bound together by treaties that create the EU's structure. The treaties provide for the EU to regulate such areas as trade and movement barriers, antitrust, employment discrimination, and some social policies. They establish legislative, executive, and judicial bodies to create rules, administer them, and enforce them. EU government actions, for example recent efforts aimed at regulating internet content, may require member nations to modify their domestic law in ways that impact constitutionally guaranteed free speech rights.

Members of the Organization of American States (OAS), including the United States, have adopted a Convention on Human Rights, which includes a free speech guarantee. The Inter–American Commission on Human Rights (ICHR), based in Washington, D.C., issues annual reports on alleged rights violations. An Inter–American Court adjudicates alleged violations, but only after the Commission refers disputes it could not resolve, and only with respect to nations that have agreed to submit to its jurisdiction, which does not include the United States. In 2000, the Commission issued a Declaration of Principles on Freedom of Expression, which it termed a "fundamental document for the defense of freedom within the inter-American system." The OAS Special Rapporteur on Freedom of Expression at the time, Santiago Canton, praised the document and noted that member nations should "begin to bring their laws into compliance with [its] principles." Press Release, Organization of American States, *OAS Issues Declaration for Protecting Freedom of Expression* (Oct 24, 2000), http://www.fas.org/sgp/news/2000/10/oas.html.

C. COMPARATIVE LAW

Comparative law is the use of foreign constitutional interpretations and legal experience as information in interpreting domestic constitutional provisions. Most high courts in other democracies look to interpretations outside their country when interpreting their own constitutional guarantees. Many high courts refer to U.S.

constitutional jurisprudence explicitly, either in adopting it or in explaining why they interpret similar provisions differently. For example, "Canadian courts [in interpreting the free speech guarantee of the 1982 Charter of Rights and Freedoms] have drawn extensively from the legal materials of other countries, including the United States, and from sources in international law. They have regarded themselves, to a degree so far uncharacteristic in the United States, as giving meaning to liberties that transcend national boundaries." Kent Greenawalt, *Free Speech in the United States and Canada,* 55 Law & Contemp. Probs. 5, 6 (1992).

The use of foreign law comparatively in U.S. constitutional interpretation is controversial. In his dissent in *Lawrence v. Texas,* 539 U.S. 558 (2003), Justice Scalia criticized the Court's references to foreign law as relevant to interpreting the scope of privacy protected by the Fourteenth Amendment's due process guarantee, terming it "[d]angerous dicta, . . . since 'this Court . . . should not impose foreign moods, fads, or fashions on Americans.' " *Id.* at 598. In a published conversation with Justice Breyer on the use of comparative law in constitutional interpretation, Justice Scalia elaborated: "[M]y theory of what to do when interpreting the American Constitution is to try to understand what it meant, what it was understood by the society to mean when it was adopted. . . . [W]hat does the opinion of a wise Zimbabwe judge or a wise member of a House of Lords law committee—what does that have to do with what Americans believe? It is irrelevant unless you really think it's been given to you to make this moral judgment, a very difficult moral judgment. And so in making it for yourself and for the whole country, you consult whatever authorities you want. Unless you have that philosophy, I don't see how it's relevant at all." *The Relevance of Foreign Legal Materials in U.S. Constitutional Cases: A Conversation Between Justice Antonin Scalia and Justice Stephen Breyer,* 3 Int'l. J. Const. L. 519, 525–29 (2005).

Justice Breyer explained, "[W]hen I refer to foreign law in cases involving a constitutional issue, I realize full well that the decisions of foreign courts do not bind American courts. . . . The practice [of looking to foreign law] involves opening your eyes to what is going on elsewhere, taking what you learn for what it is worth, and using it as a point of comparison where doing so will prove helpful. . . . If, for example, a foreign court, in a particular decision, had shown that a particular interpretation of similar language in a similar document had had an adverse effect on free expression, to read that decision might help me to apply the American Constitution. That is what is at issue. To what extent will learning what happens in other courts help a judge apply the Constitution of the United States." *Id.* at 522–537.

Notes and Questions

1. Compare the texts, enforcement mechanisms and practical impacts of the international ICCPR and the U.S. Constitution's free speech guarantees. What is the scope of the right to free speech created by each? How does Commission enforcement differ from judicial review? What is the practical impact of the ICCPR right if individuals have no ability to challenge an alleged violation of their free speech rights?

2. Why would the nations of Europe agree to a common individual rights articulation and enforcement structure? Is the ECHR free speech right just like the same right guaranteed in a national constitution? Do national constitutional free speech rights retain meaning in light of the ECHR regime? How does the OAS human rights articulation and enforcement structure differ from that of the ECHR? Why has the United States refused to submit to the jurisdiction of the Inter–American Court of Human Rights? As to these questions, consider the following:

> International constitutionalism [adopted by the countries of Europe] contemplates a constitutional order embodying universal principles that derive their authority from sources outside national democratic processes and that constrain national self-government. American or democratic national constitutionalism, by contrast, regards constitutional law as the embodiment of a particular nation's democratically self-given legal and political commitments. At any particular moment, these commitments operate as checks and constraints on national democratic will. But constitutional law is emphatically not antidemocratic. Rather, it aims at democracy over time. Hence, it requires that a nation's constitutional law be made and interpreted by that nation's citizens, legislators, and judges.

Jed Rubenfeld, *The Two World Orders, in* European and US Constitutionalism 238 (G. Nolte, ed., 2005).

3. Why do the high courts of other nations make greater use of comparative law in constitutional interpretation than the U.S. Supreme Court? What explains the disagreement between Justices Scalia and Breyer? With whom do you agree?

Chapter Two

CATEGORIES OF SPEECH

United States constitutional jurisprudence segregates categories of speech for judicial analysis. Although other countries do not generally attach the same analytical significance to the U.S. categories, this section presents the material according to U.S. system to aid comparison.

I. ANTI–GOVERNMENT SPEECH

United States free speech jurisprudence began as the Supreme Court navigated the divide between incitement to illegal action, which all governments claim the right to criminalize, and advocacy of opinions critical of government action, which is core political speech essential to maintain a healthy democracy. This work continues around the globe as the courts of other nations interpret the limits of their free speech guarantees in light of government claims that suppressing speech is necessary to maintain law and order or protect national security.

A. INCITING DRAFT RESISTANCE

In the following case, the European Court of Human Rights reviews a Turkish conviction of a newspaper editor for inciting draft resistance for consistency with the ECHR-guaranteed free speech right.

ERGIN v. TURKEY

[2006] Eur. Ct. H.R. 47533/99
available at European Court of Human Rights
http://cmiskp.echr.coe.int/tkp197/view.asp?item=38portal=hbkm&
action=html&highlight=ergin&sessionid=9625577 & skin=hudoc-en

PANEL: JUDGE BRATZA (PRESIDENT), JUDGES BONELLO, TURMEN, PELLONPAA, TRAJA, GARLICKI, AND MIJOVIC, AND MR M O'BOYLE (SECTION REGISTRAR)

THE FACTS

. . .

6. The applicant was born in 1973 and lives in Istanbul.

7. On 1 September 1997, as editor of the newspaper Gunluk Emek (Everyday Work), the applicant published in issue number 297 an article entitled "Giving the conscripts a send-off, and collective memory" signed by Baris Avsar.

8. On 4 December 1997 the public prosecutor at the Military Court of the General Staff ("the General Staff Court"), acting under art 58 of the Military Penal Code and art 155 of the Criminal Code, charged the applicant with incitement, by publication of the above article, to evade military service.

. . .

11. In its judgment the General Staff Court referred to the following passage from the offending article:

"This last week in bus stations has been a time for sending the August conscripts on their way . . . The novice soldiers setting off—"but you'll soon be back", people tell them to console them—already seemed during these ritual send-offs to be plunging into war by donning "invisible khaki". It was a time when war seemed rather attractive; the congratulations and praises made it seem like a warm nest, almost as warm as a mother's arms, into whose embrace they would have liked to run. What we saw at each of these ceremonies shows that the thing has become a collective hysteria and that this hysteria has also spawned its own indispensable attributes: the traditional drum and clarinet, the famous three-crescented flag, sometimes accompanied by the corn-ear flag of the RP [Welfare Party] or the rose-bearing flag of the BBP [Great Union Party] . . . Warm-up ceremonies are organised for those setting off for the war, the exaltation felt on killing a man is the exaltation of winning a match and, what is more, the killer justifies his act by speaking of the love he has for his fatherland and his nation. In short, it can't be said that what we're doing is right

... Those verses, written by a fallen soldier, are carved on his own tombstone. He will no longer see those who gather to give the conscripts a send-off, no longer hear the drum, the clarinet or the gunfire, not be able to read the verses written on his tombstone, on seeing which he would perhaps have felt repelled by the determinism they convey. Because from now on he is reduced to a title: a martyr ... It is because the State does not recognise as such the war which is etched deeply into the collective life and the collective memory that, apart from a small minority, those who return from it after losing an arm, a leg or an eye receive no allowance. These people who are no longer capable of meeting their own needs are being deceived by talk of fictitious jobs. 'There is a war, but not officially; you are war-wounded, but you count for nothing.'"

In its considerations the General Staff Court pointed out that military service was a constitutional duty and that the applicant, by denigrating military service had also denigrated the struggle against the PKK,[1] a terrorist organisation which killed soldiers, police officers, teachers and civil servants. It held that the offending article contained terms contrary to morality and public order.

14.   In a final judgment of 10 February 1999 the Military Court of Cassation upheld the first-instance judgment. . . .

16.   Article 155 of the Criminal Code provides:

"It shall be an offence, punishable by two months' to two years' imprisonment and a fine ... to publish articles inciting the population to break the law or weakening national security, to issue publications intended to incite others to evade military service. . . . "

THE LAW

. . .

26.   The applicant alleged that his criminal conviction had infringed his right to freedom of expression as guaranteed by art 10 of the Convention, the relevant parts of which provide:

1.   Everyone has the right to freedom of expression. This right shall include freedom to hold opinions and to receive and impart information and ideas without interference by public authority and regardless of frontiers. ...

2.   The exercise of these freedoms, since it carries with it duties and responsibilities, may be subject to such formalities,

---

1. *Editors' note*—The PPK, or Kurdistan Worker's Party, is a group of separatists, which launches military incursions into Turkey from its location in the mountains on the Iraqi border. The PPK is designated a terrorist organization by Turkey, the United States and the European Union.

conditions, restrictions or penalties as are prescribed by law and are necessary in a democratic society, in the interests of national security, territorial integrity or public safety, for the prevention of disorder or crime. . . .

28.   The Court notes that it is not disputed between the parties that the applicant's conviction constituted an interference with his right to freedom of expression, protected by art 10(1). Nor is it disputed that the interference was prescribed by law and pursued a legitimate aim for the purposes of art 10(2), namely the prevention of disorder. . . . The Court agrees with that assessment. In the present case the dispute concerns the question whether the interference was "necessary in a democratic society".

29.   The Government submitted that the applicant's conviction was necessary in a democratic society because the article was offensive to the wounded and the families of conscripts who had been killed during their military service, and that the criticisms of military service were contrary to morality and the public interest.

. . .

31.   . . . [The Court] has paid particular attention to the terms used in the article and the context in which it was published. In that connection, it has taken into account the circumstances surrounding the case submitted to it, and in particular the difficulties linked to the prevention of terrorism. . . .

32.   The offending article was a critique of the now-traditional ceremony to mark conscripts' departure for military service. In literary language the author explained that the enthusiasm surrounding these departures was a denial of the tragic end suffered by some of the conscripts concerned, namely death and mutilation.

33.   The Court notes the General Staff Court ruled that the offending article contained terms contrary to morality and public order.

34.   The Court has examined the grounds given in the decisions of the domestic courts, which cannot as they stand be regarded as sufficient to justify the interference with the applicant's right to freedom of expression. . . . It observes in particular that although the words used in the offending article give it a connotation hostile to military service, they do not exhort the use of violence or incite armed resistance or rebellion, and they do not constitute hate-speech, which, in the Court's view, is the essential element to be taken into consideration. . . . Moreover, the context in which the opinions were expressed can be distinguished, as regards their potential impact, from that of the Arrowsmith v UK case, in which the applicant, a pacifist activist, had distributed a leaflet inciting servicemen to desert at a military camp occupied by troops who

were shortly to be posted to Northern Ireland.... In the present case the offending article was published in a newspaper on sale to the general public. It did not seek, either in its form or in its content, to precipitate immediate desertion.

35.   The Court reiterates that the adjective "necessary", within the meaning of art 10(2), implies the existence of a "pressing social need". The Contracting States have a certain margin of appreciation in assessing whether such a need exists, but it goes hand in hand with a European supervision, embracing both the law and the decisions applying it, even those given by independent courts. The Court is therefore empowered to give the final ruling on whether a "restriction" is reconcilable with freedom of expression as protected by art 10.

The Court considers that the applicant's criminal conviction did not correspond to a pressing social need. The interference was accordingly not "necessary in a democratic society". There has therefore been a violation of art 10 of the Convention.

Notes and Questions

1.   United States free speech jurisprudence began in the context of speech alleged to impede execution of the national war effort. How do the facts in *Ergin*—the defendant's words, the context in which they were uttered, the defendant's likely intent and the linkage between the words and illegal action—compare to the World War I cases reviewed by the U.S. Supreme Court? What are the elements of the test applied by the ECHR to apply article 10's free speech guarantee? The test used by the U.S. Supreme Court evolved from "clear and present danger" through risk/benefit balancing to the imminent incitement test of *Brandenburg v. Ohio*, 395 U.S. 444 (1969). Which test does the article 10 test most resemble? The *Brandenburg* test requires intent, incitement, imminence and likelihood. Does the article 10 test require all of these things?

2.   The European Court of Human Rights accords member states a "margin of appreciation" when assessing whether a free speech infringement violates article 10. Why is this part of the Court's jurisprudence? Does the U.S. Supreme Court accord the government anything similar to a margin of appreciation when interpreting the free speech guarantee?

3.   Does it make a difference to the methodologies or the outcomes that the Convention's text explicitly qualifies the free speech guarantee by reference to "the interests of national security" while the U.S. Constitution's text appears to guarantee free speech absolutely?

B. SUPPORTING TERRORISM

Terrorism, perceived as prompted by speech encouraging it, has led a number of countries to revise the incitement crime to include a broader range of speech activity.

1. *Israel*

Israel does not have a constitution. In 1992, it enacted two "basic laws," intended as the framework for the ongoing creation of constitutional guarantees. One, titled Basic Law: Human Dignity and Freedom/Liberty accords certain human rights, but does not mention freedom of speech explicitly. Scholars debate whether it accords the free speech right implicitly. Nevertheless, as in England, a common law jurisprudence developed to protect free speech. In 1953, the Israeli Supreme Court articulated a standard for government suppression of potentially harmful speech, which required that the harm be "severe, serious and grave" and that its probability rise to a "near certainty." HJ. 73/53 Kol–Ha'am v. Minister of the Interior, [1953] IsrSC 7(3) 871. The assassination of Prime Minister Itzhak Rabin in 1995 following a peace rally by a law student, which was widely believed to have been fueled by a campaign of virulent anti-Rabin speech and activity, resulted both in greater enforcement of existing incitement and sedition statutes, and a statutory revision in 2002. The new law states:

Penal Law (Incitement to Violence and Terror) (Amendment No. 66), passed at the Knesset on May 15, 2002, § 144D.

(a) Any person who publishes either a call to commit a violent act or terror, or a praise, support or encouragement of violent acts or terror (for the purpose of this section: "an inciting publication") and according to its contents and the circumstances in which it was published there is a real possibility that it will lead to a violent act or terror, shall be liable to imprisonment for five years.

Several recent speech acts in Israel implicate its new Incitement to Violence provision.

(1) Islamic Movement Northern Front leader Sheikh Raed Salah was investigated and ultimately charged with incitement to violence and racism by the Israeli Attorney General for a speech in which he called for a third Palestinian intifada against Israel in response to construction work at religiously significant sites. In one speech, Salah called on Muslims to ["]save al-Aksa Mosque[,] free Jerusalem and end the occupation." *Salah to be Investigated for Incitement*, Jerusalem Post, Feb. 23, 2007, at 8.

(2) In January 2008, an ultra-Orthodox rabbi, in remarks broadcast on Israeli television said that if Israel were properly run, its Prime Minister, Ehud Olmert, should be hanging from the gallows. He continued, "The terrible traitor, Ehud Olmert, who gives these Nazis weapons, who gives money, who frees their murderous terrorists, this man, like Ariel Sharon, collaborates with the Nazis." Nathan Jeffay, *Rabbi's Incitement Against Olmert Threatens To Split Apart Chabad; Lubavitch Messianist: Prime Minister Should Be 'Hanged From the Gallows'*, Jewish Daily Forward, Jan. 9, 2008, available at http://www.forward.com/articles/12444/.

(3) The home page of a website, with six registered members, who had posted 28 entries during 2007 explains, "This website encourages Israeli terrorism against Arab terror and an iron fist against Arab terrorists. . . . The site publishes terror-and war-related material and presents practical materials pertaining to terrorism, such as the sale of weapons, various manuals for the building of certain weapons, and so forth." According to another quote, "Blessed is the hero who has the guts to do something violent against Arabs while protecting the citizens of Israel." *Israeli Website Posts Bomb-making Instructions for "Terrorism" Against Arabs*, BBC International Reports (Middle East) Sept. 2, 2007 (Westlaw; BBC–MIDEAST), quoting text of article in Israeli newspaper Ma-ariv on Sept. 2, 2007.

2. *England*

In response to the 2005 terrorist bombings of the London subways, which killed 52 people, the English Parliament amended the nation's terrorism laws with a provision it had rejected months before, which provides as follows:

1 Encouragement of terrorism

(1) This section applies to a statement that is likely to be understood by some or all of the members of the public to whom it is published as a direct or indirect encouragement or other inducement to them to the commission, preparation or instigation of acts of terrorism. . . .

(2) A person commits an offence if-

    . . .

    (b) at the time he publishes [a statement] or causes it to be published, he—

        (i) intends members of the public to be directly or indirectly encouraged or otherwise induced by the statement to commit, prepare or instigate acts of terrorism . . .; or

(ii) is reckless as to whether members of the public will be directly or indirectly encouraged or otherwise induced by the statement to commit, prepare or instigate such acts or offences.

(3) For purposes of this section, the statements that are likely to be understood by members of the public as indirectly encouraging the commission or preparation of acts of terrorism . . . include every statement which—

(a) glorifies the commission or preparation (whether in the past, in the future or generally) of such acts . . . ; and

(b) is a statement from which those members of the public could reasonably be expected to infer that what is being glorified is being glorified as conduct that should be emulated by them in existing circumstances.

. . .

(5) It is irrelevant for purposes of subsections (1) to (3)—

. . .

(b) whether any person is in fact encouraged or induced by the statement to commit, prepare or instigate any such act or offence.

Terrorism Act 2006, c. 11 (U.K.).

It is a defense for a person charged with the "glorification" offense to show "that the statement neither expressed his views nor had his endorsement" and "that is was clear, in all the circumstances of the statement's publication, that it did not express his views and . . . did not have his endorsement." Terrorism Act 2006, §§ (6)(a) & (b).

Recent applications of the new "glorification" offense include the following:

(1) In 2006, police arrested a group of leaders and recruits to terrorism for activities that included survivalist training and listening to inflammatory lectures on religion and politics. The police justified the arrest not because it would disrupt an imminent attack, but because it would interrupt the process of radicalization, which included glorification of terror and indoctrination of young people. Sean O'Neill, *New Terror Laws Used to Arrest Men 'Recruiting Suicide Cell'*, Times (London), Sept. 4, 2006, available at http://www.timesonline.co.uk/article/0,,200–2341858.00.html.

(2) Police seized and investigated the source of a sing-along children's DVD which glorified suicide bombing through cartoons and vivid imagery of a daughter watching with pride as her mother prepares and then departs to conduct a suicide attack. Chris Brooke, *British Children Targeted with Terror Sing–Along DVD for*

Would–Be Suicide Bombers, Daily Mail (London), Dec. 19, 2007, at 11.

3. *Europe*

Other countries have adopted anti-terrorism legislation that criminalizes the glorification offense. These include Denmark, Spain and France, and in 2007, the 34 countries in the Council of Europe signed its Convention on the Prevention of Terrorism, which directs each state party to criminalize "public provocation to commit a terrorist offence," defined as "the distribution, or otherwise making available, of a message to the public, with the intent to incite the commission of a terrorist offence, where such conduct, whether or not directly advocating terrorist offences, causes a danger that one or more such offences may be committed." Council of Europe, Convention on the Prevention of Terrorism, opened for signature May 16, 2005, C.E.T.S. 196, art 5.

4. *The United States*

United States federal law does not directly criminalize speech inciting terrorism or violence. Nevertheless, statutes that can capture speech acts that lead to terrorism include those that criminalize conspiracy to engage in terrorism, aiding and abetting terrorism, and providing material support to terrorism. "Material support" includes "expert advice or assistance." 18 U.S.C. §§ 2443A & B (2000). In two recent cases, the crimes alleged centered on speech inciting terrorism:

(1) Under the material support provision, among others, the federal government in 2004 prosecuted a University of Idaho graduate student, Sami Al–Hussayen, for operating and maintaining Islamic websites, which contained speech the government alleged incited terrorist activity. One site included an article titled "Provision of Suicide Operations,"which described the duty of a Mujahid or warrior to kill himself and included details of how to carry it out. Al–Hussayen argued successfully, in his defense, that he was essentially a "webmaster," providing technical assistance to create web sites, without endorsing the content of the publications posted, and the jury acquitted him of those charges. *United States v. Al–Hussayen*, No. CR03–048–C-EJL (D. Id. 2004).

(2) In 2005, the government secured a conviction against Ali Al–Timimi, a scholar who had lectured on Islam around the world. A group of his young Muslim followers, who attended a mosque in Falls Church, Virginia, had earlier been convicted of activities that included watching videos of violent jihad and playing paintball to train to participate in holy war. Al–Timimi's prosecution centered

on his speech acts, which the government alleged encouraged the group's activities. The key event occurred five days after the September 11 attacks, when Timimi told his followers "the time had come for [them] to go abroad and join the mujahideen engaged in violent jihad in Afghanistan." Several of the group left to train at terrorist camps, although none actually fought against U.S. troops in Afghanistan. *U.S. v. Al–Timimi*, No. CR04–00385–LMB (E. D. Va. 2005).

Notes and Questions

1. How do the elements of Israel's "praise of terrorism," England's "glorification of terrorism," and the European Council's "public provocation to terrorism" offenses compare to each other and to those of the U.S. *Brandenburg* test? Which formulation most appropriately balances the public interest in preventing terrorism and the individual right to free speech?

2. Do the recent speech acts in Israel constitute criminal incitement to violence under the new law? Would they constitute incitement under the *Brandenburg* test in the U.S.?

3. Do the recent speech acts in England constitute criminal incitement to violence under the new law? Would they constitute incitement under the *Brandenburg* test in the U.S.?

4. How would the examples from Israel and England fare under the European Council provision? What is the most crucial difference between the European Council provision and the other two? Does it impact the public safety/free speech balance significantly?

5. Were the juries correct in applying the *Brandenburg* test in the Al–Hussayen and Al–Timimi cases? What result under the Israeli, English and European Council provisions?

C. INSULTING GOVERNMENT OFFICIALS OR ENTITIES

In many nations around the world, statutes provide for criminal punishment for "insulting the honor" of government officials. The following describes recent enforcement of such statutes.

In Poland, two students ran afoul of the law when, after a demonstration in 1992, they shouted "down with Walesa–Communist agent." They were convicted and fined. In Indonesia, a legislator was sentenced to 34 months in prison for a speech in Germany in which he called former Indonesian presidents Suharto and Sukarno "dictators." In Romania, a journalist compared President Iliescu to a pig, and was charged with "offending State authority." In Russia, a newspaper reporter, who called Russian Defense Minister Pavel Grachev "a thief," was convicted of "insulting" Grachev, though he was promptly amnestied. A court in Azerbaijan sentenced six employees of a satirical newspaper for prison terms up to five years for "insulting the honor and dignity" of President Heydar Aliyev.

Elsewhere, journalists in Turkey have been punished for comparing parliamentary deputies to "Pavlov's dogs." Journalists in Croatia were charged with "spreading false information" for parodies highlighting President Franjo Tudjman's authoritarian tendencies. In Belarus, the opposition newspaper *Svoboda* was charged with libel for criticizing government officials and fined. . . . [I]n Ghana, journalists have been charged or threatened with criminal libel prosecutions for alleging drug peddling by the ruling party. In Slovakia, a journalist was convicted for charging that the Labor Minister's brother was involved in dishonest business practices.

Herman Schwartz, *Free Speech in Democracies: The Western Context*, Development Outreach (Summer 1999), www1.worldbank.org/devoutreach/summer99/article.asp?id + 7.

The following excerpt explains the law of insult's European heritage.

Europe inherited these laws from the Roman empire via centuries of feudalism in its heartland territories. In the feudal era, to commit lese majestè was to insult the state itself as well as its head, the two being synonymous. Since the monarch received his powers from god, he demanded "extraordinary" protection. Over the centuries, an adapted, secularised version of insult laws worked its way into the legislation of all the European monarchies.

Cases brought under these laws were often prosecuted alongside those of treason; the common factor being the fact that the accused citizen has violated the responsibility to protect his country's (monarch's, state's) image. . . .

Daria Vaisman, *Turkey's restriction, Europe's problem*, openDemocracy (Sept. 28, 2006), http://www.opendemocracy.net/democracy-turkey/free_speech_3952.jsp.

The following excerpt tracks the genesis of the insult crime in English law.

Modern criminal libel law is the product of 16th century innovations in the English Star Chamber, the secretive court that sat in closed session on cases involving state security. The Star Chamber needed a more effective method than civil defamation laws to control statements about the crown. Such control, one legal scholar said, was "an effect of overwhelming importance in an age when the peace and security of the state was manifestly precarious and when printing and the great intellectual movement of which it was one symptom had made political writings take on a new and vital importance."

The Star Chamber also premised its law on the notion that defamations breached the peace. The common belief that true statements were at least as likely to cause breaches of the peace as false ones led to the criminal punishment of both true and false statements.

In a case of libel against the deceased Archbishop of Canterbury and a living bishop in 1609, the Star Chamber used the ancient Roman code that punished certain defamations because of their anonymous character and scandalous nature. Of the case, Sir Edward Coke wrote that the Star Chamber ruled that "although libel be made against one, yet it incites all those of the same family, kindred or society to revenge, and so tends (as a consequence) to quarrels and breach of the peace, and may be the cause of the shedding of blood and great inconvenience."

So went the saying, "the greater the truth, the greater the libel."

Libels against a magistrate or other public person, the Star Chamber reasoned, should be subject to an even greater penalty because "it concerns not only the breach of the peace, but also the scandal of the Government."

Criminal Defamation Laws are 19th Century Holdover, 21 News Media and the Law (Spring 2001), http://www.rcfp.org/news/mag/25–2/lib-crimhist.html.

Human rights groups and international organizations criticize the continued existence and enforcement of criminal insult laws as inconsistent with nationally and internationally articulated free speech rights. In 2000, the Inter–American Commission on Human Rights issued a report concluding that criminal enforcement of "desacato" or "insult" laws is inconsistent with the free speech guarantee of the American Convention on Human Rights. Inter–Am. C.H.R., *Report on the Compatibility of "Desacato" Laws with the American Convention on Human Rights*, OEA/Ser. L/VIII.88, doc. 9 rev. (1995). In 2004, the Inter–American Court, located in Costa Rica, invalidated as inconsistent with the Convention's free speech guarantee the conviction in that country of a journalist who reported allegations against a former diplomat implicated in an arms sale scandal. *Repeal of "Insult" Laws Crucial for Press Freedom*, FindLaw (Apr. 20, 2007), http://news.findlaw.com/wash/s/20070420/20070420185705.html. In 2006, the Guatemalan Supreme Court invalidated its desacato law as contrary to its constitution's free speech guarantee. Eric Green, *Guatemalan Court Praised for Move to End Contry's Contempt Laws: Action called step to strength-*

ening free expressions in Americas, America.gov (Feb. 8, 2006), http://www.america.gov/st/washfile-english/2006/February/ 20060208144037AEneerG0.8583795.html. During this time period, legislative repeal of desacato laws has occurred in a number of Central and South American countries, including Argentina, Costa Rica, Nicaragua, Paraguay and Peru.

By contrast, in a 2003 judgment, the Venezuelan Supreme Court upheld the constitutionality of the insult laws, reasoning that "anyone who presents a state dignitary in an undignified light tends to weaken the functions they exercise, at least in public opinion, potentially contributing to a state of pre-anarchy." The Court further stated that Venezuela was not bound to follow the conclusions of the report by the Inter–American Commission on Human Rights. *Venezuela's Supreme Court Upholds Prior Censorship and "Insult Laws,"* Hum. Rts Watch (July 18, 2003), http:// hrw.org/english/docs/2003/07/18/venezu6239.htm. Statutory revisions in 2005 stiffened the penalties for insult and defamation, with insulting the president punishable by imprisonment for 6 to 30 months. At least three journalists were convicted and sentenced for insult-related crimes in 2006, with several others under investigation. Freedom House, *Map of Press Freedom* (2007), http://www. freedomhouse.org/template.cfm?page=251 & year=2007.

In the following case, the European Court of Human Rights reviews a recent criminal insult conviction in Poland.

SKALKA v. POLAND

38 Eur. H. R. Rep. 1 (2003)
European Court of Human Rights

[PROCEDURE

1.   The case originated in an application (no. 43425/98) against the Republic of Poland lodged with the Court under Article 34 of the Convention for the Protection of Human Rights and Fundamental Freedoms ("the Convention") by a Polish national, Mr Edward Skalka ("the applicant"), on 17 October 1997.]

The Facts

I. THE CIRCUMSTANCES OF THE CASE

9.   The applicant was born in 1941. He is currently serving a prison sentence.

10.   On 16 December 1993 the Nowy Targ District Court convicted the applicant of aggravated theft and sentenced him to imprisonment. While in prison, on unspecified dates the applicant wrote a letter to the Penitentiary Division of the Katowice Regional Court and he received a reply. Dissatisfied with that reply, on 15

November 1994 the applicant sent a letter to the President of the Katowice Regional Court, complaining about the judge who had replied to his letter. The relevant passages of the applicant's letter read:

> "(...) It cannot be excluded that further acts of that kind on the part of the Penitentiary Division of the Regional Court would make me complain to the judicial supervision about the irresponsible clowns placed in that Division.
>
> I will start by saying that any little cretin, whether he wears a gown or not, should vent his need to intimidate others by making allusions to legal responsibility [for their acts] on his mistress, if he has one, or on his dog, but not on me. I am not going to be afraid of any such clown who wants to intimidate me, but the truth is that my request of 18 August 1994 was addressed to the court, not to some fool.
>
> I expect that the President of the Katowice Regional Court will somehow convey my request to that bully and that he will, at the same time, read his reply to me (...)
>
> Not only does [the judge] write rubbish about my alleged request for a pardon, which my request was absolutely not, but he also intimidates me. If he is such a brilliant lawyer that he is able to reply to questions that were not asked–and his legal skills can be seen if the content of my letter is compared with his reply–he should find a relevant legal provision to use against me. It would not change the fact that such a limited individual, such a cretin should not take the post of a reliable lawyer who would know how to reply to a letter. A cretin he will remain and I see no reason to be afraid of any legal consequences. "You know, you understand, shut up"–that is all the education he has, as a fool does not need any better.

11.   Subsequently, on an unspecified date, the Sosnowiec District Prosecutor instituted criminal proceedings against the applicant....

12.   On 6 September 1995 the Sosnowiec District Court convicted the applicant of insulting a State authority and sentenced him to eight months' imprisonment.

II.   RELEVANT DOMESTIC LAW

23.   Article 237 of the Criminal Code 1969, applicable at the relevant time, read as follows:

"Anyone who insults a State authority at the place where it carries out its duties or in public, is liable to up to two years' imprisonment, to a restriction of personal liberty or a fine."

THE LAW

I. ALLEGED VIOLATION OF ARTICLE 10 OF THE CONVENTION

24. The applicant complained that his criminal conviction ran counter to Article 10 of the Convention.

. . .

B. *The Court's assessment*

30. It is not in dispute between the Parties that the applicant's conviction amounted to an interference with the applicant's freedom of expression and that this interference was "prescribed by law" as required by Article 10 of the Convention, namely by Article 237 of the Criminal Code 1969, applicable at the relevant time.

31. It is also a common ground that the interference pursued a legitimate aim of maintaining the authority of the judiciary within the meaning of Article 10 of the Convention.

32. The Court recalls that freedom of expression constitutes one of the essential foundations of a democratic society and one of the basic conditions for its progress and for each individual's self-fulfilment. Subject to paragraph 2, it is applicable not only to "information" or "ideas" that are favourably received or regarded as inoffensive or as a matter of indifference, but also to those that offend, shock or disturb. Such are the demands of that pluralism, tolerance and broadmindedness without which there is no "democratic society". As set forth in Article 10, this freedom is subject to exceptions, which must, however, be construed strictly, and the need for any restrictions must be established convincingly. . . .

33. The adjective "necessary", within the meaning of Article 10 § 2, implies the existence of a "pressing social need". The Contracting States have a certain margin of appreciation in assessing whether such a need exists, but it goes hand in hand with a European supervision, embracing both the legislation and the decisions applying it, even those given by an independent court. . . .

34. The work of the courts, which are the guarantors of justice and which have a fundamental role in a State governed by the rule of law, needs to enjoy public confidence. It should therefore be protected against unfounded attacks. . . .

The courts, as with all other public institutions, are not immune from criticism and scrutiny. Persons detained enjoy in this area the same rights as all other members of society. A clear distinction must, however, be made between criticism and insult. If the sole intent of any form of expression is to insult a court, or members of that court, an appropriate punishment would not, in principle, constitute a violation of Article 10 § 2 of the Convention.

35.   It is finally recalled that in exercising its supervisory jurisdiction, the Court must look at the impugned interference in the light of the case as a whole, including the content of the remarks held against the applicant and the context in which they were made. In particular, it must determine whether the interference in question was "proportionate to the legitimate aims pursued" and whether the reasons adduced by the national authorities to justify it are "relevant and sufficient". In doing so, the Court has to satisfy itself that the national authorities applied standards which were in conformity with the principles embodied in Article 10 and, moreover, that they based themselves on an acceptable assessment of the relevant facts. . . .

36.   In the present case, the applicant, while serving a prison sentence, wrote a letter to the Penitentiary Division of the Katowice Regional Court and received a reply. Obviously dissatisfied with that reply, on 15 November 1994 the applicant sent a further letter to the President of the Katowice Regional Court, complaining about the unidentified judge who had replied to his first letter. It is not open to doubt that the applicant used insulting words in his second letter. He stated that "irresponsible clowns" were placed in the Penitentiary Division of that court, and went on to shower further abuse upon the author of the reply complained of: "small-time cretin", "some fool", "a limited individual", "outstanding cretin" (see § 9 above). The Court also observes that the tone of the letter as a whole was clearly derogatory.

37.   It should also be noted that the applicant did not formulate any concrete complaints against the letter, which had so aggrieved him. He expressed his anger and frustration, but did not take reasonable care to articulate clearly why, in his view, the letter complained of deserved such a strong reaction.

38.   On the other hand, as regards the requirements that the interference must comply with, and in particular as regards the proportionality test to be applied (see § 34 above), the Court recalls that in assessing the proportionality of the interference, the nature and severity of the penalties imposed are also factors to be taken into account. . . .

39.   In this respect the Court's attention has been drawn, first and foremost, to the fact that the courts chose to impose a prison sentence of eight months on the applicant, which cannot but be regarded as a harsh measure. . . .

40.   As regards the context in which the impugned statements were uttered, the Court recalls that the phrase "authority of the judiciary" includes, in particular, the notion that the courts are, and are accepted by the public at large as being the proper forum for the settlement of legal disputes and for the determination of a

person's guilt or innocence on a criminal charge.... What is at stake as regards protection of the authority of the judiciary, is the confidence which the courts in a democratic society must inspire in the accused, as far as criminal proceedings are concerned, and also in the public at large. ...

41. In the circumstances of the present case the Court considers that the interest protected by the impugned interference was important enough to justify limitations on the freedom of expression. In consequence, an appropriate sentence for insulting both the court as an institution and an unnamed but identifiable judge would not amount to a violation of Article 10 of the Convention.

Therefore, the question in the case is not whether the applicant should have been punished for his letter to the Regional Court, but rather whether the punishment was appropriate or "necessary" within the meaning of Article 10 § 2. It is the Court's assessment that the sentence of eight months' imprisonment was disproportionately severe. Even if it is in principle, for the national courts to fix the sentence, in view of the circumstances of the case, there are common standards which this Court has to ensure with the principle of proportionality. These standards are the gravity of the guilt, the seriousness of the offence and the repetition of the alleged offences.

42. In the Court's view, the severity of the punishment applied in this case exceeded the seriousness of the offence. It was not an open and overall attack on the authority of the judiciary, but an internal exchange of letters of which nobody of the public took notice. Furthermore, the gravity of the offence was not such as to justify the punishment inflicted on the applicant. Moreover, it was for the first time that the applicant overstepped the bounds of the permissible criticism. Therefore, while a lesser punishment could well have been justified, the courts went beyond what constituted a "necessary" exception to the freedom of expression.

43. The Court therefore concludes that Article 10 has been violated.

* * *

Turkey, which has a range of criminal insult laws, including one that prohibits affronts to "Turkishness," faced an ultimatum from the European Union that it must amend or repeal it as a condition to membership. *Turkey Is Told Insult Law Must Go*, N.Y. Times, Nov. 7, 2007, at A8 (EU's enlargement commissioner, Olli Rehn ... said it was "simply not acceptable in a European democracy"), and in fact modified its law somewhat. Consider the following commentary.

In 1997, Saddam Hussein decided to sue French journalist Jean Daniel for the offence of having written that the then Iraqi president was a "Caligula-style tyrant" who had allowed thousands of children to die. Hussein was surprised to be informed by the Parisian courts that he could sue Daniel not merely (as he had planned) under the civil law, but under a French press law of 1881 which makes it a crime to insult foreign heads of state, whether or not the insult is true.

In 2004, the king of Morocco sued Spanish journalists Rosa Maria Lopez and Jose Louis Gutierrez under a 1982 Protection of Honor, Privacy and Right to a Respectful Image Law. Lopez had written that one of the king's trucks had been seized at a Spanish port and found to be carrying five tons of hashish. Spain's supreme court rejected the journalists' appeal—even though the claim was accurate—on grounds that her article "illegally disturbed His Majesty Hassan II's right to keep his honour."

These trials should sound vaguely familiar to anyone who had followed the case against Turkish novelist Orhan Pamuk (which was eventually dismissed on a legal technicality) or the less-publicised trials against other Turkish writers: among them novelist Elif Shafak (acquitted on 21 September 2006) and Armenian–Turkish journalist Hrant Dink (given a six-month suspended sentence in October 2005, and arraigned on a new set of charges on 25 September 2006). All have been accused of "insulting Turkishness" under Article 301 of the Turkish penal code, which states that insulting Turkey or its institutions is a crime. Pamuk had mentioned the mass killings of Armenians in 1915—a Turkish national taboo—in a Swiss newspaper, and Dink had written a newspaper article calling on Armenians to reject "the adulterated part of their Turkish blood."

The landscape of insult

The trials in Istanbul expose political and cultural divisions within Turkey over nationalism, secularism, the understanding of the past and the shape of the future. But they also illustrate an even more fundamental gap: between Turkey and Europe. This has to do both with the principle of freedom of speech, and with Europe's own perception of what it means to be European. That is, the trials of Turkish writers are also about Europe. For they highlight the ongoing—if largely unreported—campaign to persuade European states to repeal defamation laws in *their own* criminal codes.

This campaign has been pursued by a wide range of organisations . . .

. . .

In their defence, European Union member-states point out that in the modern era these laws are rarely, if ever, used. . . .

Old vs new Europe

But the existence of these laws points to another fundamental divide within Europe: between the established fifteen member-states and the ten which joined in May 2004. Many of the latter (Cyprus, Czech Republic, Estonia, Hungary, Latvia, Lithuania, Malta, Poland, Slovakia and Slovenia) routinely use criminal defamation laws to prosecute freedom of speech. "In central Asia and in eastern Europe, this is the single biggest reason for jailing journalists", says Haraszti. . . .

In contrast to Turkey, these cases do not receive serious publicity, nor have they served as a deterrent for these countries' EU membership. . . .

Europe's past, Turkey's future

The EU seems to be asking Turkey to play by rules that its own members break, and thus be guilty of hypocrisy. This implies that influential elements within the EU have as little real interest in seeing Turkey join as some factions in Turkey itself, and are simply using the freedom-of-speech cases to undermine Turkey's credentials. But there is another explanation for Europe's approach: that it both genuinely believes that Turkey's record on free speech and human rights is severely deficient, but that what really angers it is the content of what's being restricted rather than the principle of freedom of speech.

The David Irving case is evidence for this point. Irving, a British historian who has made a high-profile career from casting doubts about the Nazi holocaust and Hitler's knowledge of and responsibility for it, was sentenced to three years in an Austrian jail for holocaust-denial in February 2006. This was at the very time when Orhan Pamuk and Hrant Dink were being tried effectively for stating that another genocide(of Armenians) had occurred. The contradiction between Europe's protests and the actions of one of its member-states seemed stark, and shaming. But the Irving–Pamuk "contradiction", when more closely inspected, reveals the more fundamental dilemma of free speech in a democracy that Europe is grappling with: that free speech as a principle undermines the impulse to forbid what is deemed abhorrent.

In this light, the more deeply shared element of the Irving and the Pamuk–Dink–Shafak cases is Europe's discomfort with denial of the past. The idea that atonement for sins is an essential qualification to be a democracy (as evidenced in notions of "collective guilt", the genre of holocaust studies, and even the fashion among some young Germans to wear the Star of David symbol) may owe as much to modern, collective psychological conditions as to a true engagement with history, but it is effective nonetheless. After all, Germany's readiness to accept responsibility for the holocaust was the key to its rehabilitation in post-war Europe.

Against this background, official Turkey's adamant and consistent refusal openly to discuss the events of 1915 challenges a formative tenet of the EU, a shared commitment to defend a series of core human rights and to denounce their violation. Even more penetratingly, Turkey's attitude reminds Europe of its own history of colonisation, slavery, war, and genocide.

Europe can dismiss or ignore the ongoing criminal defamation cases in the newer EU countries (most of which involve accusations of corruption) as minor; but the denial of genocide is far more serious. Corruption is regrettable, a social ill—but prosecutions that appear to endorse official suppression of the past and discussion of it strike at the heart of modern European values.

In protecting its history from scrutiny as much as in restricting free speech, Turkey will have its work cut out. "(Article 301) has become a symbolic fight inside Turkey, the same way that flag-burning is an issue in the United States", says Miklos Haraszti. It is a fight that Turkey, if it wants to be part of the European club, won't be able to win.

Vaisman, *supra* p. 23.

Notes and Questions

1.   The categories of speech in U.S. constitutional jurisprudence most analogous to insult are fighting words and defamation. Do the insult prosecutions around the world meet the requirements of the fighting words category? Do they meet the standards for defamation?

2.   Could *criminal* punishment of an individual for uttering an entirely false statement with "actual malice" about a government official ever comport with the U.S. Constitution's free speech guarantee? *See Criminal Defamation Laws, supra* p. 24 (noting that some states still have criminal defamation laws on their books and a few prosecutions have occurred).

3.   What test does the ECHR apply in *Skalka v. Poland?* Which part of the test did Poland fail to meet and how exactly did it fail to meet it? The ECHR refers to a "clear distinction ... between criticism and insult." What is it and how does the Court apply it in this case? Would the defendant's words constitute either fighting words or proscribable defamation according to U.S. constitutional standards?

4. How does the history of insult laws in Europe help explain their modern-day manifestations? Does U.S. history help explain why they have never been present in U.S. law? Why, according to the commentary, are European countries more tolerant of the former soviet republics jailing journalists for reporting allegations of *current* corruption and more condemning of Turkey for jailing writers for their description of *past* acts? What does the commentator claim is the "fundamental dilemma of free speech in a democracy that Europe is grappling with" with respect to Turkey? Does the United States grapple with the same dilemma in different ways?

II. DEFAMATION

In *New York Times v. Sullivan*, 376 U.S. 254 (1964), and subsequent cases, the Supreme Court interpreted the U.S. Constitution's free speech clause to set speech-protective limits on state law actions for damage to reputation. The following excerpt describes the unfavorable reception that attempts to export U.S. defamation law have received in the rest of the world.

> Largely through the efforts of journalists, newspapers, and their lawyers, there has been an active effort to persuade other countries to adopt the American approach, and to conclude that the harm of unpublished truth about public officials and public figures is far greater than the harm of unsanctioned falsity. Yet although these efforts have been successful in moving most common law countries slightly away from the strictest version of the common law model, and in securing some modifications of analogous remedies even in civil law countries, the overwhelming reaction of the rest of the world to the American approach has been negative. In Australia, New Zealand, Canada, the United Kingdom, and a number of other countries, the unalloyed American approach has been rejected. Believing that the American model places far too much weight on the freedom of the press side of the balance, and far too little on the reputational side, the rest of even the developed democratic world has been satisfied to leave largely in place defamation remedies and standards that the United States continues to find unacceptable under the First Amendment.

Frederick Schauer, *The Exceptional First Amendment*, in American Exceptionalism and Human Rights 40–41 (Michael Ignatieff, ed., 2005).

In the following case, the Supreme Court of Canada considers whether to import the *New York Times v. Sullivan* actual malice standard into the free speech guarantee of the Charter of Rights and Freedoms, which Canada adopted in 1982.

HILL v. CHURCH OF SCIENTOLOGY

[1995] 2 S.C.R. 1130 (Can.)

Supreme Court of Canada

[At a widely reported press conference, a lawyer for the Church of Scientology, Morris Manning, falsely accused a prosecutor, Casey Hill, of misleading a court and improperly obtaining access to sealed court documents. After contempt charges against him were dismissed, Hill sued Manning and the Church of Scientology, seeking damages for defamation. Defendants argued that the free speech guarantee of the Canadian Charter of Rights and Freedoms should limit the scope of the common law defamation action.]

Judgment by: Cory J.:

. . .

(i) Freedom of Expression

101.   Much has been written of the great importance of free speech. . . .

102.   However, freedom of expression has never been recognized as an absolute right. . . .

103.   . . . Although a *Charter* right is defined broadly, generally without internal limits, the *Charter* recognizes, under s. 1, that social values will at times conflict and that some limits must be placed even on fundamental rights. [T]his Court has adopted a flexible approach to measuring the constitutionality of impugned provisions wherein "the underlying values [of the *Charter*] are sensitively weighed in a particular context against other values of a free and democratic society . . .".

106.   Certainly, defamatory statements are very tenuously related to the core values which underlie s. 2(*b*). They are inimical to the search for truth. False and injurious statement cannot enhance self-development. Nor can it ever be said that they lead to healthy participation in the affairs of the community. Indeed, they are detrimental to the advancement of these values and harmful to the interests of a free and democratic society. . . .

(ii) The Reputation of the Individual

107.   The other value to be balanced in a defamation action is the protection of the reputation of the individual. Although much has very properly been said and written about the importance of freedom of expression, little has been written of the importance of reputation. Yet, to most people, their good reputation is to be cherished above all. A good reputation is closely related to the innate worthiness and dignity of the individual. It is an attribute that must, just as much as freedom of expression, be protected by

society's laws. In order to undertake the balancing required by this case, something must be said about the value of reputation.

108. Democracy has always recognized and cherished the fundamental importance of an individual. That importance must, in turn, be based upon the good repute of a person. It is that good repute which enhances an individual's sense of worth and value. False allegations can so very quickly and completely destroy a good reputation. A reputation tarnished by libel can seldom regain its former lustre. A democratic society, therefore, has an interest in ensuring that its members can enjoy and protect their good reputation so long as it is merited.

. . .

118. In the present case, consideration must be given to the particular significance reputation has for a lawyer. The reputation of a lawyer is of paramount importance to clients, to other members of the profession and to the judiciary. A lawyer's practice is founded and maintained upon the basis of a good reputation for professional integrity and trustworthiness. It is the cornerstone of a lawyer's professional life. Even if endowed with outstanding talent and indefatigable diligence, a lawyer cannot survive without a good reputation.

. . .

120. Although it is not specifically mentioned in the *Charter*, the good reputation of the individual represents and reflects the innate dignity of the individual, a concept which underlies all the *Charter* rights. It follows that the protection of the good reputation of an individual is of fundamental importance to our democratic society.

121. Further, reputation is intimately related to the right to privacy which has been accorded constitutional protection.

. . .

(d) *Critiques of the "Actual Malice" Rule*

(i) Comments on the Decision in the United States

127. The "actual malice" rule has been severely criticized by American judges and academic writers. It has been suggested that the decision was overly influenced by the dramatic facts underlying the dispute and has not stood the test of time. . . .

128. Perhaps most importantly, it has been argued the decision has shifted the focus of defamation suits away from their original, essential purpose. Rather than deciding upon the truth of the impugned statement, courts in the U.S. now determine whether the defendant was negligent. Several unfortunate results flow from this shift in focus. First, it may deny the plaintiff the opportunity to

establish the falsity of the defamatory statements and to determine the consequent reputational harm. This is particularly true in cases where the falsity is not seriously contested. . . .

129.   Second, it necessitates a detailed inquiry into matters of media procedure. This, in turn, increases the length of discoveries and of the trial which may actually increase, rather than decrease, the threat to speech interests. . . .

130.   Third, it dramatically increases the cost of litigation. This will often leave a plaintiff who has limited funds without legal recourse. . . .

131.   Fourth, the fact that the dissemination of falsehoods is protected is said to exact a major social cost by depreciating truth in public discourse. . . .

. . .

137.   The New York Times v. Sullivan decision has been criticized by judges and academic writers in the United States and elsewhere. It has not been followed in the United Kingdom or Australia. I can see no reason for adopting it in Canada in an action between private litigants. The law of defamation is essentially aimed at the prohibition of the publication of injurious false statements. It is the means by which the individual may protect his or her reputation which may well be the most distinguishing feature of his or her character, personality and, perhaps, identity. I simply cannot see that the law of defamation is unduly restrictive or inhibiting. Surely it is not requiring too much of individuals that they ascertain the truth of the allegations they publish. The law of defamation provides for the defences of fair comment and of qualified privilege in appropriate cases. Those who publish statements should assume a reasonable level of responsibility.

. . .

139.   None of the factors which prompted the United States Supreme Court to rewrite the law of defamation in America are present in the case at bar. First, this appeal does not involve the media or political commentary about government policies. . . .

140.   Second, a review of jury verdicts in Canada reveals that there is no danger of numerous large awards threatening the viability of media organizations. Finally, in Canada there is no broad privilege accorded to the public statements of government officials which needs to be counterbalanced by a similar right for private individuals.

141.   In conclusion, in its application to the parties in this action, the common law of defamation complies with the underlying values of the *Charter* and there is no need to amend or alter it.

* * *

Germany is another democracy in which both the constitutional text and the Federal Constitutional Court's interpretive jurisprudence weigh the values of free speech versus individual reputation and privacy differently that in the United States, as the following excerpt summarizes.

> The Federal Constitutional Court has declared that the Basic Law establishes "an objective ordering of values" with some rights being more important than others. . . .
>
> The primacy of dignity leads the German Constitutional Court to reach results that appear odd to a student of the First Amendment. . . . For example, the German Constitutional Court has found that preserving the dignity of a dead man outweighed the free expression rights of a living novelist (who died before the final resolution of the case in the Federal Constitutional Court); it has prohibited the publication of a fictional interview involving the wife of the Shah of Iran; it has also enjoined distribution of a docudrama about a gay robber and refused to protect political satire that presented a politician as a rutting pig. These cases . . . demonstrate the German Constitutional Court's firm decision to weigh dignity, which encompasses the interest in personal reputation, above the freedom of speech.

Ronald J. Krotoszynski, Jr., *The First Amendment in Cross–Cultural Perspective: A Comparative Legal Analysis of the Freedom of Speech* 102–03 (2006).

LEBACH CASE

35 BVerfGE 202 (1973) (F.R.G. Fed. Const. Ct.)
German Constitutional Court
Translated in Donald P. Kommers, *The Constitutional Jurisprudence
of the Federal Republic of Germany* 416–19 (2nd ed. 1997)

[The complainant participated in an armed robbery of a German armed forces barracks in the course of which several soldiers on guard duty were killed or severely wounded. After his arrest and conviction as an accessory, he was sentenced to six years' imprisonment. The crime and trial of the defendants attracted considerable public attention. Some years later, several months before the complainant was to be released from prison, a German television station planned to run a documentary play based on the crime. The program would display Lebach's photograph, use his name, and make reference to his homosexual tendencies. The complainant sought an injunction prohibiting the television company from broadcasting the play. Citing the broadcasting freedom provision of Article 5, the Superior Court of Mainz dismissed the case. After weighing the interests of the complainant in the light of constitutional standards, the Koblenz Court of Appeals sustained the dismissal. Claiming that his right of personality under Article 2 was being infringed, the complainant filed a constitutional complaint against the decisions.]

Judgment of the First Senate. . . .

B. II. In the present case the court of appeals has held correctly that several fundamental rights affect the application of private law and that they pull in opposite directions. The right to one's personality guaranteed by Article 2 (I) in conjunction with Article I (I) of the Basic Law conflicts with the freedom of broadcasting stations to provide information under Article 5 (I) [2] of the Basic Law.

I. On the one hand, a televised broadcast of the kind at issue concerning the origin, execution, and detection of a crime which mentions the name of the criminal and contains a representation of his likeness necessarily touches the area of his fundamental rights guaranteed by Article 2 (I) in conjunction with Article I (I) of the Basic Law. The rights to the free development of one's personality and human dignity secure for everyone an autonomous sphere in which to shape one's private life by developing and protecting one's individuality. 1bis includes the right to remain alone, to be oneself within this sphere, and to exclude the intrusion of or the inspection by others. It also encompasses the right to one's own likeness and utterances, especially the right to decide what to do with pictures of oneself. In principle, everyone has the right to determine for himself whether and to what extent others may make public an account of either certain incidents from his life or his entire life story.

The decisions of the Federal Constitutional Court have not, however, extended the absolute protection of the above-mentioned fundamental rights to the entire sphere of private life. If an individual as a member of a community enters into relations with others, influences others by his existence or behavior, and thereby impinges upon the personal sphere of other people or upon the interests of communal life, his exclusive right to be master of his own private sphere may become subject to restrictions unless his inviolable, innermost sphere of life is involved. Any such social involvement, if sufficiently strong, may justify measures taken by public authorities in the interest of the public as a whole; for example, publishing pictures of a suspect in order to facilitate a criminal investigation. However, neither the state's interest in solving crimes nor any other public interest invariably justifies an infringement of the personal sphere. Instead, the preeminent importance of the right freely to develop and [command] respect for the personality, closely connected with the supreme constitutional value of human dignity, demands that any encroachment upon the right to personality which may appear necessary always be balanced against the protective rule laid down in Article 2 (I) in conjunction with Article I (I) of the Basic Law....

III. 2... In resolving the conflict [between the freedom to broadcast and the right of personality, one] must remember that ... both constitutional concerns are essential aspects of the free democratic order of the Basic Law, the result being that neither can claim precedence in principle.... In case of conflict [the court] must adjust both constitutional values, if possible; if this cannot be achieved, [the court] must determine which interest will defer to the other in the light of the nature of the case and [its] special circumstances. In so doing, the [court] must consider both constitutional values in their relation to human dignity as the nucleus of the Constitution's value system. Accordingly, the freedom to broadcast may have the effect of restricting claims based on the right to personality; however, any damage to "personality" resulting from a public broadcast may not be disproportionate to the significance of the publication to free communication.... [The court must also consider] the extent to which the [legitimate] interest served by the broadcast can be satisfied without such a far-reaching invasion of the intimate sphere.

IV. 1. In the light of these general principles the following criteria are constitutionally relevant in assessing televised broadcasts of the kind involved here.

(a) A public report of a crime in which the name, likeness, or representation of the accused is provided will always constitute a severe intrusion into his intimate sphere, given that it publicizes his misdeeds and conveys a negative image of his person in the eyes of the public....

2. On the other hand., weighty considerations suggest that the public should be fully informed of the commission of crimes, including the identity of the accused and the events which led to the act. Crimes are also part of contemporary history, the presentation of which is the quintessential task of the media....

3. In balancing these interests, ... the public interest in receiving information must generally prevail when current crimes are being reported. If someone breaches the peace by attacking or injuring fellow citizens or the legally protected interests of the community, he must not only suffer the criminal punishment provided by the law; he must also accept, as a matter of principle, that in a community committed to freedom of communication the public has an interest in receiving information through normal channels about a [criminal] act he himself caused....

However, the interest in receiving information is not absolute. The central importance of the right to personality requires not only vigilance on behalf of the inviolable, innermost personal sphere [of the accused] but also a strict regard for the principle of proportionality. The invasion of the personal sphere is limited to the need to satisfy adequately the [public's] interest in receiving information, while the harm inflicted upon the accused must be proportional to the seriousness of the offense or to its importance otherwise for the public. Consequently, it is not always permissible to disclose the name, release a picture, or use some other means of identifying the perpetrator. . . .

4.   The radiating effect of the constitutional guarantee of the right of personality does not, however, permit the media, over and above reporting on contemporary events, to intrude indefinitely upon the person and private sphere of the criminal. Instead, when the public's interest in receiving current information [about the crime] has been satisfied, the criminal's right to be left alone increases in importance, [thus] limiting the extent to which the media and the public may convert the individual sphere of his life into an object of discussion or entertainment. . . . Once a criminal court has prosecuted and convicted a defendant for an act that has attracted public attention, and he has experienced the just reaction of the community, any further or repeated invasion of the criminal's personal sphere cannot normally be justified.

5.   (a) [We] cannot generally and precisely state when the legitimate reporting of current events loses its [contemporary vitality] and is thus no longer a permissible subject of [public] discussion. . . . The decisive criterion is whether the report in question is likely to inflict upon the criminal new or additional harm, compared with information that is already available.

(b) [Courts] may treat the criminal's interest in rehabilitation or in re-covering his position in society as a decisive factor in determining the limits on broadcasting. . . .

(e) In any case, a televised report concerning a serious crime that is no longer justified by the public's interest in receiving information about current events may not be rebroadcast if it endangers the social rehabilitation of the criminal. The criminal's vital interest in being reintegrated into society and the interest of the community in restoring him to his social position must generally have precedence over the public's interest in a further discussion of the crime. . . .

V.   2.   A proper assessment of the relevant constitutional provisions involved in this case leads us to the conclusion that the petition of the complainant must prevail.[2]

* * *

2. A subsequent case modified the holding of *Lebach*. In *Lebach II,* BverfG, 1 BvR 348/98, 1 BvR 755/98, v. 25.11.1999, the Federal Constitutional

What explains the difference between the United States and German value hierarchies? Certainly, an important part of the explanation for the different text and interpretation is "the utter contempt shown towards human dignity by the Nazi regime." Donald P. Kommers, *The Constitutional Jurisprudence of the Federal Republic of Germany* 419 (2nd ed. 1997) (quoting B.S. Markesinis, *A Comparative Introduction to the German Law of Torts* 410 (3rd ed. 1994)). But the following excerpt suggests that there is more to the explanation than such recent history.

> ... [T]here are, on the two sides of the Atlantic, two different cultures of privacy, which are home to different intuitive sensibilities, and which have produced two significantly different laws of privacy.
>
> ...
>
> So why do these sensibilities differ? Why is it that French people won't talk about their salaries, but will take off their bikini tops? Why is it that Americans comply with court discovery orders that open essentially all of their documents for inspection, but refuse to carry identity cards? Why is it that Europeans tolerate state meddling in their choice of baby names? Why is it that Americans submit to extensive credit reporting without rebelling?
>
> These are not questions we can answer by assuming that all human beings share the same raw intuitions about privacy. We do not have the same intuitions, as anybody who has lived in more than one country ought to know. What we typically have is something else: We have intuitions that are shaped by the prevailing legal and social values of the societies in which we live. In particular, we have, if I may use a clumsy phrase, juridified intuitions—intuitions that reflect our knowledge of, and commitment to, the basic legal values of our culture.
>
> Indeed, to get a handle on our transatlantic privacy conflicts, we must begin by recognizing that continental European and American sensibilities about privacy grow out of much larger and much older differences over basic legal values, rooted in much larger and much older differences in social and political traditions. The fundamental contrast, in my view, is not difficult to identify. ... It is the contrast ... between privacy as an aspect of dignity and privacy as an aspect of liberty.
>
> Continental privacy protections are, at their core, a form of protection of a right to respect and personal dignity. The core

Court refused a petition by another participant in the same robbery to enjoin a television station from broadcasting a film, which portrayed the crime but did not reveal the identity of the participant. Krotoszynski, *supra* p. 37, at 109.

continental privacy rights are rights to one's image, name, and reputation, and what Germans call the right to informational self-determination—the right to control the sorts of information disclosed about oneself. These are closely linked forms of the same basic right: They are all rights to control your public image—rights to guarantee that people see you the way you want to be seen. They are, as it were, rights to be shielded against unwanted public exposure—to be spared embarrassment or humiliation. The prime enemy of our privacy, according to this continental conception, is the media, which always threatens to broadcast unsavory information about us in ways that endanger our public dignity. But of course, this concern does not end with media exposure. Any other agent that gathers and disseminates information can also pose such dangers. In its focus on shielding us from public indignity, the continental conception is typical of the continental legal world much more broadly: On the Continent, the protection of personal dignity has been a consuming concern for many generations.

By contrast, America, in this as in so many things, is much more oriented toward values of liberty, and especially liberty against the state. At its conceptual core, the American right to privacy still takes much the form that it took in the eighteenth century: It is the right to freedom from intrusions by the state, especially in one's own home. The prime danger, from the American point of view, is that "the sanctity of [our] homes," in the words of a leading nineteenth-century Supreme Court opinion on privacy, will be breached by government actors. American anxieties thus focus comparatively little on the media. Instead, they tend to be anxieties about maintaining a kind of private sovereignty within our own walls.

Such is the contrast that lies at the base of our divergent sensibilities about what counts as a "privacy" violation. On the one hand, we have an Old World in which it seems fundamentally important not to lose public face; on the other, a New World in which it seems fundamentally important to preserve the home as a citadel of individual sovereignty. What Europeans miss in Americans is a sense of the demands of public face. ... When Americans seem to continental Europeans to violate norms of privacy, it is because they seem to display an embarrassing lack of concern for public dignity—whether the issue is the public indignity inflicted upon Monica Lewinsky by the media, or the self-inflicted indignity of an American who boasts about his salary. Conversely, when continental Europeans seem to Americans to violate norms of privacy, it is because they seem to show a supine lack of resistance to invasions of the realm of private sovereignty whose main citadel is the home—whether the issue is wiretapping or [the government maintaining a list of acceptable] baby names. The question of public nudity presents the contrast in piquant form. To the continental way of seeing things, what matters is the right to control your public image—and that right may include the right to present yourself proudly nude, if you so choose. To the American mind, by contrast, what matters is sovereignty within one's own home; and people who have shucked the protection of clothing are like people who have shucked the protection of the walls of their homes, only more so. They are people who have surrendered any "reasonable expectation of privacy."

James Q. Whitman, *The Two Western Cultures of Privacy: Dignity Versus Liberty*, 113 Yale L.J. 1151, 1160–62 (2004).

Notes and Questions

1. The Canadian Supreme Court suggests that the decision in *New York Times v. Sullivan* was "overly influence by the dramatic facts underlying the dispute." What are those "dramatic facts" and why might they have influenced the standard articulated? Next, the Canadian Supreme Court offers a number of critiques of the U.S. "actual malice" standard before it declines to import it into the free speech guarantee of the Canadian Charter. Can you supply the U.S. Supreme Court's response to each critique? Has the actual malice standard withstood the test of time?

2. In three of the four briefly summarized German cases the Constitutional Court upheld suppression of, or the award of damages for, works presented as imaginary, but linked to real people in ways viewers were likely to understand (a novel with a character whose traits and actions resembled a dead man, a fabricated magazine interview parodying a real person, and a political cartoon). Would the U.S. free speech guarantee ever permit suppression of work clearly presented as fictional, either because it revealed private facts or, through savage satire, damaged the reputation of the person portrayed? Two of the cases—the imaginary interview with the Shah of Iran's wife and the case awarding damages for the political cartoon, which portrayed the Bavarian prime minister as a pig rutting another pig in judicial robes, suggest comparison with *Hustler Magazine v. Falwell*, 485 U.S. 46 (1988) in which the Supreme Court held that the U.S. free speech guarantee protects parody of public figures, unless they can meet the "actual malice" standard. Construct the arguments, based on constitutional values including free speech, which support the different results.

3. In *Lebach*, the German Constitutional Court sustained the petition for an injunction against a television station prohibiting it from broadcasting a docudrama portraying facts about a criminal's past acts. How could it do this in light of Article 5(1) of the Basic Law,

which states: "Freedom of the press and freedom of reporting by means of broadcasts and films are guaranteed. There shall be no censorship." Could a U.S. court issue such an injunction consistent with the free speech guarantee? Which aspects would pose the most problem under free speech clause principles, that the petitioner sought an injunction, that the injunction was against the media, that a criminal sought to suppress the truth about his past acts, or all three? Why don't they pose the same constitutional hurdles in Germany?

4. In fact, many European and other countries regulate what parents name their babies, requiring parents to register their chosen name, and to re-choose if the designated authority deems it unacceptable. Professor Whitman offers a colorful example:

> Continental governments reserve to themselves the right to refuse to register certain given names that parents have chosen for their infants. This is done differently in different countries. In Germany, the local registry office, the Standesamt, maintains a list of permissible names. After reforms in 1993, the state has more limited powers in France. Today, local French officials can issue a complaint if parents choose a name that those officials deem to be not in the best interests of the newborn child. A court will then be seized of the matter, and will decide if the name is an acceptable one. If it rejects the parents' choice, the court itself is to choose a name for the infant in question, if necessary.

> These are practices that seem strange indeed to Americans—how can a judge name your baby?—but they are widely defended by Europeans. Most commonly, Europeans say that the state simply must intervene to protect children against the stupidities of their parents. Indeed, to judge from my own conversations, the popular mind is vividly conscious of the problem of parental stupidity. It is a problem that is exemplified in particular, for ordinary Europeans, by the case of a French child named by her parents "Megane Renaud." "Megane" is the French version of the American name "Megan," one of a number of American names that became popular in France in the 1980s and 1990s. "Megane" is however also the name of a popular car model marketed by the French manufacturer Renault (pronounced in the same way as "Renaud"). Thus two bits of French popular culture came together in an unfortunate way when parents with the surname "Renaud" chose to call their newborn daughter "Megane." Local officials made a highly publicized (though ultimately unsuccessful) intervention, apparently believing that it was too much to saddle a child with a name something like the equivalent of "Camry Toyota."

> There are other recent cases, too, in which parents have been prevented from giving their children names that are "ridiculous, pejorative, or in bad taste." One Belgian woman, for example, was recently forbidden to name her newborn "Anakin," after the character in the Star Wars movie series. Despite her threat to go on a hunger strike, officials decreed that her child was to be called "Dorian." There is even European human rights law on the issue.

The case in question involved a French couple that chose to name their child "Fleur de Marie" ("Mary's Flower"), a name rejected by local officials on the ground that it was not a proper saint's name. That decision was litigated all the way to the European Court of Human Rights, which held, in 1996, with a Canadian judge dissenting, that the law of names did not represent a cognizable violation of the right of privacy.

Whitman, *supra* p. 43, at 1160–62.

How can *government* regulation of baby names be consistent with the protection of *personal* dignity and control of public image, which influences European law and free speech jurisprudence?

III. HATE SPEECH

The United States is also a "free speech outlier" in the arena of hate speech, as the following excerpt explains.

Practically every European country, along with other English-speaking countries like Canada, has embraced some form of hate speech legislation. Norway's law is typical. It forbids "publicly stirring one part of the population against another" and any utterance that "threatens, insults, or subjects to hatred, persecution, or contempt any person or group of persons because of their creed, color, race, or national origins . . . or homosexual bent." In Canada, hate speech principles are enshrined in several statutes. The criminal code includes a section that makes it a criminal act to advocate genocide, publicly incite hatred, or "willfully promote hatred." The Canadian human rights law outlaws the spreading of hate through telecommunications, including the internet. This policy applies to a lengthy list of categories: race, ethnicity, national origin, color, religion, age, sex, sexual orientation, marital status, family status, disability, or pardoned criminals. Furthermore, legislation banning hate speech is incorporated into Canada's broadcasting regulation laws. These laws have been invoked on a number of occasions. To take two examples, a newspaper was fined for publishing biblical citations-not the actual text-condemning homosexuality, and a teacher was suspended for writing a letter to the editor contending that homosexuality is not a fixed condition, but something that can be changed over time.

In addition to hate speech laws, legislation that explicitly outlaws Holocaust denial has been adopted by a number of European countries. Germany and Austria are most notable here, but similar laws also exist in France and 11 other countries.

As these examples suggest, many of the hate expression incidents that have reached the level of criminal prosecution or other types of formal action involve statements that are deemed anti-Semitic or pro-Nazi or deny or belittle the Holocaust experience. Muslims in Europe have been known to complain that hate speech codes are applied unfairly, with prosecutions brought in cases of anti-Semitic statements while anti-Muslim remarks are ignored. In fact, the past few years have brought several high-profile cases in which prominent European writers were accused of making statements that slandered Muslims or their faith. A noted French author was the defendant in a case brought by four Muslim organizations for having declared that Islam is the "stupidest religion." He was acquitted; had he been convicted, he faced a sentence of up to eighteen months in prison and a fine of over US$70,000. A similar case has been brought against Oriana Fallaci, the Italian journalist, for a book that, in polemical fashion, criticizes Muslim culture and warns of the dangers of the Islamization of Europe. As Europe becomes more racially diverse, demands for the implementation of hate speech legislation can be expected to increase. Once a state adopts laws regulating speech or expression, it creates an expectation among the public that it will intervene on behalf of groups that regard themselves as aggrieved.

It is true, however, that the initial rationale for Europe's hate speech regimen derives from the continent's experience in World War II, when the Nazis set the stage for genocide through virulent campaigns of demonization that sought to blame the country's troubles on the Jews.

This helps explain the laws that specifically outlaw Holocaust denial, a wedge issue for anti-Semites. Beyond the question of anti-Semitism, hate speech laws are part of a mosaic of agreements and understandings that Europeans have woven together to discourage the rise of the kind of extreme nationalism that led to two catastrophic world wars during the twentieth century. These laws also reflect the European attitude that gives priority to collective rights over individual rights.

... Europeans find incomprehensible American court rulings that permit neo-Nazis to march through Jewish neighborhoods or racist organizations to parade through black districts. European irritation with America's libertarian policies has actually increased with the growth of the internet. Europeans speak of the "commercialization of the First Amendment," by which they mean the circulation of hate speech through the internet for profit. Europeans also complain that most of the hate speech that filters through the internet has its origins in the United States, which prohibits child pornography but not hate material. Indeed, some racist organizations whose principal audience lies in Europe locate their sites in the United States precisely to avoid criminal prosecution by European authorities.

Arch Puddington, *Freedom of Expression after the "Cartoon Wars,"* *in* Freedom of the Press 2006: a global survey of media independence 22–24 (Karin Deutsch Karlekar, ed., 2006).

South Africa adopted its Constitution in 1996, as part of the peaceful transition from a government-imposed system of white supremacy called Apartheid to a representative democracy. Drafters of South Africa's new Constitution consciously surveyed the world's constitutions, picking and choosing the government structures and rights guarantees that best fit with the nation they wanted to create. Similarly, and according to explicit constitutional instruction, South Africa's Constitutional Court looks to foreign and international law when interpreting its rights guarantees, including, in the case that follows, the right to free speech and the exception of hate speech from that guarantee.

THE ISLAMIC UNITY CONVENTION v. THE INDEPENDENT BROADCASTING AUTHORITY

2002 (4) SA 294 (CC) at 34 (S. Afr.)
Constitutional Court of South Africa

LANGA DCJ:

INTRODUCTION

[1]   The applicant, the Islamic Unity Convention, runs a community radio station known as Radio 786 under a broadcasting licence issued to it by the first respondent, the Independent Broadcasting Authority (the IBA). On 8 May 1998 the station broadcast a programme entitled "Zionism and Israel: An in-depth analysis" in which an interview with one Dr Yaqub Zaki, described as an historian and author, was featured. In the interview, Dr Zaki dealt with the historical, political, social and economic factors which, according to him, played a role in the establishment of the state of Israel. He expressed views which, among other things, questioned the legitimacy of the state of Israel and Zionism as a political ideology, asserted that Jewish people were not gassed in concentration camps during the Second World War but died of infectious diseases, particularly typhus and that only a million Jews had died.

[2]   Following the broadcast, fourth respondent, the South African Jewish Board of Deputies (the Board), lodged a formal complaint with the second respondent, the Head: Monitoring and

Complaints Unit, claiming that the material that had been broadcast contravened clause 2(a) of the Code of Conduct for Broadcasting Services (the Code), in that it was "likely to prejudice relations between sections of the population, i.e. Jews and other communities." . . .

. . .

[5] . . . [A]pplicant asked the High Court to grant an order declaring that clause 2(a) of the Code is unconstitutional and therefore invalid because of its inconsistency with the right of freedom of expression in Section 16 of the Constitution. . . .

. . .

The Constitutional Issue

[21] Although the matter has its origins in the complaint by the Board in respect of a specific broadcast, the function of this Court in the present proceedings is to adjudicate on the question of the constitutionality of clause 2(a) of the Code in relation to that complaint as an abstract and objective one. The contents of the particular statement in respect of which the Board complains are not relevant to the enquiry. What the Court is concerned with is whether the provision on which the complaint was based is consistent with the right to freedom of expression in section 16 of the Constitution.

[22] Clause 2(a) provides that-

"Broadcasting licensees shall . . . not broadcast any material which is indecent or obscene or offensive to public morals or offensive to the religious convictions or feelings of any section of a population or likely to prejudice the safety of the State or the public order or relations between sections of the population."

. . .

[24] The complaint was based entirely on the portion of clause 2(a) that refers to material that is "likely to prejudice relations between sections of the population." It is this part of the clause, therefore, that is the relevant portion for the purposes of this judgment. . . .

Freedom of Expression

[25] Section 16 of the Constitution provides as follows:

(1) Everyone has the right to freedom of expression, which includes—

   (a) freedom of the press and other media;

   (b) freedom to receive or impart information or ideas;

(c) freedom of artistic creativity; and

(d) academic freedom and freedom of scientific research.

(2) The right in subsection (1) does not extend to-

(a) propaganda for war;

(b) incitement of imminent violence; or

(c) advocacy of hatred that is based on race, ethnicity, gender or religion, and that constitutes incitement to cause harm.

This Court has held that—

"... freedom of expression is one of a 'web' of mutually supporting rights' in the Constitution. It is closely related to freedom of religion, belief and opinion (s 15), the right to dignity (s 10), as well as the right to freedom of association (s 18), the right to vote and to stand for public office (s 19), and the right to assembly (s 17) ... The rights implicitly recognise the importance, both for a democratic society and for individuals personally, or the ability to form and express opinions, whether individually or collectively, even where those views are controversial."

[citation omitted]

[27]   Notwithstanding the fact that the right to freedom of expression and speech has always been recognised in the South African common law, we have recently emerged from a severely restrictive past where expression, especially political and artistic expression, was extensively circumscribed by various legislative enactments. The restrictions that were placed on expression were not only a denial of democracy itself, but also exacerbated the impact of the systemic violations of other fundamental human rights in South Africa. Those restrictions would be incompatible with South Africa's present commitment to a society based on a "constitutionally protected culture of openness and democracy and universal human rights for South Africans of all ages, classes and colours".

[28]   South Africa is not alone in its recognition of the right to freedom of expression and its importance to a democratic society. The right has been described as "one of the essential foundations of a democratic society; one of the basic conditions for its progress and for the development of every one of its members ..." As such it is protected in almost every international human rights instrument. In *Handyside v The United Kingdom* the European Court of Human Rights pointed out that this approach to the right to freedom of expression is—

"applicable not only to 'information' or 'ideas' that are favourably received or regarded as inoffensive or as a matter of indifference, but also to those that offend, shock or disturb.... Such are the demands of that pluralism, tolerance and broadmindedness without which there is no 'democratic society' ".

[29]   The pluralism and broadmindedness that is central to an open and democratic society can, however, be undermined by speech which seriously threatens democratic pluralism itself. Section 1 of the Constitution declares that South Africa is founded on the values of "human dignity, the achievement of equality and the advancement of human rights and freedoms." Thus, open and democratic societies permit reasonable proscription of activity and expression that pose a real and substantial threat to such values and to the constitutional order itself.

[30]   There is thus recognition of the potential that expression has to impair the exercise and enjoyment of other important rights, such as the right to dignity, as well as other state interests, such as the pursuit of national unity and reconciliation. The right is accordingly not absolute; it is, like other rights, subject to limitation under section 36(1) of the Constitution. Determining its parameters in any given case is therefore important, particularly where its exercise might intersect with other interests. Thus in *Mambolo,* the following was said in the context of the hierarchical relationship between the rights to dignity and freedom of expression:

"With us the right to freedom of expression cannot be said automatically to trump the right to human dignity. The right to dignity is at least as worthy of protection as the right to freedom of expression. How these two rights are to be balanced, in principle and in any particular set of circumstances, is not a question that can or should be addressed here. What is clear though and must be stated, is that freedom of expression does not enjoy superior status in our law." [footnote omitted.]

[31]   Section 16 is in two parts. Subsection (1) is concerned with expression that is protected under the Constitution. It is clear that any limitation of this category of expression must satisfy the requirements of the limitations clause to be constitutionally valid. Subsection (2) deals with expression that is specifically excluded from the protection of the right.

[32]   How is section 16(2) to be interpreted? The words "[t]he right in subsection (1) does not extend to ..." imply that the categories of expression enumerated in section 16(2) are not to be regarded as constitutionally protected speech. Section]6(2) therefore defines the boundaries beyond which the right to freedom of expression does not extend. In that sense, the subsection is definitional. Implicit in its provisions is an acknowledgment that certain

expression does not deserve constitutional protection because, among other things, it has the potential to impinge adversely on the dignity of others and cause harm. Our Constitution is founded on the principles of dignity, equal worth and freedom, and these objectives should be given effect to.

[33] Three categories of expression are enumerated in section 16(2). They are expressed in specific and defined terms. Section 16(2)(a) and (b) are respectively concerned with "propaganda for war" and "incitement of imminent violence". Section 16(2)(c) is directed at what is commonly referred to as hate speech. What is not protected by the Constitution is expression or speech that amounts to "advocacy of hatred" that is based on one or other of the listed grounds, namely race, ethnicity, gender or religion and which amounts to "incitement to cause harm". There is no doubt that the state has a particular interest in regulating this type of expression because of the harm it may pose to the constitutionally mandated objective of building the nonracial and non-sexist society based on human dignity and the achievement of equality. There is accordingly no bar to the enactment of legislation that prohibits such expression. Any regulation of expression that falls within the categories enumerated in section 16(2) would not be a limitation of the right in section 16.

[34] Where the state extends the scope of regulation beyond expression envisaged in section 16(2), it encroaches on the terrain of protected expression and can do so only if such regulation meets the justification criteria in section 36(1) of the Constitution.

[35] The prohibition against the broadcasting of material that is "likely to prejudice relations between sections of the population" self-evidently limits the right in section 16 of the Constitution. The phrase "section of the population" in this part of clause 2(a) is less specific than "race, ethnicity, gender or religion" as spelt out in section 16(2)(a). The prohibition clearly goes beyond the categories of expression enumerated in section 16(2). It does not, for instance, require that the material prohibited should amount to advocacy of hatred, least of all hatred based on race, ethnicity, gender or religion, nor that it should have any potential to cause harm.

[39] ... The Board submitted that if the prohibition against the broadcasting of material "likely to prejudice relations between sections of the population" were given a narrow interpretation, I t is reasonably capable of a meaning which renders it justifiable in terms of section 36(1).

[The Court disagreed that such a narrowing interpretation was plausible]

[45] The Board has submitted that the limitation of the right to freedom of expression may be justifiable in the interests of

human dignity and equality, which are founding values of the Constitution, and national unity, which is an important and legitimate objective. ...

[46]   ... That purpose is undermined by the prohibition in so far as it inhibits the right to "freedom to receive or impart information or ideas."

. . .

[50]   The effect of the limitation in this case is substantial, affecting as it does the right of broadcasters to communicate and that of the public to receive information, views and opinions. Could less restrictive means have been used to achieve the purpose of the regulation in this instance? ...

[51]   There is no doubt that the inroads on the right to freedom of expression made by the prohibition on which the complaint is based are far too extensive and outweigh the factors considered by the Board as ameliorating their impact. ... It has [] not been shown that the very real need to protect dignity, equality and the development of national unity could not be adequately served by the enactment of a provision which is appropriately tailored and more narrowly focussed. I find therefore that the relevant portion of clause 2(a) impermissibly limits the right to freedom of expression and is accordingly unconstitutional.

. . .

ORDER

[60]   The following order is accordingly made

. . .

4.   Clause 2(a) of the said Code of Conduct for Broadcasting Services is declared to be inconsistent with section 16 of the Constitution and invalid to the extent that it prohibits the broadcasting of material that is "likely to prejudice relations between sections of the population"; provided that this order does not apply to (i) propaganda for war; (ii) incitement of imminent violence; or (iii) advocacy of hatred that is based o n race, ethnicity, gender or religion, and that constitutes incitement to cause harm.

. . .

Chaskalson CJ, Ackermann J, Kriegler J, Madala J, Mokgoro J, O'Regan J, Sachs J, Yacoob J, Du Plessis AJ and Skweyiya AJ concur in the judgment of Langa DCJ.

In the following decision, the Broadcasting Complaints Commission of South Africa applied the free speech standards articulated by the Constitutional Court in *Islamic Unity Convention* in ruling on a complaint alleging that a subsequent broadcast contained hate speech.

TAM v. SABC3

Case No: 2004/15 (BCCSA) Broadcasting Complaints Commission, South Africa
http://www.bccsa.co.za/templates/judgement_template_225.asp

Tribunal: Prof Kobus van Rooyen SC(Chairperson),Prof Ravi Nayagar (Viewer Listener Representative),Dr Linda Venter (Co–Opted member)

For Complainant: Dr Tam in person

For Respondent: Mr Fakir Hassen, Manager: Broadcast Compliance, Policy and Mrs Dorothy van Tonder, Consultant, Regulatory Affairs, SABC.

. . .

JUDGMENT JCW VAN ROOYEN (Chairperson)

[1]   The issue in this matter is whether the reference to a Chinese person as a "Chinaman" amounts to hate speech. On SABC3, during a regular overnight TV feed from BBC World, a sports presenter from an independent (non-BBC) production house was heard to comment that a Chinese person, who was taking part in a golf tournament, was the first "Chinaman" to have taken part in such an international golfing event. The comment was not made by a BBC presenter.

[2]   Dr Tam, a South Africa citizen of Chinese descent, argued that the term was extremely derogatory and that the broadcast amounted to hate speech based on race. The SABC argued that the use of the term was not attributable to the SABC, since it had no control over the content of the BBC programme and, in fact, the person who had uttered the word was not a BBC presenter either.

[3]   The question is whether the material, judged within context, amounted to the advocacy of hatred based on race, ethnicity, gender or religion and that constituted incitement to cause harm. Our approach to derogatory racial terms has been a strict one. Racial peace in this country, where racial oppression and superiority were part of the Apartheid policy and legislation of the past, demands that race should not, in any manner, form the basis of discrimination or be used to insult. In fact, the test for incitement is that even if the person addressed did not hear the derogatory word, the language nevertheless amounts to incitement if the words were directed at him or her. The mere fact that such a word is broadcast, already supports a prima facie case which should be answered by a broadcaster. Where public interest requires that derogatory language be broadcast, for example in news items direct-

ed at informing the public of racial abuse, such broadcasts have been held not to have amounted to a contravention of the Code—see Williams, Snyman, Logie & Others v SABC 54/2003. This approach is based on an instructive judgment of the European Court of Human Rights in Jersild v Denmark (36/1993/431/510), where the Court held that a journalist, Jersild, had been wrongly convicted by Danish Courts for furthering racial hostility by broadcasting an interview with racists. The interview included racially derogatory language of the worst kind—coarse language and terminology that also directly accused immigrants from Africa as intellectually inferior. The Court held that it had been in the public interest to reveal the shocking attitude of the group interviewed and that the public had the right to be informed thereof. Compare Johanessen 1995 South African Journal of Human Rights 123.

[4] In Islamic Unity Convention v Independent Broadcasting Authority and Others the Constitutional Court emphasised that expression should not be allowed to impair the exercise and enjoyment of other important rights, such as the right to dignity, other state interests and the pursuit of national unity and reconciliation. Furthermore, on other occasions, it has been emphasised by the Constitutional Court that the protection of the rights of minorities is an integral part of our new democracy. The fact that such a minority is constituted by a small group is irrelevant. It is entitled to equal protection in terms of the Constitution. Compare Christian Education South Africa v Minister of Education Prince v President Cape Law Society, and Others where the majority states: "The fact that they are a very small group within the larger South African community [the Court was referring to members of the Rastafarian religion] is no reason to deprive them of the protection to which they are entitled under the Bill of Rights. On the contrary their vulnerability as a small and marginalised group means that the Bill of Rights has particular significance for them. The interest protected [in that case by s 15(1) and s 31 of the Constitution] is 'not a statistical one dependent on a counter-balancing of numbers, but a qualitative one based on respect for diversity'."

[5] I have referred to these judgments, not to equate the Chinese community with any marginalised group, which it is not, but to accentuate the importance of the recognition of diversity and the protection of a minority in the pursuit of national unity and reconciliation. The dignity and vulnerability of members of any minority must, at all times, be protected against derogatory language. This principle is, of course, also applicable to a majority. Inherent in dignity also lies the right to security of the person. Security of the person is explicitly protected by section 14 of the Bill of Rights, where the right to privacy is stated to include "to be free from all forms of violence from either public or private

sources." This would include derogatory language, which could be defined as a form of verbal violence. In our judgment in South African Human Rights Commission v SABC we held that "harm" in the hate speech provision is a subjective requirement and that the likely emotional harm should be serious. The "harm" in the hate speech provision includes harm to dignity.

[6]   The evidence before us is that the term "Chinaman" is a seriously derogatory term—comparable to the word "kaffir", which is utterly unacceptable–base on race and that, in the circumstances, there was no justification for the use of the word. It amounted to hate speech within the definition and although the "advocacy" was not explicit and pronounced, the mere reference to a person as a "Chinaman" amounts to hate speech as a result of its likely serious impact on the dignity of a Chinese person. Of course, there would be circumstances where the term would not be derogatory as a result of the context. There was nothing in the broadcast which suggested that the term was contextually used otherwise than in its derogatory sense. Whether the person who used it knew that it was derogatory is unknown. Nevertheless, objectively it is derogatory and is not the kind of language which should be used in broadcasts, unless the broadcast is in the public interest or the word is dramatically or documentarily justified.

[7]   We accordingly hold that the term amounted to hate speech. The question is, however, whether the SABC should be held responsible for this hate speech. Is it not too far removed from its sphere of control? The term was used by an independent presenter commenting on the BBC about the unique event. In the circumstances we have decided that it would be unfair to hold the SABC responsible for what had been said by an outsider on a BBC broadcast. ... A written apology was extended by the BBC via the SABC to the complainant. The complainant was not happy with the letter since it had not been signed. The SABC's representative undertook to obtain the signed apology and send it to the Complainant. The complaint is not upheld. The Registrar is directed to ensure that the CEO's of all the broadcasters under our jurisdiction are informed of the derogatory nature of the term involved. JCW van Rooyen SC Chairperson The Commissioners on the Tribunal concurred 7 June 2004.

Notes and Questions

1.   What explains the outlier position of the U.S. with respect to the constitutional protection of hate speech? What is the result as communications become increasingly rapid and global? Will the permissive U.S. position win out as hate speech protected domestically seeps outside its borders, or might another result obtain? Consider the proposals in the following strategy piece aimed at EU members.

With respect to racism and xenophobia, one of the specific challenges arises from the fundamental clash between the U.S. and Europe. . . .

. . .

It is not long ago that, *de facto*, the Internet was escaping from any anti-racist regulation. The hate sites, for the most part hosted in the U.S., were considered as unreachable and the general policy was to put up with the situation. . . .

At the same time, European authorities, as well as national governments and NGOs fighting racism and discrimination have been confronted with the dramatic growth of the hate business online. . . .

. . .

National States have accordingly tried to apply their own legislations to the Internet, upon the principle "what is illegal off-line is illegal online". Then again, there is a huge gap between the national scope of States' sovereignty and the universality of cyber-space where national borders have been until now of little relevance. In this respect, the *Yahoo! case* is a major instance. In 2000, a French judge ordered Yahoo! Inc. to take all appropriate measures in order to prevent people located on the French territory from accessing its auction sales of Nazi paraphernalia and, more broadly, from accessing any pro-Nazi site hosted on its servers (mainly, on *Geocities*). In November 2001, at the request of Yahoo! Inc., a U.S. federal District Court declared that the First Amendment precludes enforcement within the U.S. of the French ruling. . . . When considering the *Yahoo! case*, it is quite patent that the coexistence of conflicting forums leads to a legal chaos and a jurisdiction dead-end. . . .

. . .

A logical way to escape this jurisdiction dead-end would be to agree on international standards regarding racist and xenophobic speech. As a matter of fact, international law provides such standards. . . .

However, these international provisions do not bind the United States of America, which have consistently made constitutional reservations regarding the obligation to outlaw racist speech. . . .

A last solution is to ask the Internet Services Providers (ISPs) to self-regulate racist and xenophobic material posted on-line or to co-regulate such content in collaboration with public authorities. . . .

The combination of the E.U. Directive provisions, on the one hand, [which immunize ISPs from liability if they remove offensive content once they receive notice] and the U.S. "Good Samaritan" provision, on the other hand, [which immunizes ISPs whether they choose to remove or retain offensive content] allows the Europeans to play behind the back of the Constitution of the United States of America. It strongly incites U.S. based ISPs operating internationally to apply an anti-hate speech policy consistent with the standards of international law.

Up to now, we have seen that the e-commerce Directive induces two strategies for the Member States to get rid of racist material online: either, they ask the European-based access providers to filter the illegal content, or they manage to convince the U.S.-based hosting provider to remove the illegal content from the Net altogether.

But there is a third possible strategy, which consists neither to block access nor to urge for a take down but to target and to pressure the search engines (like Google, Altavista, *etc.*). [T]his strategy seems quite straightforward to implement, as there are only a handful of powerful search engines in use amongst Internet surfers around the world, and especially in Europe. Therefore, search engines are increasingly becoming the key-players in the regulation of illegal content online.

A report from the Berkman Center for Internet and Society of Harvard University, released on October 24, 2002, shows that the famous California based company Google has *quietly* excluded 65 sites from listings available at Google.de. and 113 from listings available at Google.fr. Most of these sites are anti-Semitic, pro-Nazi or related to white supremacy (e.g. *stormfront.org*). It has also been banned *"Jesus-is-lord.com"*, a fundamentalist Christian site that is adamantly opposed to abortion. In a press interview, Google spokesman, Nate Tyler, said: *"To avoid legal liability, we removed sites from Google.de search results pages that may conflict with German law"*. He indicated that each site that was de-listed came after a specific complaint from a foreign government, but he refused to hand down a list of the targeted websites.

Isabelle Rorive, *Strategies to Tackle Racism and Xenophobia on the Internet—Where are We in Europe?*, 7 Int'l J. Comm. L. & Pol'y 1–9 (2002/2003).

2. Why do "Europeans find incomprehensible American court rulings that permit neo-Nazis to march through Jewish neighborhoods or racist organizations to parade through black districts"? How do they respond to the free speech justifications offered by the U.S. Supreme Court for these results? Why does U.S. law permit criminalization of child pornography but not hate material? Why don't Europeans (or others) see the same distinction?

3. South Africa and the United States share histories of institutionalized racism, yet they adopt different positions with respect to the constitutionality of criminalizing hate speech: the South African Constitution explicitly excepts it from free speech clause protection while the U.S. jurisprudence categorizes it as protected speech. What ex-

plains the difference? Despite the different constitutional text, do you see elements of U.S. constitutional jurisprudence in the South African Constitutional Court's opinion in *Islamic Unity Convention?*

4.   U.S. jurisprudence permits the government to criminalize hate speech undertaken "with an intent to intimidate." *Virginia v. Black,* 538 U.S. 343 (2003). How different is this standard than the "incitement to cause harm" that the South African Constitution requires? Why it is that the single reference to a golfer as a "Chinaman" constitutes prohibitable hate speech in the judgment of the South African Broadcasting Complaints Commission, but an extended interview with racists mouthing "derogatory language of the worst kind" does not? How is it that the single reference meets the twin requirements that it constitute "advocacy of hatred" and "incitement to cause harm?" Is an apology an appropriate remedy for hate speech or is something different required? Consider the following.

> Within the category of civility, . . ., it is important to [distinguish] between rules that require what can be called the outward show of respect and rules that call for the sincere acknowledgment of the equality of others. . . . The stuff of the outward show of respect is direct interaction between two individuals, the deployment of polite forms of address (such as "Sir," "Madam," "Your Grace," or "Your Majesty"), polite inquiries (such as "How are you?" and "How are [various members of your family]?"), polite formulas attached to the exchange of goods or services ("Thank you," "much obliged," or "your servant"), and polite deportment. . . .
>
> The show of respect is, indeed, a realm of socially sanctioned lying: One is being most polite when one disguises one's actual lack of respect for another. . . .
>
> . . . The world of the show of respect, . . ., is a world purely of ceremony, not of substance. The use of the apology as a remedy also reflects the character of the outward show of respect as involving interaction between two individuals. Because the victim of a failure to show respect has been insulted by one person, the wound to that victim's subjective sense of dignity can ordinarily be salved by an individual apology.
>
> . . .
>
> Unlike rules guaranteeing the outward show of respect, rules requiring the sincere acknowledgment of the equality of others do not necessarily involve direct interaction between individuals at all. On the contrary, it is a striking fact that it may violate those rules to tell an ethnic joke even when no individual who is a target of the joke is present at all. There is a reason for this: While the outward show of respect aims to create or affirm a ritual relationship of respect between two individuals, the sincere acknowledgment of the equality of others aims to create or affirm a deeper dignitary structure for society at large. This contrast is manifested in the sort of remedy called for by a breach of rules requiring the sincere acknowledgment of the equality of others. Because the

victim of an ethnic slur has been confronted by a larger social pattern of disrespect, an individual apology will typically do little to restore his or her subjective sense of dignity. It is small comfort to the victim to hear what may seem a "merely polite" or hypocritical disavowal of prejudiced views. On the contrary, the victim tends to wish that the joke-teller would undergo some sort of transformation of inner state of mind—some experience of conversion or reeducation. This highlights a revealing, and very large, contrast between these two kinds of rules. While a kind of hypocrisy is in the spirit of the outward show of respect, the drive of rules requiring the sincere acknowledgment of the equality of others is precisely to root out hypocrisy. Substance, and not ceremony, does matter here. Indeed, one of the most deeply felt injuries of those who complain about the absence of a social commitment to dignity equality is the injury occasioned by hypocritical shows of tolerance. (This suggests that advocates of the apology as a remedy for offensive hate speech, . . . have not fully considered the underlying phenomenology of the kind of disrespect involved.)

Whitman, *supra* p. 43, at 1290.

IV. SEX SPEECH

The United States and Canada share a common English heritage with respect to criminalization of obscenity, which looked to the "corruption of public morals" as the justification for suppression. A more modern justification asserted in both U.S. and Canadian courts, is that the harm caused to women by degrading sex speech justifies government regulation. The Seventh Circuit Court of Appeals in *American Booksellers Ass'n v. Hudnut*, 771 F.2d 323 (7th Cir. 1985) rejected this justification in striking down an Indianapolis anti-pornography ordinance, and the U.S. Supreme Court affirmed. *Hudnut v. American Booksellers Association*, 475 U.S. 1001 (1986). The Canadian Supreme Court addresses this justification in considering the constitutionality of criminalizing various forms of sex speech in the case below.

R. v. BUTLER

[1992] 1 S.C.R. 452 (Can.)
Supreme Court of Canada

[The accused owned a shop selling and renting "hard core" video-tapes and magazines as well as sexual paraphernalia. He was charged with various counts of selling obscene material, possessing obscene material for the purpose of distribution or sale, and exposing obscene material to public view, contrary to s. 159 (now s. 163) of the *Criminal Code*. Section 163(8) of the *Code* provides that "any publication a dominant characteristic of which is the undue exploitation of sex, or of sex and any one or more of ... crime, horror, cruelty and violence, shall be deemed to be obscene". The trial judge concluded that the obscene material was protected by the guarantee of freedom of expression in s. 2(*b*) of the *Canadian Charter of Rights and Freedoms*, and that *prima facie* only those materials which contained scenes involving violence or cruelty intermingled with sexual activity or depicted lack of consent to sexual contact or otherwise could be said to dehumanize men or women in a sexual context were legitimately proscribed under s. 1. He convicted the accused on eight counts relating to eight films and entered acquittals on the remaining charges. The Crown appealed the acquittals. The Court of Appeal, in a majority decision, allowed the appeal and entered convictions with respect to all the counts. The majority concluded that the materials in question fell outside the protection of the *Charter* since they constituted purely physical activity and involved the undue exploitation of sex and the degradation of human sexuality.]

The judgment of Lamer C.J. and La Forest, Sopinka, Cory, McLachlin, Stevenson and Iacobucci was delivered by

Sopinka J.—This appeal calls into question the constitutionality of the obscenity provisions of the *Criminal Code*, R.S.C., 1985, c. C–46, s. 163. They are attacked on the ground that they contravene s. 2(*b*) of the *Canadian Charter of Rights and Freedoms*. The case requires the Court to address one of the most difficult and controversial of contemporary issues, that of determining whether, and to what extent, Parliament may legitimately criminalize obscenity.

Pornography can be usefully divided into three categories: (1) explicit sex with violence, (2) explicit sex without violence but which subjects people to treatment that is degrading or dehumanizing, and (3) explicit sex without violence that is neither degrading nor dehumanizing. Violence in this context includes both actual physical violence and threats of physical violence. Relating these three categories to the terms of s. 163(8) of the *Code*, the first, explicit sex coupled with violence, is expressly mentioned. Sex coupled with crime, horror or cruelty will sometimes involve violence. Cruelty, for instance, will usually do so. But, even in the absence of violence, sex coupled with crime, horror or cruelty may fall within the second category. As for category (3), subject to the exception referred to below, it is not covered.

Some segments of society would consider that all three categories of pornography cause harm to society because they tend to undermine its moral fibre. Others would contend that none of the categories cause harm. Furthermore there is a range of opinion as to what is degrading or dehumanizing. See *Pornography and Prostitution in Canada: Report of the Special Committee on Pornography and Prostitution* (1985) (the Fraser Report), vol. 1, at p. 51. Because this is not a matter that is susceptible of proof in the traditional way and because we do not wish to leave it to the individual tastes of judges, we must have a norm that will serve as an arbiter in determining what amounts to an undue exploitation of sex. That arbiter is the community as a whole.

The courts must determine as best they can what the community would tolerate others being exposed to on the basis of the degree of harm that may flow from such exposure. . . .

In making this determination with respect to the three categories of pornography referred to above, the portrayal of sex coupled with violence will almost always constitute the undue exploitation of sex. Explicit sex which is degrading or dehumanizing may be undue if the risk of harm is substantial. Finally, explicit sex that is not violent and neither degrading nor dehumanizing is generally tolerated in our society and will not qualify as the undue exploitation of sex unless it employs children in its production.

. . .

C. *Does s. 163 Violate s. 2(b) of the Charter?*

. . .

[T]he content of a video movie, the content of a magazine and the imagery of a sexual gadget are all within the freedom of expression.

. . .

In this case, both the purpose and effect of s. 163 are specifically to restrict the communication of certain types of materials based on their content. In my view, there is no doubt that s. 163 seeks to prohibit certain types of expressive activity and thereby infringes s. 2(b) of the *Charter*.

D. *Is s. 163 Justified Under s. 1 of the Charter?*

(a) Prescribed by Law

[The Court finds the limit on speech is prescribed by law.]

. . .

(b) Objective

The respondent argues that there are several pressing and substantial objectives which justify overriding the freedom to distribute obscene materials. Essentially, these objectives are the avoidance of harm resulting from antisocial attitudinal changes that exposure to obscene material causes and the public interest in maintaining a "decent society". On the other hand, the appellant argues that the objective of s. 163 is to have the state act as "moral custodian" in sexual matters and to impose subjective standards of morality.

The obscenity legislation and jurisprudence prior to the enactment of s. 163 were evidently concerned with prohibiting the "immoral influences" of obscene publications and safeguarding the morals of individuals into whose hands such works could fall ... In this sense, its dominant, if not exclusive, purpose was to advance a particular conception of morality. Any deviation from such morality was considered to be inherently undesirable, independently of any harm to society ...

I agree with Twaddle J.A. of the Court of Appeal that this particular objective is no longer defensible in view of the *Charter*. To impose a certain standard of public and sexual morality, solely because it reflects the conventions of a given community, is inimical to the exercise and enjoyment of individual freedoms, which form the basis of our social contract ... The prevention of "dirt for dirt's sake" is not a legitimate objective which would justify the violation of one of the most fundamental freedoms enshrined in the *Charter*.

On the other hand, I cannot agree with the suggestion of the appellant that Parliament does not have the right to legislate on the basis of some fundamental conception of morality for the purposes of safeguarding the values which are integral to a free and democratic society ...

As the respondent and many of the interveners have pointed out, much of the criminal law is based on moral conceptions of right and wrong and the mere fact that a law is grounded in morality does not automatically render it illegitimate. In this regard, criminalizing the proliferation of materials which undermine another basic *Charter* right may indeed be a legitimate objective.

In my view, however, the overriding objective of s. 163 is not moral disapproval but the avoidance of harm to society. In *Towne Cinema*, Dickson C.J. stated, at p. 507:

It is harm to society from undue exploitation that is aimed at by the section, not simply lapses in propriety or good taste.

The harm was described in the following way in the Report on Pornography by the Standing Committee on Justice and Legal Affairs (MacGuigan Report) (1978), at p. 18:4:

The clear and unquestionable danger of this type of material is that it reinforces some unhealthy tendencies in Canadian society. The effect of this type of material is to reinforce male-female stereotypes to the detriment of both sexes. It attempts to make degradation, humiliation, victimization, and violence in human relationships appear normal and acceptable. A society which holds that egalitarianism, non-violence, consensualism, and mutuality are basic to any human interaction, whether sexual or other, is clearly justified in controlling and prohibiting any medium of depiction, description or advocacy which violates these principles.

. . .

This being the objective, is it pressing and substantial? Does the prevention of the harm associated with the dissemination of certain obscene materials constitute a sufficiently pressing and substantial concern to warrant a restriction on the freedom of expression? In this regard, it should be recalled that in *Keegstra*, *supra*, this Court unanimously accepted that the prevention of the influence of hate propaganda on society at large was a legitimate objective.

In reaching the conclusion that legislation proscribing obscenity is a valid objective which justifies some encroachment on the right to freedom of expression, I am persuaded in part that such legislation may be found in most free and democratic societies . . . The advent of the *Charter* did not have the effect of dramatically depriving Parliament of a power which it has historically enjoyed. It is also noteworthy that the criminalization of obscenity was considered to be compatible with the *Canadian Bill of Rights*.

The enactment of the impugned provision is also consistent with Canada's international obligations (*Agreement for the Suppression of the Circulation of Obscene Publications* and the *Convention for the Suppression of the Circulation of and Traffic in Obscene Publications*).

Finally, it should be noted that the burgeoning pornography industry renders the concern even more pressing and substantial than when the impugned provisions were first enacted. I would therefore conclude that the objective of avoiding the harm associated with the dissemination of pornography in this case is sufficiently pressing and substantial to warrant some restriction on full exercise of the right to freedom of expression. The analysis of whether the measure is proportional to the objective must, in my view, be undertaken in light of the conclusion that the objective of the impugned section is valid only in so far as it relates to the harm to society associated with obscene materials. Indeed, the section as interpreted in previous decisions and in these reasons is fully consistent with that objective. The objective of maintaining conventional standards of propriety, independently of any harm to society, is no longer justified in light of the values of individual liberty which underlie the *Charter*. This, then, being the objective of s. 163, which I have found to be pressing and substantial, I must now determine whether the section is rationally connected and proportional to this objective. As outlined above, s. 163(8) criminalizes the exploitation of sex and sex and violence, when, on the basis of the community test, it is undue. The determination of when such exploitation is undue is directly related to the immediacy of a risk of harm to society which is reasonably perceived as arising from its dissemination.

(c) Proportionality

(i) *General*

The proportionality requirement has three aspects:

(1) the existence of a rational connection between the impugned measures and the objective;

(2) minimal impairment of the right or freedom; and

(3) a proper balance between the effects of the limiting measures and the legislative objective.

In assessing whether the proportionality test is met, it is important to keep in mind the nature of expression which has been infringed.

. . .

The objective of the impugned provision is not to inhibit the celebration of human sexuality. However, it cannot be ignored that the realities of the pornography industry are far from the picture which the B.C. Civil Liberties Association would have us paint. Shannon J., in *R. v. Wagner*, *supra*, described the materials more accurately when he observed, at p. 331:

Women, particularly, are deprived of unique human character or identity and are depicted as sexual playthings, hysterically and instantly responsive to male sexual demands. They worship male genitals and their own value depends upon the quality of their genitals and breasts.

In my view, the kind of expression which is sought to be advanced does not stand on an equal footing with other kinds of expression which directly engage the "core" of the freedom of expression values.

This conclusion is further buttressed by the fact that the targeted material is expression which is motivated, in the overwhelming majority of cases, by economic profit. This Court held in *Rocket v. Royal College of Dental Surgeons of Ontario*, [1990] 2 S.C.R. 232, at p. 247, that an economic motive for expression means that restrictions on the expression might "be easier to justify than other infringements".

I will now turn to an examination of the three basic aspects of the proportionality test.

(ii) *Rational Connection*

The message of obscenity which degrades and dehumanizes is analogous to that of hate propaganda. As the Attorney General of Ontario has argued in its factum, obscenity wields the power to wreak social damage in that a significant portion of the population is humiliated by its gross misrepresentations.

Accordingly, the rational link between s. 163 and the objective of Parliament relates to the actual causal relationship between obscenity and the risk of harm to society at large.

. . .

While a direct link between obscenity and harm to society may be difficult, if not impossible, to establish, it is reasonable to presume that exposure to images bears a causal relationship to changes in attitudes and beliefs ... In the face of inconclusive social science evidence, the approach adopted by our Court in *Irwin Toy* is instructive. In that case, the basis for the legislation was that television advertising directed at young children is *per se* manipulative. The Court made it clear, at p. 994, that in choosing its mode of intervention, it is sufficient that Parliament had a reasonable basis.

. . .

... the Court also recognized that the government was afforded a margin of appreciation to form legitimate objectives based on somewhat inconclusive social science evidence.

... Parliament was entitled to have a "reasoned apprehension of harm" resulting from the desensitization of individuals exposed to materials which depict violence, cruelty, and dehumanization in sexual relations.

Accordingly, I am of the view that there is a sufficiently rational link between the criminal sanction, which demonstrates our community's disapproval of the dissemination of materials which potentially victimize women and which restricts the negative influence which such materials have on changes in attitudes and behaviour, and the objective.

(iii) *Minimal Impairment*

In determining whether less intrusive legislation may be imagined, this Court stressed in the *Prostitution Reference, supra,* that it is not necessary that the legislative scheme be the "perfect" scheme, but that it be appropriately tailored in the context of the infringed right (at p. 1138).

. . .

There are several factors which contribute to the finding that the provision minimally impairs the freedom which is infringed.

First, the impugned provision does not proscribe sexually explicit erotica without violence that is not degrading or dehumanizing. It is designed to catch material that creates a risk of harm to society. It might be suggested that proof of actual harm should be required. It is apparent from what I have said above that it is sufficient in this regard for Parliament to have a reasonable basis for concluding that harm will result and this requirement does not demand actual proof of harm.

Second, materials which have scientific, artistic or literary merit are not captured by the provision. As discussed above, the court must be generous in its application of the "artistic defence". For example, in certain cases, materials such as photographs, prints, books and films which may undoubtedly be produced with some motive for economic profit, may nonetheless claim the protection of the *Charter* in so far as their defining characteristic is that of aesthetic expression, and thus represent the artist's attempt at individual fulfilment. The existence of an accompanying economic motive does not, of itself, deprive a work of significance as an example of individual artistic or self-fulfilment.

Third, in considering whether the provision minimally impairs the freedom in question, it is legitimate for the court to take into account Parliament's past abortive attempts to replace the definition with one that is more explicit ... The attempt to provide exhaustive instances of obscenity has been shown to be destined to fail (Bill C–54, 2nd Sess., 33rd Parl.). It seems that the only practicable alternative is to strive towards a more abstract definition of obscenity which is contextually sensitive and responsive to progress in the knowledge and understanding of the phenomenon to which the legislation is directed ...

Fourth, while the discussion in this appeal has been limited to the definition portion of s. 163, I would note that the impugned section, with the possible exception of subs. 1, which is not in issue here, has been held by this Court not to extend its reach to the private use or viewing of obscene materials. ...

Finally, I wish to address the arguments of the interveners, the Canadian Civil Liberties Association and Manitoba Association for Rights and Liberties, that the objectives of this kind of legislation may be met by alternative, less intrusive measures. First, it is submitted that reasonable time, manner and place restrictions would be preferable to outright prohibition. I am of the view that this argument should be rejected. Once it has been established that the objective is the avoidance of harm caused by the degradation which many women feel as "victims" of the message of obscenity, and of the negative impact exposure to such material has on perceptions and attitudes towards women, it is untenable to argue that these harms could be avoided by placing restrictions on access to such material. Making the materials more difficult to obtain by increasing their cost and reducing their availability does not achieve the same objective. Once Parliament has reasonably concluded that certain acts are harmful to certain groups in society and to society in general, it would be inconsistent, if not hypocritical, to argue that such acts could be committed in more restrictive conditions. The harm sought to be avoided would remain the same in either case.

It is also submitted that there are more effective techniques to promote the objectives of Parliament. For example, if pornography is seen as encouraging violence against women, there are certain activities which discourage it—counselling rape victims to charge their assailants, provision of shelter and assistance for battered women, campaigns for laws against discrimination on the grounds of sex, education to increase the sensitivity of law enforcement agencies and other governmental authorities. In addition, it is submitted that education is an under-used response.

It is noteworthy that many of the above suggested alternatives are in the form of responses to the harm engendered by negative attitudes against women. The role of the impugned provision is to control the dissemination of the very images that contribute to such attitudes. Moreover, it is true that there are additional measures which could alleviate the problem of violence against women. However, given the gravity of the harm, and the threat to the values at stake, I do not believe that the measure chosen by Parliament is equalled by the alternatives which have been suggested . . .

(iv) *Balance Between Effects of Limiting Measures and Legislative Objective*

The final question to be answered in the proportionality test is whether the effects of the law so severely trench on a protected right that the legislative objective is outweighed by the infringement. The infringement on freedom of expression is confined to a measure designed to prohibit the distribution of sexually explicit materials accompanied by violence, and those without violence that are degrading or dehumanizing. As I have already concluded, this kind of expression lies far from the core of the guarantee of freedom of expression. It appeals only to the most base aspect of individual fulfilment, and it is primarily economically motivated.

The objective of the legislation, on the other hand, is of fundamental importance in a free and democratic society. It is aimed at avoiding harm, which Parliament has reasonably concluded will be caused directly or indirectly, to individuals, groups such as women and children, and consequently to society as a whole, by the distribution of these materials. It thus seeks to enhance respect for all members of society, and non-violence and equality in their relations with each other.

I therefore conclude that the restriction on freedom of expression does not outweigh the importance of the legislative objective.

* * *

The Convention on Cybercrime is an international treaty, which seeks to harmonize national laws and coordinate enforcement mechanisms for cybercrime and Internet crimes. It was drafted by the Council of Europe, with participation from its observer states Canada, Japan and the United States. More than 45 countries have signed the convention. The U.S. Senate ratified it in August 2006 and it entered into force on January 1, 2007. The Convention does not address obscenity or adult pornography, and addresses racist speech in a protocol, which the United States did not sign. The Convention provides as follows with respect to child pornography:

Article 9: Offences related to child pornography

1.   Each Party shall adopt such legislative and other measures as may be necessary to establish as criminal offences under its domestic law, when committed intentionally and without right, the following conduct:

> a.   producing child pornography for the purpose of its distribution through a computer system;
>
> b.   offering or making available child pornography through a computer system;
>
> c.   distributing or transmitting child pornography through a computer system;
>
> d.   procuring child pornography through a computer system for oneself or for another person;
>
> e.   possessing child pornography in a computer system or on a computer-data storage medium.

2.   For the purpose of paragraph 1 above, the term "child pornography" shall include pornographic material that visually depicts:

> a.   a minor engaged in sexually explicit conduct;
>
> b.   a person appearing to be a minor engaged in sexually explicit conduct;
>
> c.   realistic images representing a minor engaged in sexually explicit conduct.

3.   For the purpose of paragraph 2 above, the term "minor" shall include all persons under 18 years of age. A Party may,

however, require a lower age-limit, which shall be not less than 16 years.

4.   Each Party may reserve the right not to apply, in whole or in part, paragraphs 1, sub-paragraphs d. and e, and 2, sub-paragraphs b. and c.

Council of Europe, Convention on Cybercrime, C.E.T.S. No. 185 (Nov. 23, 2001), available at http://conventions.coe.int/Treaty/EN/Treaties/Html/185.htm.

Notes and Questions

1.   What test does the Canadian Supreme Court apply to determine the ability of government to criminalize sex speech? How does it compare to U.S. constitutional jurisprudence?

2.   The Canadian Supreme Court in *R. v. Butler* rejects the ability of Parliament "[t]o impose a certain standard of public and sexual morality, solely because it reflects the conventions of a given community," but affirms its "right to legislate on the basis of some fundamental conception of morality for the purposes of safeguarding the values which are integral to a free and democratic society." How are these two statements about Parliament's ability to enacts morals legislation consistent?

3.   Compare the Canadian Supreme Court's reasoning with the following summary of the Seventh Circuit's reasoning in *Hudnut*:

> We do not try to balance the arguments for and against an ordinance such as this. The ordinance discriminates on the ground of the content of the speech. Speech treating women in the approved way—in sexual encounters "premised on equality" ... is lawful no matter how sexually explicit. Speech treating women in the disapproved way—as submissive in matters sexual or as enjoying humiliation—is unlawful no matter how significant the literary, artistic, or political qualities of the work taken as a whole. The state may not ordain preferred viewpoints in this way. The Constitution forbids the state to declare one perspective right and silence opponents.

771 F.3d at 325. Trace the different conclusions to their different starting points. What explains the different choices in the paths of reasoning? Is it different constitutional text? Different constitutional ages and histories? Different cultural values? The existence in Canada of a history of parliamentary supremacy?

4.   Review the text of the Cybercrime Treaty, particularly the definition of child pornography that signatory states are directed to criminalize. Can the United States do so consistent with its Constitution's free speech guarantee? Can you guess which provisions might be a result of United States' participation in the Convention's drafting?

V. COMMERCIAL SPEECH

While the U.S. Constitution has been interpreted to protect commercial speech, including advertising, for over three decades, such constitutional restrictions on government's right to regulate generally do not pertain around the world, as the following excerpt explains.

> In the name of constitutionally protected "commercial speech," advertising in the United States operates with very few limitations and minimal government oversight. In Europe, it is different. In 1989, two officials from J. Walter Thompson described the problem of promoting a theoretical low-fat diet candy bar, "Jupiter." A commercial designed for TV use across Europe would emphasize three points: "Your waistline will like it, and you get a free tape measure to prove it"; "It's an after-school treat that won't spoil your evening meal"; and "When your doctor says cut down, reach for Jupiter, with one-third of the calories of other chocolate bars." Here are some of the obstacles the campaign would encounter:
>
> > In Belgium, commercials may not refer to dieting. In France, premiums can't be worth more than one percent of the sale price, which rules out the tape measure, and children can't give endorsements, which means no child eating a Jupiter after school. In West Germany, any comparisons with another candy bar would be illegal; in Denmark, ads can't make nutritional claims; in Britain, candy must be presented as only an occasional snack–and no doctors in the commercial.

Stevenson, *Freedom of the Press Around the World* 24 (quoting Martin Mayer, *Whatever Happened to Madison Avenue? Advertising in the '90s* 204 (1991)). The Parliament of the European Union has issued a number of directives relating to advertising and unfair competition, but these establish minimum consumer protections, and so the laws impacting commercial speech within the member states still vary widely. *See EC Consumer Law Compendium— Comparative Analysis* (Hans Schulte–Nolke, Christain Twigg–Flesner & Martin Ebers, eds., 2008).

The issues with respect to commercial speech, which have been an active part of U.S. constitutional jurisprudence for decades, have entered the case law of other countries more recently, as those subject to advertising restrictions or penalties imposed for acts of allegedly unfair competition increasingly raise free speech claims. Like the U.S. Supreme Court, other national high courts have struggled both to identify commercial speech and articulate the extent to which it is entitled to constitutional protection as compared to other types, such as "core" political speech. As one commentator observes, "[Although t]he European lawyer is not familiar with the notion of commercial speech.... Closer investigation of the European jurisprudence shows ... that [it] has already and increasingly does give the European courts and scholars a splitting headache." Joanna Krzeminska, *Freedom of Commercial Speech in Europe* 1 (2005) (conference paper, European Union Studies Association), available at http://aei.pitt.edu/3043/02/JKrzeminska_EUSA_paper.doc. In the following case, the eighteen judges of European Court of Human Rights divided 9:9 in addressing a claimed violation of the Convention's Article 10 free speech right, which had split the national courts as well.

MARKT INTERN AND BEERMANN v. GERMANY

165 Eur. Ct. H.R. (ser. A) (1989)
European Court of Human Rights

As to the Facts

8. The first applicant, markt intern, is a publishing firm, whose registered office is at Düsseldorf. The second applicant, Mr Klaus Beermann, is its editor-in-chief.

9. Markt intern, which was founded and is run by journalists, seeks to defend the interests of small and medium-sized retail businesses against the competition of large-scale distribution companies, such as supermarkets and mail-order firms. It provides the less powerful members of the retail trade with financial assistance in test cases, lobbies public authorities, political parties and trade associations on their behalf and has, on occasion, made proposals for legislation to the legislature.

However, its principal activity in their support is the publication of a number of bulletins aimed at specialised commercial sectors such as that of chemists and beauty product retailers ... These are weekly news-sheets which provide information on developments in the market and in particular on the commercial practices of large-scale firms and their suppliers. ...

10. On several occasions undertakings which had suffered from the applicants' criticism or their calls for boycotts instituted proceedings against them for infringement of the Unfair Competition Act of 7 June 1909 ...

11. On 20 November 1975 an article by Mr Klaus Beermann appeared in the information bulletin for chemists and beauty product retailers. It described an incident involving an English mail-order firm, Cosmetic Club International ("the Club"), in the following terms:

" 'I ordered the April beauty set ... from Cosmetic Club International and paid for it, but returned it a few days later because I was not satisfied. Although the order-form clearly and expressly stated that I was entitled to return the set if I was dissatisfied, and that I would be reimbursed, I have not yet seen a pfennig. There was also no reaction to my reminder of 18 June, in which I gave them until 26 June to reply.' This is the angry report of Maria Lüchau, a chemist at Celle, concerning the commercial practices of this English Cosmetic Club.

On 4 November we telexed the manager of the Club, Doreen Miller, as follows: 'Is this an isolated incident, or is this part of your official policy?' In its swift answer of the following day, the Club claimed to have no knowledge of the set returned by Mrs Lüchau or of her reminder of June. It promised however to carry out a prompt investigation of the case and to clarify the matter by contacting the chemist in Celle.

Notwithstanding this provisional answer from Ettlingen, we would like to put the following question to all our colleagues in the chemists and beauty product trade: Have you had similar experiences to that of Mrs Lüchau with the Cosmetic Club? Do you know of similar cases? The question of whether or not this incident is an isolated case or one of many is crucial for assessing the Club's policy."

12.   Previously, on 20 September and 18 October 1974 and on 29 October 1975, markt intern had already published articles on the Club and advised retailers and manufacturers to be cautious in their dealings with it because the Club had failed to respect certain dates and promises. On 29 October 1975 markt intern described as correct the Club's statement in a legal pleading that "a change in the attitude of the industry show[ed] that the call for a boycott [had] not failed to make an impression".

[The Hamburg Regional Court ruled in favor of the Club, issuing an injunction prohibiting markt intern from repeating the statements published on 20 November and imposing a fine for disseminating untruthful statements to the Club's commercial disadvantage. The Court of Appeal ruled in favor the applicants, quashing the Regional Court's judgment, reasoning that by publishing its article on 20 November 1975, markt intern had not acted from competitive motives and that the statements were truthful. The Federal Court of Justice set aside the Court of Appeal's judgment and reinstated the injunction and imposition of fines. The Federal Court of Justice based its judgment on a civil code section, according to which: "Any person who in the course of business commits, for purposes of competition, acts contrary to honest practices may be enjoined from further engaging in those acts and held liable in damages." The Federal Constitutional Court dismissed the appeal, reasoning "the requirements which must be satisfied in order for freedom of expression and of the press to override other legal interests protected under statutes of general application are not fulfilled where an item published in the press is intended to promote, in the context of commercial competition, certain economic interests to the detriment of others." The European Commission on Human Rights disagreed with the German Federal Constitutional Court, finding a violation of Article 10 of the Convention and noting the importance of distinguishing "between advertising by competitors on the one hand and information imparted by the press on the other." [cite]].

As to the Law

A. Applicability of Article 10

25. The Government primarily disputed the applicability of Article 10. Before the Court they argued that if the case were examined under that provision, it would fall, by reason of the contents of the publication of 20 November 1975 and the nature of markt intern's activities, at the extreme limit of Article 10's field of application. The wording and the aims of the information bulletin in question showed that it was not intended to influence or mobilise public opinion, but to promote the economic interests of a given group of undertakings. In the Government's view, such action fell within the scope of the freedom to conduct business and engage in competition, which is not protected by the Convention.

. . .

26. The Court recalls that the writer of the article in question reported the dissatisfaction of a consumer who had been unable to obtain the promised reimbursement for a product purchased from a mail-order firm, the Club; it asked for information from its readers as to the commercial practices of that firm. It is clear that the contested article was addressed to a limited circle of tradespeople and did not directly concern the public as a whole; however, it conveyed information of a commercial nature. Such information cannot be excluded from the scope of Article 10 § 1 . . . which does not apply solely to certain types of information or ideas or forms of expression . . .

B. Compliance With Article 10

27. In the Court's view, the applicants clearly suffered an "interference by public authority" in the exercise of the right protected under Article 10, in the form of the injunction issued by the Federal Court of Justice restraining them from repeating the statements appearing in the information bulletin of 20 November 1975. Such an interference infringes the Convention if it does not

satisfy the requirements of paragraph 2 of Article 10. It should therefore be determined whether it was "prescribed by law", whether it pursued one or more of the legitimate aims set out in that paragraph and whether it was "necessary in a democratic society" to achieve such aims.

1.   "Prescribed by law"

[The Court found the interference to be prescribed by law.]

2.   Legitimate aim

31.   ... The Court finds that the interference was intended to protect the reputation and the rights of others, legitimate aims under paragraph 2 of Article 10.

3.   "Necessary in a democratic society"

32.   The applicants argued that the injunction in question could not be regarded as "necessary in a democratic society". The Commission agreed with this view.

The Government, however, disputed it. In their view, the article published on 20 November 1975 did not contribute to a debate of interest to the general public, but was part of an unlawful competitive strategy aimed at ridding the beauty products market of an awkward competitor for specialist retailers. The writer of the article had sought, by adopting aggressive tactics and acting in a way contrary to usual practice, to promote the competitiveness of those retailers. The Federal Court of Justice and the Federal Constitutional Court had ruled in accordance with well established case-law, having first weighed all the interests at stake.

In addition, in the field of competition, States enjoyed a wide discretion in order to take account of the specific situation in the national market and, in this case, the national notion of good faith in business. The statements made "for purposes of competition" fell outside the basic nucleus protected by the freedom of expression and received a lower level of protection than other "ideas" or "information".

33.   The Court has consistently held that the Contracting States have a certain margin of appreciation in assessing the existence and extent of the necessity of an interference, but this margin is subject to a European supervision as regards both the legislation and the decisions applying it, ... Such a margin of appreciation is essential in commercial matters and, in particular, in an area as complex and fluctuating as that of unfair competition. Otherwise, the European Court of Human Rights would have to undertake a re-examination of the facts and all the circumstances of each case. The Court must confine its review to the question

whether the measures taken on the national level are justifiable in principle and proportionate . . .

34.   In this case, in order to establish whether the interference was proportionate it is necessary to weigh the requirements of the protection of the reputation and the rights of others against the publication of the information in question . . .

Markt intern published several articles on the Club criticising its business practices and these articles, including that of 20 November 1975, were not without a certain effect (see paragraph 12 above). On the other hand, the Club honoured its promises to reimburse dissatisfied customers and, in 1975, 11,870 of them were reimbursed (see paragraph 20 above).

The national courts did weigh the competing interests at stake. . . .

35.   In a market economy an undertaking which seeks to set up a business inevitably exposes itself to close scrutiny of its practices by its competitors. Its commercial strategy and the manner in which it honours its commitments may give rise to criticism on the part of consumers and the specialised press. In order to carry out this task, the specialised press must be able to disclose facts which could be of interest to its readers and thereby contribute to the openness of business activities.

However, even the publication of items which are true and describe real events may under certain circumstances be prohibited: the obligation to respect the privacy of others or the duty to respect the confidentiality of certain commercial information are examples. In addition, a correct statement can be and often is qualified by additional remarks, by value judgments, by suppositions or even insinuations. It must also be recognised that an isolated incident may deserve closer scrutiny before being made public; otherwise an accurate description of one such incident can give the false impression that the incident is evidence of a general practice. All these factors can legitimately contribute to the assessment of statements made in a commercial context, and it is primarily for the national courts to decide which statements are permissible and which are not.

36.   In the present case, the article was written in a commercial context; markt intern was not itself a competitor in relation to the Club but it intended—legitimately—to protect the interests of chemists and beauty product retailers. The article itself undoubtedly contained some true statements, but it also expressed doubts about the reliability of the Club, and it asked the readers to report "similar experiences" at a moment when the Club had promised to carry out a prompt investigation of the one reported case.

. . .

37. In the light of these findings and having regard to the duties and responsibilities attaching to the freedoms guaranteed by Article 10, it cannot be said that the final decision of the Federal Court of Justice—confirmed from the constitutional point of view by the Federal Constitutional Court—went beyond the margin of appreciation left to the national authorities. It is obvious that opinions may differ as to whether the Federal Court's reaction was appropriate or whether the statements made in the specific case by markt intern should be permitted or tolerated. However, the European Court of Human Rights should not substitute its own evaluation for that of the national courts in the instant case, where those courts, on reasonable grounds, had considered the restrictions to be necessary.

38. Having regard to the foregoing, the Court reaches the conclusion that no breach of Article 10 has been established in the circumstances of the present case.

For These Reasons, The Court

Holds, by nine votes to nine, with the casting vote of the President (Rule 20 § 3 of the Rules of Court), that there has been no violation of Article 10 (art. 10) of the Convention.

... JOINT DISSENTING OPINION OF JUDGES GÖLCÜKLÜ, PETTITI, RUSSO, SPIELMANN, DE MEYER, CARRILLO SALCEDO AND VALTICOS

I.

In the field of human rights, it is the exceptions, and not the principles, which "[are] to be interpreted narrowly."

This proposition is especially true in relation to the freedom of expression.

In any event, in the light of the criteria which the Court has applied hitherto, the "necessity" of the measures taken against the applicants was not "convincingly established."

It is just as important to guarantee the freedom of expression in relation to the practices of a commercial undertaking as it is in relation to the conduct of a head of government, . . .

The fact that a person defends a given interest, whether it is an economic interest or any other interest, does not, moreover, deprive him of the benefit of freedom of expression.

In order to ensure the openness of business activities, it must be possible to disseminate freely information and ideas concerning the products and services proposed to consumers. Consumers, who are exposed to highly effective distribution techniques and to advertising which is frequently less than objective, deserve, for their part too, to be protected, as indeed do retailers.

In this case, the applicants had related an incident which in fact occurred, as has not been contested, and requested retailers to supply them with additional information. They had exercised in an entirely normal manner their basic right to freedom of expression.

This right was, therefore, violated in their regard by the contested measures.

II.

Having said this, we consider it necessary to make three further observations in relation to the present judgment.

We find the reasoning set out therein with regard to the "margin of appreciation" of States a cause for serious concern. As is shown by the result to which it leads in this case, it has the effect in practice of considerably restricting the freedom of expression in commercial matters.

By claiming that it does not wish to undertake a re-examination of the facts and all the circumstances of the case, the Court is in fact eschewing the task, which falls to it under the Convention, of carrying out "European supervision" as to the conformity of the contested "measures" "with the requirements" of that instrument.

On the question of the need to "weigh the competing interests at stake", it is sufficient to note that in this case the interests which the applicants sought "legitimately" to protect were not taken into consideration at all.

INDIVIDUAL DISSENTING OPINION OF JUDGE PETTITI

In addition to the observations put forward in the joint dissenting opinion, I wish to make the following comments.

Freedom of expression is the mainstay of the defence of fundamental rights. Without freedom of expression, it is impossible to discover the violation of other rights.

In this field the States have only a slight margin of appreciation, which is subject to review by the European Court. Only in rare cases can censorship or prohibition of publication be accepted. This has been the prevailing view in the American and European systems since 1776 and 1789 (cf. First Amendment, United States Constitution; case-law of the supreme courts of the United States, Canada, France, etc.).

This is particularly true in relation to commercial advertising or questions of commercial or economic policy, in respect of which the State cannot claim to defend the general interest because the interests of consumers are conflicting. In fact, by seeking to support pressure groups—such as laboratories—the State is defending a specific interest. It uses the pretext of a law on competition or on prices to give precedence to one group over another. The protection of the interests of users and consumers in the face of dominant positions depends on the freedom to publish even the harshest criticism of products. Freedom must be total or almost total, except where an offence is committed (for example misleading advertising) or where an action is brought for unfair competition, but in those circumstances the solution is not censorship but criminal prosecution or civil proceedings between the undertakings. The arsenal of laws caters for the punishment of misleading advertising.

. . .

The problem is all the more serious because often the States which seek to restrict the freedom use the pretext of economic infringements or breaches of economic legislation such as anti-competition or anti-trust provisions to institute proceedings for political motives or to protect "mixed" interests (State—industrial) in order to erect a barrier to the freedom of expression (the Eastern block countries provide numerous examples, but the States of the Council of Europe follow this practice too). The economic pressure which groups or laboratories can exert should not be underestimated. In certain cases this pressure has been such that it has delayed the establishment of the truth and therefore put back the prohibition of a medicine or substance dangerous for the public health.

The economic press of numerous member States publishes each day articles, millions of copies of which are circulated, containing criticism of products in terms a hundred times stronger than those in question in the markt intern case. It is this freedom accorded to that press which ensures the protection of the public at large.

DISSENTING OPINION OF JUDGE MARTENS,
APPROVED BY JUDGE MACDONALD

1. I am entirely convinced of the correctness of the Court's view that the contested article published by markt intern is in principle protected by the freedom of expression secured under Article 10 (art. 10) of the Convention. The socio-economic press is just as important as the political and cultural press for the progress of our modern societies and for the development of every man. . . .

3. The Federal Court takes the view that the question whether the contested article published by markt intern was acceptable is to be classified under the law on unfair competition and it is this classification, and the assessments inferred therefrom, which the European Court has endorsed . . . In so doing, the European Court has subscribed to an approach which, in my view, is incompatible

with the right to the freedom of expression, which the Convention also guarantees to a partisan press organ.

4.   The law on unfair competition governs the relationships between competitors on the market. It is based on the assumption that in engaging in competition the competitors seek only to serve their own interests, while attempting to harm those of others. That is why (as the Federal Court notes in its judgment) the German law on unfair competition prohibits persons from engaging in competition by making denigrating statements about their competitors. It is permissible for a competitor to criticise another publicly only if he has sufficient reasons for so doing and if the nature and scope of his criticism remain within the limits required by the situation. In this field, the prohibition on publishing criticism is therefore the norm and it falls to the person who takes the risk of publishing such criticism to show that there were sufficient grounds for his criticism and that it remains within the strictest limits. In considering whether this proof has been furnished, the court weighs up only the interests of the two competitors.

In the field of freedom of expression the converse is true. In this field the basic assumption is that this right is used to serve the general interest, in particular as far as the press is concerned, and that is why in this context the freedom to criticise is the norm. Thus in this field it falls to the person who alleges that the criticism is not acceptable to prove that his claim is well-founded. In determining whether he has done so, the court must weigh up the general interest, on the one hand, and the individual interests of the party who claims to have been injured, on the other.

5.   It follows that to classify under the law on unfair competition the question whether an article published by an organ of the press is acceptable is to place that organ of the press in a legal position which is fundamentally different from that to which it is entitled under Article 10 of the Convention and one which is clearly unfavourable to it. That is why, in my view, for that organ of press, such a classification constitutes a considerable restriction on the exercise of the freedoms guaranteed to it under Article 10. It should therefore be asked whether it can be necessary in a democratic society to restrict the rights and fundamental freedoms of an organ of the press in this way solely because that organ has espoused the cause of specific economic interests, namely those of a particular sector of a specialised trade. I am in no doubt that this question must be answered in the negative. This is clear from the fact that, as far as I know, such a rule extending the scope of the law on unfair competition to the detriment of freedom of the press is unknown in the other member States of the Council of Europe, and rightly so because, in certain respects, all newspapers may be

regarded as partisan, having espoused the cause of certain specific interests.

6.   In my view, it follows from the foregoing that the Court ought to have considered that in this instance it had to examine a case in which the assessment of the national authorities suffered from a fundamental defect and that, accordingly, it ought itself to have determined whether the interference was necessary in a democratic society . . .

7.   In my view—and here too I find myself in agreement with the joint dissenting opinion—it is necessary to ask whether it was established convincingly . . . that the private interests of the Club were more important than the general interest, in accordance with which not only the specialised reader but also the public as a whole should have been able to acquaint themselves with facts having a certain importance in the context of the struggle of small and medium-sized retail undertakings against the large-scale distribution companies. In answering this question, I, like the authors of the joint dissenting opinion, reach the conclusion that the reply must be negative. Like the Court . . . , I take into account the fact that in a market economy an undertaking which seeks to set up a business inevitably exposes itself to close scrutiny of its practices. That is why the Club, which was in that situation, cannot in principle complain that the specialised press, which has given itself the task of defending the interests of its competitors on that market, analyses its commercial strategy and publishes its criticisms thereof. Such criticism contributes, as the Court stressed, to the openness of business activities. Since the freedom of expression also applies to "statements" which hurt, care should be taken not to find such criticism unacceptable too quickly simply because it harms the undertaking criticised. In this instance, it cannot be denied that the article published by markt intern is unfavourable to the Club and reveals a very critical attitude in the latter's regard. On the other hand, it reported an incident which, as has not been contested, in fact occurred and it did not purport to offer a definitive assessment of the Club's commercial practices, but invited retailers to supply additional information. For my part, I am not convinced that it is truly necessary to prohibit such an article in a democratic society.

8.   It is for the above reasons that I voted in favour of finding a violation of Article 10.

Notes and Questions

1.   How does the European Court of Human Rights define commercial speech? Why is the article at issue commercial speech? What test does the European Court of Human Rights apply to determine

whether the German law's restriction of commercial speech comports with Article 10's free speech guarantee? Is it the same test that applies to other forms of speech? If not, what is different?

2.   Compare the reasoning of the joint dissenting opinion with that of the majority. Do the joint dissenters agree that statements made "for the purposes of competition" fall outside the basic nucleus of free speech protection and should receive less protection than other types of speech? Would the joint dissenters follow the same multi-part test set out by the majority? If so, why would the dissenters come out differently?

3.   Consider the specific points Judge Pettiti makes in his dissent. What does he imply about the degree of free speech protection commercial speech should receive vis-a-vis other types of speech? Why does he say that censorship is particularly dangerous in the context of commercial speech?

4.   What is the fundamental error in the analysis of the German courts that Judges Martens and MacDonald identify in their dissent? According to these judges, how do the assumptions and analyses in the law of unfair competition and the field of freedom of expression differ? How would these judges apply Article 10's multi-part test?

VI.   ELECTIONS, POLITICAL SPEECH AND FREEDOM OF ASSEMBLY

Although adhering to the values of pluralism and democratic self-determination, many modern constitutional democracies tolerate limits on elections, political speech and assembly that would likely violate the United States Constitution.

A.   CONTRIBUTION AND SPENDING LIMITS

All democracies impose some limits on the election process to achieve the goals of fairness and undermining the reality and perception of official corruption. In the following decision, the Canadian Supreme Court reviews the constitutionality of provisions of the Canada Elections Act 2000, which limit third party election advertising to $3,000 per electoral district and $150,000 nationally, and ban third party advertising entirely on election day.

HARPER v. CANADA (ATTORNEY GENERAL)
[2004] 1 S.C.R. 827
Supreme Court of Canada

Per Iacobucci, Bastarache, Arbour, LeBel, Deschamps and Fish JJ.:

. . . In promoting the equal dissemination of points of view by limiting the election advertising of third parties who are influential participants in the electoral process, the overarching objective of the spending limits is electoral fairness. This egalitarian model of elections seeks to create a level playing field for those who wish to engage in the electoral discourse, enabling voters to be better informed. . . .

The limits on third party election advertising expenses set out in s. 350 infringe the right to freedom of political expression guaranteed by s. 2(*b*) of the *Charter* but they do not infringe the right to vote protected by s. 3. The right to meaningful partic- ipation in s. 3 of the *Charter* cannot be equated with the exercise of freedom of expression. The two rights are distinct and must be reconciled. Under s. 3, the right of meaningful participation in the electoral process is not limited to the selection of elected represen- tatives and includes a citizen's right to exercise his or her vote in an informed manner. In the absence of spending limits, it is possible for the affluent or a number of persons pooling their resources and acting in concert to dominate the political discourse, depriving their opponents of a reasonable opportunity to speak and be heard, and undermining the voter's ability to be adequately informed of all views. Equality in the political discourse is thus necessary for meaningful participation in the electoral process and ultimately enhances the right to vote. This right, therefore, does not guarantee unimpeded and unlimited electoral debate or expres- sion. Spending limits, however, must be carefully tailored to ensure that candidates, political parties and third parties are able to convey their information to the voter; if overly restrictive, they may undermine the informational component of the right to vote. Here, s. 350 does not interfere with the right of each citizen to play a meaningful role in the electoral process.

The harm that Parliament seeks to address in this case is electoral unfairness. Given the difficulties in measuring this harm, at the stage of the justification analysis a reasoned apprehension that the absence of third party election advertising limits will lead to electoral unfairness is sufficient. Furthermore, on balance, the contextual factors favour a deferential approach to Parliament in determining whether such limits are demonstrably justified in a free and democratic society. While the right to political expression lies at the core of the guarantee of free expression and warrants a high degree of constitutional protection, there is nevertheless a danger that political advertising may manipulate or oppress the voter. Parliament had to balance the rights and privileges of all the participants in the electoral process. The difficulties of striking this balance are evident and, given the right of Parliament to choose Canada's electoral model and the nuances inherent in implement- ing this model, a court must approach the justification analysis with deference.

Section 350 is justified under s. 1 of the *Charter*. While the overarching objective of the third party advertising expense limits is electoral fairness, more narrowly characterized, the objectives of the scheme are threefold: (1) to promote equality in the political discourse; (2) to protect the integrity of the financing regime applicable to candidates and parties; and (3) to ensure that voters have confidence in the electoral process. In view of the findings of the Lortie Commission, the central piece of the evidential record in this case, these three objectives are pressing and substantial. Section 350 also meets the proportionality test. First, the third party advertising expense limits are rationally connected to the objectives. They prevent those who have access to significant financial resources, and are able to purchase unlimited amount of advertising, to dominate the electoral discourse to the detriment of others; they create a balance between the financial resources of each candidate or political party; and they advance the perception that the electoral process is substantively fair as it provides for a reasonable degree of equality between citizens who wish to participate in that process. Second, s. 350 minimally impairs the right to free expression. Third party advertising is unrestricted prior to the commencement of the election period, and third parties may freely spend money or advertise to make their views known or to persuade others. Further, the definition of "election advertising" in s. 319 only applies to advertising that is associated with a candidate or party. The limits set out in s. 350 allow third parties to inform the electorate of their message in a manner that will not overwhelm candidates, political parties or other third parties while precluding the voices of the wealthy from dominating the political discourse. Third, the s. 350's salutary effects of promoting fairness and accessibility in the electoral system and increasing Canadians' confidence in it outweigh the deleterious effect that the spending limits permit third parties to engage in informational but not necessarily persuasive campaigns.

. . . *Per* McLachlin C.J. and Major and Binnie JJ. (dissenting in part): The third party advertising spending limits in s. 350 of the *Canada Elections Act* are inconsistent with the s. 2(*b*) *Charter* guarantees and, hence, invalid. The effect of third party limits for spending on advertising is to prevent citizens from effectively communicating their views on issues during an election campaign. The denial of effective communication to citizens violates free expression where it warrants the greatest protection—the sphere of political discourse. Section 350 puts effective radio and television communication beyond the reach of "third party" citizens, preventing citizens from effectively communicating their views on election issues, and restricting them to minor local communication. Effective expression of ideas thus becomes the exclusive right of registered political parties and their candidates.

Because citizens cannot mount effective national television, radio and print campaigns, the only sustained messages voters see and hear during the course of an election campaign are from political parties. The right of a citizen to hold views not espoused by a registered party and to communicate those views is essential to the effective debate upon which our democracy rests, and lies at the core of the free expression guarantee. Any limits to this right must be justified under s. 1 of the *Charter* by a clear and convincing demonstration that they serve a valid objective, do not go too far, and enhance more than harm the democratic process. Promoting electoral fairness by ensuring the equality of each citizen in elections, preventing the voices of the wealthy from drowning out those of others, and preserving confidence in the electoral system, are pressing and substantial objectives in a liberal democracy.

However, the infringement of the right to free expression is not proportionate to these objectives. There is no evidence to support a connection between the limits on citizen spending and electoral fairness, and the legislation does not infringe the right to free expression in a way that is measured and carefully tailored to the goals sought to be achieved. The limits imposed on citizens amount to a virtual ban on their participation in political debate during the election period, except through political parties.... [T]he Attorney General has not demonstrated that limits this draconian are required to meet the perceived dangers.

. . .

Notes and Questions

1.   Compare the result and reasoning of *Harper v. Canada* with those of *Buckley v. Valeo*, 424 U.S. 1 (1976) and its progeny. What explains the different results? Would a "reasoned apprehension" of electoral unfairness in the absence of expenditure limits be enough to justify them in the U.S.? Would concrete proof of a link between unlimited expenditures and unfairness be enough? Why or why not? What explains the greater deference of the Canadian Supreme Court to the legislative judgment?

2.   In countries where expenditure limits are permissible and in fact imposed through national legislation, such as England, contribution limits may be less employed to combat the reality or appearance of corruption than in the United States. For example, while both aimed at this objective, "the rules adopted in the UK and US could fairly be described as virtual polar opposites. Thus, on the question of donations, the UK allows registered donors to make unlimited contributions and relies upon the obligation to disclose as sufficient to safeguard the

goal of political integrity ... The one major point of congruence is the emphasis upon transparency in reporting and disclosure provisions. Both sets of electorate, it seems, are entrusted to seek out and use donation and expenditure information to inform their political judgments." Ian Cram, *Contested Words* 93–94 (2006). What might explain the different choices made by England? Recall that England does not have a written constitution, and so does not have a free speech guarantee that trumps parliamentary legislation. Does anything limit England's choices of means of regulating elections?

B. POLITICAL PARTIES AND SAFEGUARDING DEMOCRACY

A number of constitutions establish certain fundamental attributes of the state and authorize the dissolution of political parties that threaten to destroy it. The following excerpt describes Germany's "militant democracy."

Donald P. Kommers
The Constitutional Jurisprudence of the Federal Republic of Germany

217–18 (2d ed. 1997)

The German Constitution requires the defense of the "free democratic basic order." These terms appear in numerous provisions of the Basic Law, serving generally as a limitation on the exercise of certain freedoms. Fundamental rights may be limited or even forfeited ... if they are used to combat or to abolish the constitutional order. For example, Article 9(2) of the Basic Law prohibits associations whose "purposes or activities ... are directed against the constitutional order or the concept of international understanding." Even the freedom to teach "shall not absolve from loyalty to the Constitution" (Article 5[3]). In short, the exercise of several guaranteed rights under the Basic Law is predicated on certain principles of political obligation.

Article 21(I) ... established the so-called party privilege, the principle that secures to all political parties th freedom to organize and mobilize the electorate. This freedom, however, is limited by the terms of Paragraph 2: "Parties which, by reason of their aims or the behavior of their adherents, seek to impair or abolish the free democratic basic order or endanger the existence of the Federal Republic of Germany, shall be unconstitutional. The Federal Constitutional Court shall decide on the question of unconstitutionality." This provision was designed to repair a central failing of the Weimar Republic; namely, its tolerance of extremist parties bent on destroying democracy. Recalling the conditions that led to the

Hitler state, the founders resolved that the Federal Republic could never be neutral in the face of its mortal enemies.

. . .

In a passage that marked the birth, jurisprudentially, of West Germany's militant democracy, the court set forth the essential meaning of Article 21(2):

> The Basic Law represents a conscious effort to achieve a synthesis between the principle of tolerance with respect to all political ideas and certain inalienable values of the political system. Article 21(2) does not contradict any basic principle of the Constitution; it expresses the conviction of the [founding fathers], based on their concrete historical experience, that the state could no longer afford to maintain an attitude of neutrality toward political parties. [The Basic law] has in this sense created a "militant democracy," a constitutional [value] decision that is binding on the Federal Constitutional Court.

The Communist Party Case, 5 BVerfGE 85, 139 (1956), translated in *Id.* at 223.

* * *

As a result of the German Constitution's Article 21(2), "three parties have been banned . . . the neo-Nazi *Sozialistiche Reichspartei* in 1951; the Communist Part (KPD) after much delay in 1956, and the Nationalist Front in 1992. Claims that the far right National Democratic Party (NPD) was implicated in a spate of physical attacks on disabled persons and immigrants prompted Chancellor Schroeder's Social Democratic Government in December 2000 to apply to the federal Constitutional Court to have the NPD banned. Although the ban had been agreed by the Bundestag, proceedings in the Constitutional Court were postponed in 2003 when doubts emerged about the reliability of the evidence supplied by a leading witness." Cram, *supra* p. 74, at 49.

In this same time period, Turkey's Constitutional Court dissolved an Islamic political party as it threatened to take power as the dominant player in a coalition government. The European Court of Human Rights, in a unanimous decision excerpted below, upheld the dissolution against a claim that it violated the ECHR's free speech and assembly guarantees.

REFAH PARTISI (THE WELFARE PARTY) AND OTHERS v. TURKEY

2003–II Eur. Ct. H.R. 267
European Court of Human Rights

Procedure

1. The case originated in four applications (nos. 41340/98, 41342/98, 41343/98 and 41344/98) against the Republic of Turkey lodged with the European Commission of Human Rights ("the Commission") under former Article 25 of the Convention for the Protection of Human Rights and Fundamental Freedoms ("the Convention") by a Turkish political party, Refah Partisi (the Welfare Party—"Refah") and three Turkish nationals, Mr Necmettin Erbakan, Mr Şevket Kazan and Mr Ahmet Tekdal ("the applicants") on 22 May 1998.

2. The applicants alleged in particular that the dissolution of Refah by the Turkish Constitutional Court and the suspension of certain political rights of the other applicants, who were leaders of Refah at the material time, had breached Articles 9, 10, 11, 14, 17 and 18 of the Convention and Articles 1 and 3 of Protocol No. 1.

. . .

The Facts

I. THE CIRCUMSTANCES OF THE CASE

A. The Applicants

10. The first applicant, Refah Partisi (the Welfare Party—"Refah"), was a political party founded on 19 July 1983 . . .

11. Refah took part in a number of general and local elections . . .

Ultimately, Refah obtained approximately 22% of the votes in the general election of 24 December 1995 and about 35% of the votes in the local elections of 3 November 1996.

The results of the 1995 general election made Refah the largest political party in Turkey with a total of 158 seats in the Grand National Assembly (which had 450 members at the material time). On 28 June 1996 Refah came to power by forming a coalition government with the centre-right True Path Party (Doğru Yol Partisi), led by Mrs Tansu Ciller. According to an opinion poll carried out in January 1997, if a general election had been held at that time, Refah would have obtained 38% of the votes. The same poll predicted that Refah might obtain 67% of the votes in the general election to be held roughly four years later.

B.   Proceedings in the Constitutional Court

. . .

12.   On 21 May 1997 Principal State Counsel at the Court of Cassation applied to the Turkish Constitutional Court to have Refah dissolved on the grounds that it was a "centre" (mihrak) of activities contrary to the principles of secularism. . . .

4.   The Constitutional Court's judgments

. . .

23.   On 16 January 1998 the Constitutional Court dissolved Refah on the ground that it had become a "centre of activities contrary to the principle of secularism" . . .

25.   With regard to the merits, the Constitutional Court held that while political parties were the main protagonists of democratic politics their activities were not exempt from certain restrictions. In particular, activities by them incompatible with the rule of law could not be tolerated. The Constitutional Court referred to the provisions of the Constitution which imposed respect for secularism on the various organs of political power. It also cited the numerous provisions of domestic legislation requiring political parties to apply the principle of secularism in a number of fields of political and social life. The Constitutional Court observed that secularism was one of the indispensable conditions of democracy. In Turkey the principle of secularism was safeguarded by the Constitution, on account of the country's historical experience and the specific features of Islam. The rules of sharia were incompatible with the democratic regime. The principle of secularism prevented the State from manifesting a preference for a particular religion or belief and constituted the foundation of freedom of conscience and equality between citizens before the law. Intervention by the State to preserve the secular nature of the political regime had to be considered necessary in a democratic society.

26.   The Constitutional Court held that the following evidence proved that Refah had become a centre of activities contrary to the principle of secularism . . .

[The Court cited numerous positive references in public statements of Refah members to creation of a regime of sharia in Turkey, to distinctions among people based on religion and to the necessity of "jihad" or "holy war" to achieve regime change.]

40.   The Constitutional Court observed that it had taken into consideration international human-rights protection instruments, including the Convention. It also referred to the restrictions authorised by the second paragraph of Article 11 and Article 17 of the Convention. It pointed out in that context that Refah's leaders and members were using democratic rights and freedoms with a view to

replacing the democratic order with a system based on sharia. The Constitutional Court observed:

"Democracy is the antithesis of sharia . . .

The Constitutional Court held that where a political party pursued activities aimed at bringing the democratic order to an end and used its freedom of expression to issue calls to action to achieve that aim, the Constitution and supranational human-rights protection rules authorised its dissolution.

. . .

43. Judges Haşim Kılıç and Sacit Adalı expressed dissenting opinions stating, inter alia, that in their view the dissolution of Refah was not compatible either with the provisions of the Convention or with the case-law of the European Court of Human Rights on the dissolution of political parties. They observed that political parties which did not support the use of violence should be able to take part in political life and that in a pluralist system there should be room for debate about ideas thought to be disturbing or even shocking.

. . .

II. RELEVANT DOMESTIC LAW

A. The Constitution

45. The relevant provisions of the Constitution read as follows:

Article 2

"The Republic of Turkey is a democratic, secular and social State based on the rule of law, respectful of human rights in a spirit of social peace, national solidarity and justice, adhering to the nationalism of Atatürk and resting on the fundamental principles set out in the Preamble."

. . .

Article 24 § 4

"No one may exploit or abuse religion, religious feelings or things held sacred by religion in any manner whatsoever with a view to causing the social, economic, political or legal order of the State to be based on religious precepts, even if only in part, or for the purpose of securing political or personal interest or influence thereby."

Article 68 § 4

"The constitutions, rule books and activities of political parties shall not be incompatible with the independence of the State, the integrity of State territory and of the nation, human rights, the principles of equality and the rule of law, national sovereignty or the principles of a democratic, secular republic. No political party may be founded with the aim of advocating and establishing the domination of one social class or group, or a dictatorship in any form whatsoever. ..."

Article 69 § 4

"... The Constitutional Court shall give a final ruling on the dissolution of political parties on an application by Principal State Counsel at the Court of Cassation."

Article 69 § 6

"... A political party may not be dissolved on account of activities contrary to the provisions of Article 68 § 4 unless the Constitutional Court has held that the political party concerned constitutes a centre of such activities."

This provision of the Constitution was added on 23 July 1995.

...

The Law

I. ALLEGED VIOLATION OF ARTICLE 11 OF THE CONVENTION

49. The applicants alleged that the dissolution of Refah Partisi (the Welfare Party) and the temporary prohibition barring its leaders–including Mr Necmettin Erbakan, Mr Şevket Kazan and Mr Ahmet Tekdal–from holding similar office in any other political party had infringed their right to freedom of association, guaranteed by Article 11 of the Convention, the relevant parts of which provide:

"1. Everyone has the right to freedom of peaceful assembly and to freedom of association ...

2. No restrictions shall be placed on the exercise of these rights other than such as are prescribed by law and are necessary in a democratic society in the interests of national security or public safety, for the prevention of disorder or crime, for the protection of health or morals or for the protection of the rights and freedoms of others. ..."

A. Whether there was an interference

50. The parties accepted that Refah's dissolution and the measures which accompanied it amounted to an interference with the applicants' exercise of their right to freedom of association. The Court takes the same view.

B.   Whether the interference was justified

51.   Such an interference will constitute a breach of Article 11 unless it was "prescribed by law", pursued one or more of the legitimate aims set out in paragraph 2 of that provision and was "necessary in a democratic society" for the achievement of those aims.

1.   "Prescribed by law"

. . .

59.   The parties did not dispute that activities contrary to the principles of equality and respect for a democratic, secular republic were undoubtedly unconstitutional under Article 68 of the Constitution. Nor did they deny that the Constitutional Court had sole jurisdiction, on an application by Principal State Counsel, to dissolve a political party which had become a centre of activities contrary to Article 68 of the Constitution. Moreover, Article 69 of the Constitution (amended in 1995) explicitly confirms that the Constitutional Court alone is empowered to determine whether a political party constitutes a centre of anti-constitutional activities. The Court notes that Refah's MPs took part in the work of the parliamentary committee concerned and the debate in the Grand National Assembly on the 1995 amendments to the Constitution (see paragraph 11 above).

. . .

64.   Consequently, the interference was "prescribed by law".

2.   Legitimate aim

. . .

67.   The Court considers that the applicants have not adduced sufficient evidence to establish that Refah was dissolved for reasons other than those cited by the Constitutional Court. Taking into account the importance of the principle of secularism for the democratic system in Turkey, it considers that Refah's dissolution pursued several of the legitimate aims listed in Article 11, namely protection of national security and public safety, prevention of disorder or crime and protection of the rights and freedoms of others.

3.   "Necessary in a democratic society"

. . .

(b) The Court's assessment

(i) General principles

(α) Democracy and political parties in the Convention system

86.   On the question of the relationship between democracy and the Convention, the Court has already ruled . . . as follows:

"Democracy is without doubt a fundamental feature of the European public order . . .

87.   The Court has also confirmed on a number of occasions the primordial role played in a democratic regime by political parties enjoying the freedoms and rights enshrined in Article 11 and also in Article 10 of the Convention . . .

88.   Moreover, the Court has previously noted that protection of opinions and the freedom to express them within the meaning of Article 10 of the Convention is one of the objectives of the freedoms of assembly and association enshrined in Article 11. That applies all the more in relation to political parties in view of their essential role in ensuring pluralism and the proper functioning of democracy. . . .

89.   The Court considers that there can be no democracy without pluralism. It is for that reason that freedom of expression as enshrined in Article 10 is applicable, subject to paragraph 2, not only to "information" or "ideas" that are favourably received or regarded as inoffensive or as a matter of indifference, but also to those that offend, shock or disturb. . . . Inasmuch as their activities form part of a collective exercise of the freedom of expression, political parties are also entitled to seek the protection of Article 10 of the Convention. . . .

(β) Democracy and religion in the Convention system

90.   For the purposes of the present case, the Court also refers to its case-law concerning the place of religion in a democratic society and a democratic State. It reiterates that, as protected by Article 9, freedom of thought, conscience and religion is one of the foundations of a "democratic society" within the meaning of the Convention. It is, in its religious dimension, one of the most vital elements that go to make up the identity of believers and their conception of life, but it is also a precious asset for atheists, agnostics, sceptics and the unconcerned. The pluralism indissociable from a democratic society, which has been dearly won over the centuries, depends on it. That freedom entails, inter alia, freedom to hold or not to hold religious beliefs and to practise or not to practise a religion. . . .

. . .

(γ) The possibility of imposing restrictions, and rigorous European supervision

96.   The freedoms guaranteed by Article 11, and by Articles 9 and 10 of the Convention, cannot deprive the authorities of a State in which an association, through its activities, jeopardises that State's institutions, of the right to protect those institutions. In this connection, the Court points out that it has previously held that

some compromise between the requirements of defending democratic society and individual rights is inherent in the Convention system . . .

. . .

98.   . . . [T]he Court considers that a political party may promote a change in the law or the legal and constitutional structures of the State on two conditions: firstly, the means used to that end must be legal and democratic; secondly, the change proposed must itself be compatible with fundamental democratic principles. It necessarily follows that a political party whose leaders incite to violence or put forward a policy which fails to respect democracy or which is aimed at the destruction of democracy and the flouting of the rights and freedoms recognised in a democracy cannot lay claim to the Convention's protection against penalties imposed on those grounds . . .

99.   The possibility cannot be excluded that a political party, in pleading the rights enshrined in Article 11 and also in Articles 9 and 10 of the Convention, might attempt to derive therefrom the right to conduct what amounts in practice to activities intended to destroy the rights or freedoms set forth in the Convention and thus bring about the destruction of democracy . . . In view of the very clear link between the Convention and democracy (see paragraphs 86–89 above), no one must be authorised to rely on the Convention's provisions in order to weaken or destroy the ideals and values of a democratic society. Pluralism and democracy are based on a compromise that requires various concessions by individuals or groups of individuals, who must sometimes agree to limit some of the freedoms they enjoy in order to guarantee greater stability of the country as a whole . . .

In that context, the Court considers that it is not at all improbable that totalitarian movements, organised in the form of political parties, might do away with democracy, after prospering under the democratic regime, there being examples of this in modern European history.

100.   The Court reiterates, however, that the exceptions set out in Article 11 are, where political parties are concerned, to be construed strictly; only convincing and compelling reasons can justify restrictions on such parties' freedom of association. In determining whether a necessity within the meaning of Article 11 § 2 exists, the Contracting States have only a limited margin of appreciation. Although it is not for the Court to take the place of the national authorities, which are better placed than an international court to decide, for example, the appropriate timing for interference, it must exercise rigorous supervision embracing both the law and the decisions applying it, including those given by

independent courts. Drastic measures, such as the dissolution of an entire political party and a disability barring its leaders from carrying on any similar activity for a specified period, may be taken only in the most serious cases ... Provided that it satisfies the conditions set out in paragraph 98 above, a political party animated by the moral values imposed by a religion cannot be regarded as intrinsically inimical to the fundamental principles of democracy, as set forth in the Convention.

...

(ε) The appropriate timing for dissolution

102.   In addition, the Court considers that a State cannot be required to wait, before intervening, until a political party has seized power and begun to take concrete steps to implement a policy incompatible with the standards of the Convention and democracy, even though the danger of that policy for democracy is sufficiently established and imminent. The Court accepts that where the presence of such a danger has been established by the national courts, after detailed scrutiny subjected to rigorous European supervision, a State may "reasonably forestall the execution of such a policy, which is incompatible with the Convention's provisions, before an attempt is made to implement it through concrete steps that might prejudice civil peace and the country's democratic regime" ...

...

(ζ) Overall examination

...

(α) Pressing social need

...

132.   ... [T]he Court finds that the acts and speeches of Refah's members and leaders cited by the Constitutional Court were imputable to the whole of the party, that those acts and speeches revealed Refah's long-term policy of setting up a regime based on sharia within the framework of a plurality of legal systems and that Refah did not exclude recourse to force in order to implement its policy and keep the system it envisaged in place. In view of the fact that these plans were incompatible with the concept of a "democratic society" and that the real opportunities Refah had to put them into practice made the danger to democracy more tangible and more immediate, the penalty imposed on the applicants by the Constitutional Court, even in the context of the restricted margin of appreciation left to Contracting States, may reasonably be considered to have met a "pressing social need".

(β) Proportionality of the measure complained of

133.   After considering the parties' arguments, the Court sees no good reason to depart from the following considerations in the Chamber's judgment:

> "82.   ... The Court has previously held that the dissolution of a political party accompanied by a temporary ban prohibiting its leaders from exercising political responsibilities was a drastic measure and that measures of such severity might be applied only in the most serious cases (see the previously cited Socialist Party and Others v. Turkey judgment, p. 1258, § 51). In the present case it has just found that the interference in question met a 'pressing social need'. It should also be noted that after [Refah's] dissolution only five of its MPs (including the applicants) temporarily forfeited their parliamentary office and their role as leaders of a political party. The 152 remaining MPs continued to sit in Parliament and pursued their political careers normally. ... The Court considers in that connection that the nature and severity of the interference are also factors to be taken into account when assessing its proportionality. ..."

. . .

4.   The Court's conclusion regarding Article 11 of the Convention

135.   Consequently, following a rigorous review to verify that there were convincing and compelling reasons justifying Refah's dissolution and the temporary forfeiture of certain political rights imposed on the other applicants, the Court considers that those interferences met a "pressing social need" and were "proportionate to the aims pursued". It follows that Refah's dissolution may be regarded as "necessary in a democratic society" within the meaning of Article 11 § 2.

136.   Accordingly, there has been no violation of Article 11 of the Convention . . . .

* * *

Professor Samuel Issacharoff comments on the *Refah Partisi* decision as follows:

> On first impression, the opinion jars many democratic sensibilities, particularly those formed in the free speech environment of the United States. The condemnation of all sharia likely was far too sweeping and almost certainly applied a different standard to Islamic religious belief than would have been applied to any Christian faith. Further, the use of a deferential "reasonableness" standard for the political exclusion of a party with broad popular support gives a great deal of latitude to national determinations that are necessarily problematic. Nonetheless,

the effect of the court's ruling seemed the best that anyone could have hoped for. Under the pressure of prohibitions for its proclaimed aim of imposing clerical rule, the Welfare Party fractured.

Unlike the earlier prohibitions, which simply declared the various incarnations of Professor Erbakan's movement illegal through either court action or military intervention, the Turkish Constitutional Court decision upheld by the ECHR targeted certain electoral objectives more surgically. The decision left in place a sizeable block of the former Refah Party in Parliament, still with tremendous authority over national politics. Under these circumstances, ... the prospect of reintegration into Turkish politics remained present subject to a tempering of the perceived threats to continued democratic order.

The result was that a moderate wing led by former Istanbul mayor Recep Tayyip Erdogan, himself a former protege of Professor Erbakan, broke off to form the Justice and Development Party, a far more moderate Islamic party. In 2002, Erdogan became Prime Minister when Justice and Development emerged as the largest bloc in Parliament. Under his tutelage, Turkey has pursued its efforts at EU integration and remains a bastion of moderation in the Middle East. Far from creating an insuperable barrier to an Islamic voice in Turkish politics, the dissolution of the Welfare Party appears to have sparked a realignment in which committed democratic voices from the self-proclaimed Islamic communities found a means of integration into mainstream Turkish political life.... Undoubtedly, this is not the last word in the struggle between a constitutional commitment to secularism and significant popular support for Islamic politics. But under the circumstances, it is difficult to imagine a better outcome.

Samuel Issacharoff, *Fragile Democracies*, 120 Harv. L. Rev. 1405, 1446–47 (2007). The following excerpt contains Professor Issacharoff's more general evaluation of electoral speech and assembly restrictions imposed to preserve democracy.

Samuel Issacharoff
Fragile Democracies
120 Harv. L. Rev. 1405, 1409–1467 (2007)

Democracies are not powerless to respond to the threat of being compromised from within. At the descriptive level, the prime method of response is the prohibition on extremist participation in the electoral arena, a practice which exists with surprising regularity across democratic societies. Some states restrict speech within the electoral arena, as India has done with its prohibition on any campaign appeals to religious intolerance or ethnic enmity. Other states forbid the formation of parties hostile to democracy, as Germany has done in banning any successors in interest to the Nazi or Communist parties and in more recently banning an Islamic fundamentalist movement, the Califate State. Still others impose content restrictions on the views that parties may hold, as with the requirement in Turkey of fidelity to the principles of secular democracy as a condition of eligibility for elected office. Similarly, Israel, through its Basic Law, excludes from the electoral arena any party that rejects the democratic and Jewish character of the state, as well as any party whose platform is deemed an incitement to racism. Other states specifically ban designated parties, as evidenced by the practice in several of the former Soviet Republics of barring their local communist parties from seeking elected office; the United States has taken similar steps. Finally, some states prohibit parties that are deemed to be fronts for terrorist or paramilitary groups. Thus, Spain has recently banned Batasuna, a political party sharing the objectives of the Basque separatist ETA insurgents, from any participation in Spanish or European parliamentary elections.

The list of types of restrictions could go on at some length, and the scope of these restrictions has expanded in the aftermath of September 11 and the press of Islamic militancy. The key point, however, is not the ubiquity of the prohibitions, but the rationale for them. All these societies recognize that the electoral arena is not simply a forum for the recording of preferences, but a powerful situs for the mobilization of political forces. Elections serve to amplify the ability of all political forces to disseminate their views. They also provide a natural medium for partisans to have their passions raised and to provoke frenzied mob activity. If elected to parliamentary office, even fringe extremist groups typically enjoy parliamentary immunity for incitement from the halls of power. Under most national laws, they can command official resources for their electoral propaganda. And, as with the fascist rise to power in Europe, they can use their positions in parliament to cripple any prospect of effective governance, destabilize the state, and launch themselves as successors to a failing democracy.

Whatever the inherent difficulties in the use of state authority to enforce codes of democratic exchange, the problems are presented most acutely in the electoral arena. Seemingly, the world has learned something from the use of that arena as the springboard for fascist mobilizations to power in Germany and Italy. Perhaps as well, the world has learned that appeals to communal intolerance in countries like India, even if conducted from within the safe harbor of democratic processes, lead almost invariably to communal violence in which election rhetoric is a rostrum from which antidemocratic forces rally the faithful. At some level, all these countries grapple with an intuition that democratic elections require, as a precondition to the right of participation, a commitment to the preservation of the democratic process.

At the same time, limiting the scope of democratic deliberation necessarily calls into question the legitimacy of the political process. When stripped down to their essentials, all definitions of democracy rest ultimately on the primacy of electoral choice and the presumptive claim of the majority to rule. It is of course true that this thin definition of democracy cannot stand alone, for all electoral systems must assume a background set of rules, institutions, and definitions of eligible citizenship that serve as preconditions to the exercise of any meaningful popular choice. Moreover, all democracies of the modern era have constitutional constraints that cabin, through substantive limits and procedural hurdles, what the majority may do at any given point. However, a distinct set of problems emerges whenever a society decides that certain viewpoints may not find expression in the political arena and may never be considered as contenders for popular support . . .

. . . Much of this discussion will sound antithetical to core First Amendment principles in American law, and it is likely that American courts would not tolerate most, or perhaps any, of the measures discussed and endorsed [here]. One of the points of engagement with American law will be the use of the clear and present danger test that originated in American law to describe how democracies have responded to a subset of the threats they face (as with armed insurrectionist parties and military splinter groups, for example). While the terminology may be similar, it is vital to understand the limits of the parallels between the threats that democracy faces in the United States and in other countries.

. . .

It is possible that the seeming doctrinal attachment to strong protections of political organization in the United States may be attributable to some unique variables, beginning with the comparative political stability of twentieth-century America relative to more embattled, more fragile democracies. That stability is enhanced by the distinct electoral structures in the United States that marginalize minor parties from governance. Further, as a doctrinal matter, it is quite likely that the propensity toward criminal prosecution of political dissidents in the United States has also contributed to the lack of an administrative law of electoral exclusion. All of these features are important, and the uniqueness of our national setting dictates caution in attempting to export the clear and present

danger test to the administrative prohibition on political participation in much more fragile institutional settings.

The clear and present danger test aptly captures what is at
stake in the criminal prohibition of organizations whose aims are
fundamentally antithetical to democracy and who are being
charged, in effect, with unlawful conduct. As is developed below,
the threat of criminal conduct by marginal groups captures only a
subset of the threats faced by democracies, particularly in far less
stable national settings. In such circumstances, unfortunately, fo-
cusing on the immediacy of the threat of unlawful activity is
insufficient to reflect the gravity of the threat.

. . .

Rather than starting from the question whether a prohibition
of antidemocratic forces is permissible, I prefer to start by asking
what kinds of prohibitions are being contemplated. Here, I depart
considerably from American case law, which tends to collapse the
question of what prohibitions on political parties are acceptable into
the debate over what criminal sanctions on political speech are
justified. [I] therefore consider[] the forms of political restraint that
operate outside the bounds of the criminal justice system. The
inquiry concerns the existence of a space between the standards
that justify incarceration and those that might suffice to justify a
prohibition on electoral participation. Put simply, are there methods to suppress antidemocratic political mobilizations that are
distinct from criminally prosecuting their adherents, and can those
methods be justified even if we would not tolerate incarceration for
those who share the antidemocratic viewpoints?

In rough form, then, we should consider three different approaches to antidemocratic mobilizations in the electoral arena that
are distinct from criminal prosecutions of the advocates of the
underlying positions: first, an electoral code governing the content
of political appeals; second, the proscription of political parties that
fail to accept some fundamental tenet of the social order; and third,
a ban on electoral participation for some political parties, even if
they are permitted to maintain a party organization. The first two
approaches represent the general range of established responses to
antidemocratic agitation, stretching from regulations of electoral
conduct to proscriptions on the organization of political parties.
The third option—the ban on electoral eligibility but not on party
formation—is less established as a form of party regulation. Nonetheless, this intermediate form of regulation offers an intriguing,
less restrictive means of addressing the unique problems of antidemocratic mobilization through electoral activity.

. . .

It is by now well established that all constitutional orders retain emergency powers, either formally or informally. Justice Jackson's firm admonition that the Constitution is not "a suicide pact" well sums up the sense that even a tolerant democratic society must be able to police its fragile borders. The discussion [here] rests on many premises that are, thus far, largely alien to the American experience, or at least the last hundred years of it. [I begin] by noting that some democratic societies are more fragile, and have political structures more porous to antidemocratic elements, than the United States. That porousness requires an ability to restrict the capture of governmental authority by those who would subvert democracy altogether. The next step is to envision a realm of electoral politics with rules of conduct distinct from the rules that apply to broader constitutional rights of assembly, petition, and speech. In order to manage the unique threats that arise from that distinct political realm, fragile democracies need the ability to discipline electoral activity without regard to the imminence of criminal or insurrectionary conduct, the accepted standard for the criminalization of political speech. Finally, independent oversight of the political process is required to prevent the dangerous powers here argued for from being deployed in the name of the self-serving preservation of incumbent political power.

As an empirical matter, it is entirely possible that democracy faces greater dangers from the promiscuous use of police powers than from domestic enemies. With respect to more stable democracies, I am willing to concede that this is likely the case and that the main task of legal oversight may very well be the preservation of civil liberties. That reality does little to address the problems faced by societies that are more menaced by the indisputable emergence from time to time of mass-based movements seeking to destroy democratic life.

The international experience also cautions against readily assuming that any restraints in the political process necessarily lead to a collapse of democratic rights or a fundamental compromising of democratic legitimacy. Virtually all democratic societies define some extremist elements as beyond the bounds of democratic tolerance. Despite errors of overreaching, likely inevitable in human affairs, it appears that this power is largely used with restraint and hesitation. With the benefit of hindsight, therefore, the question that needs to be addressed is whether Weimar Germany could have assembled the tools necessary to fight off the Hitlerian challenge within the bounds of democratic legitimacy. One certainly must hope so.

Notes and Questions

1.   Germany's Constitutional Court describes its Basic Law as an attempt "to achieve a synthesis between the principle of tolerance with respect to all political ideas and certain inalienable values of the political system." *The Communist Party Case,* 5 BVerfGE 85, 139 (1956), translated in Donald P. Kommers, *The Constitutional Jurisprudence of the Federal Republic of Germany* 223. Does the U.S. Constitution embody the principle of tolerance with respect to all political ideas? Does it embrace certain values of the political system? Are those values "inalienable"? Does the U.S. Constitution achieve a synthesis between the two principles? If so, what is it? How does it differ from the German synthesis?

2.   The decision of the European Court of Human Rights in *Refah Partisi* was unanimous. Had there been a dissent, what would its reasoning be? Is it indeed difficult to imagine a better outcome than what occurred in Turkish politics after the decision? In 2001, the Turkish Constitutional Court dissolved the Virtue Party, which it deemed a successor to the banned Welfare party. In early 2008, the Turkish government (with control of Parliament and the offices of Prime Minister and President held by the Justice and Development Party, the moderate offshoot of the Welfare Party described in the above excerpt) approved amendments to the constitution, which would allow women in universities to wear head scarves, a symbol of the Islamic faith. Protests ensued from committed secularists, as well as praise from those who welcomed recognition of Islam in public life, and the Supreme Court Chief Public Prosecutor filed an application to dissolve the Justice and Development Party, alleging that, like its predecessors, it had become a "center" of anti-democratic activity. *Top Court Sees Application to Close AKP*, Turkish Daily News, Mar. 17, 2008, http://www.turkish dailynews.com.tr/article.php?enewsid=99132. In a very close decision, Turkey's Constitutional Court rejected the application. Sabrina Tavernise and Sebnem Arsu, Turkish Court Calls Ruling Party Constitutional, N.Y. Times, July 31, 2008, at A6. In Iran, a group of clerics called the Guardian Council reviews candidates seeking to participate in elections, barring those who are not loyal to the "principles of Islam" and the "values of the revolution." *See* Nazila Fathi, *Iran's Religious Conservatives Are Expected to Solidify Power at Polls*, N. Y. Times, Mar. 6, 2008, at A8. Is there a principled difference between the standards used to dissolve political parties in Germany and Turkey and those used to disqualify candidates in Iran?

3.   How does Professor Issacharoff explain the difference between U.S. constitutional jurisprudence with respect to electoral speech and that in other countries, which permit more wide-reaching and viewpoint-based restrictions? Are you convinced? What is democratic legitimacy? Why does it matter? How do a nation's rules with respect to freedom of speech impact its democratic legitimacy?

Chapter Three

MEDIA FREEDOM

I. SCOPE OF THE FREE PRESS RIGHT

Many constitutions, like the U.S. Constitution's First Amendment, guarantee both freedom of speech, and of the press, but high courts in different nations have interpreted the relationship of the press to the speech guarantee differently.

Eric Barendt
Freedom of Speech 419–24 (2005)

[There are] three perspectives on the relationship of press freedom to freedom of speech. The first is that the two freedoms are really equivalent. They have broadly the same meaning; freedom of the press simply refers to the free speech rights of owners, editors, and journalists . . .

There are advantages to this approach. It treats ordinary individual speakers and writers in the same way as the press and other media, so avoiding any charge of discrimination in favor of the latter. Secondly, it does not face the definitional problems which are inevitable when a legal regime recognizes special press or media rights: what, for instance, is the 'press' and does it include book publishers or the publishers of circulars and leaflets? Finally, the traditional perspective does make sense in many contexts. If a government bans a television program or a court awards libel damages against a newspaper, freedom of speech and media freedom are equally implicated. It is immaterial whether the channel controller or editor claims a violation of the right to freedom of expression or a right to press freedom.

But there are shortcomings to this approach. First, it means that any explicit mention in the constitutional text of freedom of the press or freedom of the broadcasting media is redundant, for it does not add anything to freedom of speech. That would seem particularly hard to accept where the constitution covers the press and broadcasting media separately from the individual right to freedom of expression. ... Secondly, th[is] perspective does not meet the powerful argument that the press is entitled to some legal privileges because it performs a vital constitutional role. For instance, newspapers may claim that freedom of the press gives them immunity from taxation and other laws which endanger their existence or which make it impossible for them to perform their function effectively. Equally, the media may argue that, as a matter of constitutional law, they are entitled under the free press guarantee to acquire information or to attend public events, even though the general free speech clause does not give individuals comparable access rights.

From the second perspective, freedom of the press would bear a meaning distinct from freedom of speech (or expression). Press freedom exists to protect mass media institutions which may enjoy special rights and privileges going beyond freedom of speech. The guarantee of this freedom is a structural provision of the constitution, giving the media, uniquely among private institutions, protection in recognition of its role as a check on government. ...

But this argument is open to criticism, at least insofar as it is understood to suggest a privileged position for the press. There are serious objections of principle to giving the traditional print and broadcasting media special rights which are not shared by individual writers and artists on whose work they often rely. Why should a journalist enjoy, say, access rights to interview prisoners or to report prison riots, when a novelist or penal reformer is denied them? Admittedly, the media as a whole may play a more substantial role than any particular individual in disseminating information and ideas to the public. But this seems a thin basis for conferring on every press and broadcasting institution a wide range of privileges and immunities beyond the rights covered by freedom of speech, irrespective of the outlet's contribution to this process. Moreover, all sorts of institutions such as banks, financial services, and credit agencies now provide information to their customers and subscribers, while Internet service providers actually or potentially reach as many people as newspapers and broadcasters. There seems no obvious basis for distinguishing the position of these information providers from that of the traditional media. On the other hand, if the benefit of 'media freedom' were extended to all information providers, the term would really cease to have any clear or distinct meaning.

Another objection to recognition of a broad constitutional guarantee for the institutional media is that it might be interpreted as allowing them to act incompatibly with free speech itself, or at least in a manner prejudicial to free speech interests or values. For example, one likely implication of a distinct press freedom is that the owner of a newspaper has an absolute right to determine its contents. He could exploit that right to damage the readers' interests in pluralism of information—a value underlying freedom of speech—by, say, dictating the political line of the newspaper irrespective of the editor's views, or by arbitrarily refusing to publish readers' letters in reply to what they considered inaccurate allegations printed in the paper. A similar clash might occur if press barons resisted the application of competition and anti-concentration laws with the argument that it would violate their free press rights. In these circumstances, it can be argued, the owner is really exercising a freedom to determine the use of his property, the newspaper, or a commercial freedom, although of course he may claim to be exercising freedom of speech. . . .

These arguments lead to a third perspective on the relationship of press freedom and freedom of speech. The former is not a right which is distinct from the latter and which is recognized to protect media institutions and their proprietors as such; rather, press freedom should be protected only to 'the degree to which it promotes certain values at the core of our interest in freedom of expression generally.' Media freedom is an instrumental, rather than a primary or fundamental human right. Press claims to special privileges and immunities should only be recognized insofar as they promote the values of freedom of speech, in particular the public interest in pluralism in its sources of information.

This perspective . . . fits well with the underlying rationale for extending free speech guarantees to mass media speech: the essential role of the media in disseminating ideas and information to the public. It enables courts to resolve conflicts between the rights of the press and other media, on the one hand, and the claims by individuals to assert their right to free speech against the media on the other. Secondly, it does not involve the drawing of a bright or sharp line between the rights of the institutional media and the rights of other information providers; the claims, say, of both journalists and novelists to interview prisoners or visit hospitals might be recognized, insofar as that step would give the public more information about significant social problems. It is, however, less clear whether recognition of those rights should primarily be a matter for the courts in their interpretation of a free speech or press clause or for the legislature. It may be better for statutes or other regulations to provide for access and other specific press rights. In the first place, the framing of these rights should be sensitive to particular circumstances; secondly, it is easier to introduce or amend legislation to meet new claims or to extend existing entitlements to new media outlets.

Donald P. Kommers
The Constitutional Jurisprudence of the Federal Republic of Germany

397–403 (2d. ed. 1997)

The right to a free press is a separate and independent freedom under Article 5 [of Germany's Basic Law.] . . .

The *Spiegel* case (1966) set forth the general principle governing the role of the press in a democratic society as well as some of the conditions under which it might be regulated in the public interest. . . .

SPIEGEL CASE

20 BVerfGE 162 (1966)

German Constitutional Court

[The German Constitutional Court split on the merits of the claim, which involved a police raid on the offices of the widely-read weekly magazine, *Der Spiegel*, but united in the articulation of the basis of the Basic Law's press right.]

Judgment of the First Senate . . .

C. 1. A free press, untrammeled by governmental control and censorship, is an essential element of a free society; a free, politically active, regularly published press is particularly indispensable in a modern democracy. If citizens are to make political decisions, they must be thoroughly informed; they must also be acquainted with the opinions of others in order to weigh alternative courses of action. The press enlivens this continuing discussion; it supplies information and takes positions with respect to it, and thereby orients public debate. The press articulates public opinion and clarifies public issues, facilitating the citizen's judgment. . . .

This "public task" of the press is important; it cannot be fulfilled by established governmental authority. Publishing companies must be able to organize freely within the social sphere. They operate according to the principles of the free market and in the organizational form of private enterprise. They compete intellectually and economically with other publishing enterprises, a process in which the state must not intervene.

2. The function of a free press in the democratic state corresponds to its legal position under the Basic Law. Article 5 guarantees freedom of the press. The location of the guarantee within the system of the Basic Law, together with the traditional meaning of

[this guarantee], underscores the subjective character of the right. This means that persons and companies are free to function without official interference. [The subjective aspect of this right] confers upon the press, in certain respects, a favored legal position. Freedom of the press also has an objective side; i.e., it guarantees the existence of the institution of a "free press." Independent of the personal rights of individuals, the state is duty-bound in all areas of the legal system to respect the principle of a free press wherever a regulation might concern it. The freedom to engage in a publishing enterprise, free access to the journalistic profession, and the duty of public agencies to divulge information are all manifestations of this principle. In addition, the state may have a positive duty to take action against the development of monopolies of opinion.

The independence of the press guaranteed by Article 5 of the Basic Law extends from the accumulation of information to the dissemination of news and opinion. Thus the protection of the relationship of trust between the press and its private informants is an integral part of a free press. Because the press cannot function without private sources of information, this protection is indispensable. Sources of information will flow freely only when editorial privilege is respected.

3. Freedom of the press carries with it the possibility of conflict with other values also protected by the Basic Law; it can come into conflict with the rights of individuals, groups, or the community in general. The Basic Law gives the legal system, to which the press is also subject, the task of regulating this conflict; it must respect the legal rights and interests of others as well as of the general public whenever those interests are at least as worthy of protection as those of the press. The privileged position of the members of the press is granted them solely because of their function and only so far as this function reaches. It is not a question of personal privileges; the freeing of individuals from generally valid norms must be justified against this background.

. . .

NOTE: THE RIGHTS AND RESPONSIBILITIES OF THE PRESS. The *Spiegel* case is important for underscoring the objective character of the right to a free press. Article 5 not only incorporates a subjective right of the press against governmental encroachment but also confers on the press an affirmative constitutional right to institutional autonomy and independence. The press enjoys this special status under the Basic Law because it performs a critical "public role" in the life of a liberal democracy. Its primary purposes are to collect information, distribute the news, and contribute to the development of public opinion. Indeed, it is government's responsibility to legislate norms designed to maintain and facilitate these institutional functions. The *Television I* case (1961 ...) suggests that the legislature may in certain instances even be obliged to protect the press from societal forces or pressures likely to endanger its freedom.

Each of the German Lander, including the five states of the old GDR, has enacted laws defining the rights and duties of the press. Many of these laws have codified a number of the Constitutional Court's holdings, including those that protect editorial secrecy and the right of journalists not to disclose, even in criminal proceedings, their sources of information. Hamburg's Press Act, some of whose provisions would be constitutionally suspect in the United States, exemplifies these statutes. It affirms the principle of a free press by prohibiting licensing or equivalent measures; it defines the public role of the press, emphasizing its responsibility to procure and disseminate the news as well as to voice its opinion on public policy; it imposes a correlative duty on the part of public officials to supply the press with information of value to it in the fulfillment of its public role; it obligates the press in turn to check the content, origin, and truth of all the news prior to its publication; it sets forth the conditions under which publishers and editors are to grant citizens a right of reply; finally, it defines in great detail the responsibility of the press under the Criminal Code.

. . .

One ... provision of the Criminal Code prohibits the press from publishing the exact wording of a criminal charge before it is presented in a public trial. The statute does not bar other comments about a case or even a summary of an indictment. The *Stern* case, decided in 1985, arose from an action against the weekly magazine *Stern* for publishing, before trial, the text of a criminal charge in the famous Flick parry-funding affair. The Hamburg District Court, before which the magazine was haled for violating the code provision, referred the question of its validity to the Constitutional Court, which sustained the rule as a valid limitation on freedom of the press under the general-law clause of Article 5 (2). The court explained:

> By forbidding the publication of the exact wording of court records in criminal proceedings before their disclosure at trial, the legislature was concerned that such publications would be more prejudicial to defendants and other participants in the trial than the mere reporting of the case in other than direct quotations.... The literal reproduction of statements knowingly uttered as such is a particularly sharp weapon in the battle of opinions. Such quotations add credence to the charge, almost serving as a statement of fact .... This is true not only of the literal reproduction of expressions of opinion but also of the

literal reproduction of communications based on fact. A word-for-word reproduction of parts of documents conveys, and rightly so, the impression of official authenticity to the disadvantage of defendant in a criminal suit.

Notes and Questions

1.　Into which perspective on the relationship of press freedom to freedom of speech does U.S. constitutional jurisprudence fall? What perspective does the German Constitutional Court adopt? What might explain the difference?

2.　In what ways might the provisions of Hamburg's Press Act be suspect in the United States? Would a U.S. law prohibiting reproduction of the exact wording of an indictment comport with the free speech guarantee? Would such a restriction be content-based under U.S. constitutional doctrine?

II.　THE GAP BETWEEN THE RIGHT AND THE REALITY OF MEDIA FREEDOM

Freedom of speech, and of the press, either explicitly or implicitly, are almost universally guaranteed in national constitutions and international human rights treaties. The following excerpts report a continuing gap between the guarantee of media speech free from government influence and its effectuation.

Reporters Without Borders[3] Press Freedom Round-up 2007

86 journalists killed in 2007—up 244% over five years (Jan. 2, 2008),
http://www.rsf.org/article.php3?id_article=24909

At least 86 journalists were killed around the world in 2007. The figure has risen steadily since 2002—from 25 to 86 (+ 244%)—and is the highest since 1994, when 103 journalists were killed, nearly half of them in the Rwanda genocide, about 20 in Algeria's civil war and a dozen in the former Yugoslavia.

More than half those killed in 2007 died in Iraq. . . .

All 47 journalists killed in Iraq were, except for a Russian reporter, Iraqis who mostly worked for the local media and were deliberately targeted. The motive was often hard to pinpoint but was always linked to their work or the media outlet that employed them.

3.　Reporters Without Borders is an international organization registered in France, which is dedicated to protecting and defending the rights of journalists around the world.

. . .

About 90% of murders of journalists go entirely or partly unpunished.

. . .

135 journalists were in prison around the world on 1 January 2008 and the figure has hardly shrunk for several years. Those freed are immediately replaced by new journalist prisoners. At least 887 were arrested in 2007, mostly in Pakistan (195), Cuba (55) and Iran (54).

. . .

China (with 33 in jail) and Cuba (24) have been the world's two biggest prisons for journalists over the past four years.

. . .

65 cyber-dissidents are also in prison for speaking out on the Internet, with China the main culprit (50 imprisoned).

. . .

[A]t least 67 media workers were kidnapped in 15 countries in 2007. The worst place to be was still Iraq, where 25 were seized. Ten were executed by their kidnappers.

. . .

At least 14 journalists are still being held as hostages, all of them in Iraq.

. . .

At least 2,676 websites were shut down or suspended around the world in 2007, most of them discussion forums.

Freedom House[4]
MAP OF PRESS FREEDOM (2007),

http://www.freedom house.org/template.cfm?page=251 & year=2007

The state of global press freedom declined in 2006, with particularly worrisome trends evident in Asia, the former Soviet Union, and Latin America. Despite notable improvements in a number of countries, gains were generally overshadowed by a continued, relentless assault on independent news media in a group of geopolitically crucial states, including Russia, Venezuela, Iran, and China,

---

4. Freedom House is a U.S.-based nongovernmental organization dedicated to promoting the spread of democracy. Beginning in 1979, it has published a yearly global survey of media independence, which includes rating the level of press freedom in each country. Introductory materials to each volume explain its methodology.

as well as declines in countries with more open press environments, such as Argentina, Brazil, the Philippines, Sri Lanka, and Thailand. Moreover, a growing number of governments moved in 2006 to restrict internet freedom by censoring, harassing, or shutting down sites that provide alternative sources of news and commentary.

. . .

The Global Picture

Out of 195 countries and territories assessed, 74 countries (38 percent) were rated Free, 58 (30 percent) were rated Partly Free, and 63 (32 percent) were rated Not Free. . . .

In terms of population, the survey found that only 18 percent of the world's inhabitants live in countries that enjoy a Free press, while 39 percent have a Partly Free press and 43 percent have a Not Free press. The relatively negative picture painted by these population figures is due to the impact of two countries—China, with a Not Free rating, and India, with a Partly Free rating—which together account for some two billion of the world's six billion people. . . .

A growing drive to neutralize or eliminate all potential sources of political opposition has emerged in countries as diverse as Russia, Venezuela, and Zimbabwe in recent years. Along with the institutions of civil society, the press has been a principal target of this movement for near absolute political domination and is often one of the first targets of authoritarian regimes. The methods used tend to be legalistic: print or broadcast outlets are taken over by the state or by forces aligned with the political leadership; license renewals are denied; journalists are jailed or hit with heavy fines for libel or defamation . . .

Governments Target Internet–Phenomenon Youtube BBC International Reports (Media)

Mar. 11, 2008 (Westlaw, BBCMONM)

Since its launch in February 2005, YouTube has been blocked or banned by a number of countries, among others China, Iran (and several other Middle East countries), Pakistan, Turkey, Burma and Brazil. The issue was highlighted in late February when Pakistan caused an international four-day outage in its most recent attempt to block the site. As can be expected, the reasons for banning the Google-owned video-sharing site vary from country to country.

Pakistan: Religious or political control

The Pakistan government has, since early 2006, blocked 12 web sites (among them YouTube) that displayed controversial cartoons of the Prophet Muhammad. The Pakistan Telecommunication Authority (PTA) orders the nation's 70 internet service providers (ISPs) to block targeted sites.

YouTube was barred on 22 February over a "blasphemous" clip which purported to be a trailer for the anti-Quran film by Dutch politician Geert Wilders, "Fitna" ("Sedition"). Although Pakistani officials insisted the move was due to the presence of offensive, anti-Islamic material, many commentators in the Pakistani press and cyberspace saw it as an attempt to suppress videos about election rigging. The videos, which were subsequently broadcast on Geo TV, were apparently shot with hidden cameras and showed vote-tampering at polling stations.

Sites other than YouTube have been affected by the PTA-ordered blackouts. The blogspot.com domain was blocked, according to Don't Block the Blog, a group of Pakistani activists. In February 2006, the ISPs' mass blackout blocked access to millions of popular web sites including Google.com, Download.com, Microsoft.com, Gmail.com and Yahoo.com.

China: Full set of censorship tools

Internet censorship in the People's Republic of China is conducted under a wide variety of regulations (over 60) and they are vigorously implemented by provincial branches of state-owned ISPs and businesses. The internet police task force is estimated at more than 30,000. Critical comments on internet forums are usually erased within minutes.

The Golden Shield Project (referred to outside China as the Great Firewall of China), owned by the Ministry of Public Security, was launched in 1998. According to Wikipedia, China uses the full toolbox of censoring methods: IP blocking, Domain Name Service filtering and redirection, URL filtering, Packet filtering, Connection reset, web feed blocking and reverse surveillance.

On 31 January, China's state media regulator imposed tough new rules governing the control of audio-visual content on the internet. According to a notice posted on the State Administration of Film, Radio and Television website, only state-controlled entities holding a three-year broadcast licence will have the right to operate websites containing professionally published audio-visual content. The regulation has been widely seen as a move by China to restrict online videos to state-controlled sites, and to require internet providers to delete and report a variety of content.

. . .

In October 2007, the internet was abuzz with speculation that YouTube had been blocked by the Chinese authorities. . . .

Some attributed the blackout to the 17th Communist National Congress being held in Beijing (from 15 October 2007). Others attributed it to the fact that YouTube had launched a Chinese-language version of the site, for Hong Kong and Taiwan, on 18 October. (Reuters reported on 6 February 2008 that "YouTube is often blocked during high-level political events in China, while online encyclopaedia Wikipedia and Yahoo's photo-sharing network Flickr have also been periodically blocked").

Blogspot, Wikipedia, Flickr and Livejournal have all been blocked by the Chinese authorities at one time or another. The websites of foreign media such as CNN, NBC and the Washington Post have also been blocked.

'Taboo topics' inevitably censored include anything related to the Dalai Lama/Tibet independence movement, the outlawed Falun Gong, and the Tiananmen Square protest.

Blocked websites are re-routed to Chinese search engines such as Baidu. According to a Harvard study, at least 18,000 websites are blocked.

. . .

Iran: Host of foreign sites banned

Iran is considered to have one of the most repressive internet-censorship regimes in the world, and is given the worst ranking by watchdog bodies such as Reporters Without Borders and OpenNet Initiative. Critics accuse Iran of using filtering technology to censor more sites than any country apart from China. Censorship is aimed at purging the country of all Western cultural influences.

YouTube is banned in Iran, along with Flickr and a number of blogging platforms, PersianBlog to name one.

In a clampdown in December 2006, Iran shut down some of the most popular sites, including Amazon.com, the International Movie Database (imdb.com), Wikipedia and most other informational databases and search engines. Anyone attempting to access these is met with a page reading: "The requested page is forbidden". Most forms of media are vetted by the Ministry of Culture and Islamic Guidance.

. . .

Burma: Ban during protests

In Burma, YouTube was banned during protests [in 2007]. Mizzima News (www.mizzima.com) reported on 7 September that the site, which featured video of protests against the military junta, had been banned. The site was blocked by the country's two ISPs.

The military government, which took power in a coup d'etat in 1988, controls all media in the country and in 1996 passed several repressive laws to control the flow of information. Protests are banned and information that undermines "state security, national solidarity and culture" is a criminal offence.

Television, video and film are all regulated. Even satellites, video-cassette recorders and computer equipment are controlled.

In 2000, the Internet Law, which prohibits postings that are harmful to state interests, was issued by the State Peace and Development Council.

According to a study conducted by OpenNet Initiative in 2005, internet censorship is mostly confined to websites related to pro-democracy groups or pornography. In addition, 85% of email service provider sites are blocked. The Myanmar Information Communications Technology Development Corporation licenses cybercafés. Users are required to register, and owners are required to save screen shots of user activity every 5 minutes and, upon request, deliver them to MICTDC.

During the 2007 protests, cybercafés prohibited users from browsing banned sites, including news websites such as www.cnn.com and dissident websites, including Mizzima.

Censorship for all reasons

The wide range of reasons advanced for blocking YouTube around the globe reveals how exposed it is to many agendas and vested interests.

Turkey has banned YouTube several times over insults to their founding father, Mustafa Kemal Ataturk, or "insulting Turkishness"—a serious crime under the controversial Article 301 of the penal code. The Turkish Telecommunications Board is ordered by court order to block any site falling foul of this law. Turkish authorities claim it is not government censorship, but legal process. However, critics say the law is used to silence government critics.

In the United Arab Emirates, YouTube was blocked because it presented a seven-part documentary "Desert Nights", on the trafficking of Armenian women for the prostitution industry in Dubai. Ara Manoogian, the Armenian journalist who made the documentary (along with Edik Baghdasaryan), claimed in a blog (aramanoogian.blogspot) on 19 June 2006 that police and migration service officials in Dubai were involved in the prostitution racket. News site Hetq Online, which reported the claims, was also blocked.

In Morocco, users were unable to access YouTube because of, it was reported, videos critical of the government's treatment of the people of Western Sahara, a territory that Morocco took control of in 1975. YouTube was unavailable for five days from 25 to 30 May 2007. According to reports, footage of Moroccan police beating female independence protestors in Laayoune was featured. Global Voices advocacy reported on 26 May 2007: "This is the third major site blocked by the Moroccan filtering regime after Google Earth and Livejournal.''

In Brazil, YouTube was blocked for several days in January 2007 as a result of a private action by the model Daniela Cicarelli, on the grounds that a video clip (depicting a sexual encounter at the beach, shot by a paparazzo) was being used without her permission. Some of the country's ISPs implemented a court order that the site be blocked, making YouTube inaccessible in some parts of Brazil. The ban was reversed by the Supreme Court after a few days.

In Thailand, the government last year banned the site for about four months because of clips that were considered offensive to King Bhumibol Adulyadej.

In Syria, YouTube was blocked in August 2007, apparently over a satirical video featuring the First Lady in Marilyn Monroe-style, with her dress blown up, bidding farewell to a foreign dignitary at the airport.

Moral justification for censorship

University of Toronto-based Nart Villeneuve (www.nartv.org), who monitors internet censorship, points out that, ''It is often under the rubric of morality and public order and/or national security that internet censorship is framed by those who seek its implementation or seek to justify its ongoing practice. The practice of filtering ... is growing. Increasingly, it is not the practice of filtering that is being challenged, the debate is about what content is being filtered. . . .''

Notes and Questions

1. How does the imprisonment of journalists around the world relate to the constitutional free speech right? Does the U.S. free speech right prohibit the government from imprisoning journalists for what they investigate or publish? How do the murder of journalists around the world and the constitutional free speech and free press rights relate? Does the U.S. free speech right impose an obligation on the government to protect journalists from violence or to investigate and prosecute the perpetrators if it occurs? Could a constitutional free speech right impose such an obligation?

2. What kinds of free speech challenges does the Internet pose that are different from those posed by print or broadcast publications? Does a robust free speech guarantee mean that a government may impose no restrictions on Internet content? Are there circumstances under which the U.S. free speech guarantee would allow the government to block access to a site like YouTube? What would distinguish the justification from the justification that other governments now use for Internet filtering?

PART II

FREEDOM OF RELIGION

Chapter Four

RELIGIOUS LIBERTY—A
GLOBAL OVERVIEW

I. THE DISTINCTIVE NATURE OF NATIONAL CHURCH–STATE RELATIONSHIPS

A. CHURCH–STATE RELATIONSHIPS IN NORTH AMERICA

The relationship between church and state in virtually every nation is a product of that country's distinctive history, culture and demography. That is why it is so difficult to generalize about constitutional provisions relating to religion in different jurisdictions. Any attempt to draw comparisons between legal systems inevitably requires some discussion and understanding of the historical and cultural backgrounds of the countries in question.

To illustrate the importance of this reality, consider the church-state relationships of three countries in North America: the United States, Canada, and Mexico. The United States, of course, enforces both the Free Exercise Clause and the Establishment Clause of the First Amendment as well as the No Religious Test Clause of Article VI. To some considerable extent, it requires the separation of church and state. The conventional explanation for the United States' constitutional commitment to religious freedom and equality focuses on the religious pluralism of American society in the late 1700s. Given the diversity of belief among the colonies, and the all too recent memories of religious warfare and persecution in Europe, protecting religious freedom seemed to have both a principled and a pragmatic justification.

If we compare the United States' system to that of Canada, it seems clear that Canada is also a religiously pluralistic western democracy. While the Canadian Charter does not contain an estab-

116

lishment clause, it does have a provision protecting religious liberty. Moreover, Section 15, the equality rights provision of the Charter, explicitly prohibits discrimination based on religion, as well as other characteristics, and Section 27 requires that interpretations of the Charter must take account of the "multicultural heritage of Canadians." Yet in 1996, in *Adler v. Ontario*, [1996] 3 S.C.R. 609, the Canadian Supreme Court upheld a provincial law that provided public funding for private Catholic religious schools but did not fund Jewish schools or schools of other Christian denominations. This kind of a discriminatory funding arrangement would have been summarily struck down by a United States court. Given the Canadian commitment to religious liberty and equality, what explains the Supreme Court's decision to uphold a funding scheme that prefers one faith over others?

No answer based on abstract principles of law can provide a persuasive response to this question. But an answer based on Canada's unique history and demography is straightforward and easy to understand. At the time of the Confederation that established Canada as a unified country in the mid–1860s, Canadian society reflected two national identities, one British and the other French, that had to be brought together to form a working, unified polity. One of the differences dividing these two populations was religion: the British were predominantly Protestant and the French predominantly Catholic. Education was a major area of controversy. Roman Catholics in areas with an overwhelming Protestant majority and Protestants in areas with an overwhelming Catholic majority feared that the public schools in their communities would reflect the religious beliefs of the majority. Accordingly, negotiators worked out "an historical compromise which was a crucial step along the road leading to Confederation," *id.* ¶ 29, that was codified in Section 93 of the Constitution Act of 1867. This provision in essence guaranteed public support for Roman Catholic denominational schools in a province, such as Ontario, with a Protestant majority. The equality rights of the Canadian Charter adopted in 1982 were not intended to and could not undercut the terms of this historic compromise.

A comparison between the United States' constitutional system and that of Mexico illustrates the importance of history and culture from a different perspective. Unlike the United States, Mexico is a homogenous country with regard to the religion of its people, the great majority of whom are Roman Catholics. Yet Mexico's constitution imposed a far stricter mandate separating church and state than anything ever envisioned under the United States Constitution. Public manifestations of religion were restricted, clergy could neither vote nor hold office, churches and religious associations could not be involved in political activity, and religious references were barred from public ceremonies. Even after the constitutional regime was substantially altered in 1992, clergy were still denied the right to run for elected office, and political associations could not have ties to religious organizations. Given the lack of religious pluralism in Mexico, what explains its extreme commitment to the separation of church and state and so many establishment clause-type prohibitions in its Constitution?

Again, the answer is clear from history. From the time of the conquest of Mexico, the Catholic Church and the State were closely intertwined. Opposition to early royalist regimes and opposition to the Church became similarly inter-connected. The Catholic Church in Mexico sided with conservative forces and opposed the populist republican revolutions during the 1800s that resulted in the country's first constitution in 1857. Indeed, the Church went so far as to join with French forces in an unsuccessful attempt to create a monarchy in Mexico to be led by the Emperor Maximilian. The constitutional provisions restricting the Church's influence reflect the government's antagonism toward an historical adversary and concern about the Church's power in a society that lacks religious diversity.

B. VARIATIONS AMONG CHURCH–STATE RE-LATIONSHIPS IN EUROPE

Leszek Lech Garlicki,
Perspectives on Freedom of Conscience and Religion in the Jurisprudence of Constitutional Courts
2001 BYU L. Rev. 467, 468–69

From the European perspective, the Christian tradition is of fundamental significance. Therefore, most European constitutions and jurisprudence assume a predominantly Christian audience, since other religions have always been in the minority.

Even assuming this largely Christian audience, individual European nations have adopted vastly different schemes, which flow from their different histories and traditions. Consequently, along with traditionally Protestant states (e.g., Great Britain and the Scandinavian countries) and traditionally Catholic states (e.g., Austria, France, Spain, Ireland, Liechtenstein, Slovenia, Poland, Portugal, and Italy), there are European countries of mixed religious structure (e.g., Germany and Switzerland). Historically speaking, almost all countries formerly had a state church, and the political elite were more interested in establishing and maintaining religious peace than ensuring religious equality. In countries where historical development focused on evolution rather than revolution, there may still be found a very close linkage between a dominant religion and the state, namely Scandinavian countries and the Anglican Church in England. However, in a majority of Continental countries, the official relationship between church and state eventually broke down. This separation of church and state is not meant to result in a lack of assistance or cooperation by the state to churches and does not foreclose the existence of some churches remaining closer to the state than other religious organizations or groups.

Laura Barnett
Freedom of Religion and Religious Symbols in the Public Sphere

PARLIAMENTARY INFORMATION AND RESEARCH SERVICE,
LIBRARY OF PARLIAMENT (CANADA), 2–3, 26–28 (2006)

While some European countries have well established religious identities within their society–British and German Protestantism, Italian and French Catholicism–most countries today are reluctant to establish any clear connection between church and state. In moving definitively away from the religious nature of European politics, a few countries, most particularly France, have gone so far as to proclaim themselves "laic" states. An ambiguous term that is equivalent neither to "secularity" nor "neutrality," at its most general level, laïcité refers to an official separation of church and state. Yet beyond this, laïcité indicates a specific state policy with respect to religion, although it varies broadly between countries. In the more extreme example of countries such as France and Turkey, laïcité indicates an active program whereby the country is promoted as fundamentally politically independent of any religious authority and in which a need for public order can be used to justify interference with freedom of religion–a form of anti-religion to deal with the excesses of religion.

. . .

Of all states in the Western world, France's conception of secularism is the most rigidly defined, with strictly enforced policies that keep religion out of the public sphere. One of the crucial aspects of the French interpretation of the right to freedom of religion is that right's definition as a *liberté publique*, rather than as a civil right (as the term is understood in most other countries). In France, civil rights do not exist as natural rights that an individual may assert against the state; rather, they are the "natural right to enjoy freedoms defined and delimited exclusively" by state law. Citizens must profess allegiance to the state first and religious institutions second; religion belongs to the private sphere, and freedom of religion exists within the confines prescribed by state laïcité. Clearly, recognition of freedom of religion within a laïc state is full of contradictory tensions, with the end result that although France may have very strong notions of negative freedom, positive freedoms can be significantly restrained.

. . .

State laïcité essentially means that the state supports no belief or particular ideology and cannot discriminate based on religion. This is a notion that fits well with France's policy of immigrant assimilation. While France may be open to newcomers, its policy is to insist on the homogeneity of French culture, with assimilation as a condition of membership. . . .

This bounded notion of freedom of religion is tightly linked to a larger cultural and historical phenomenon in France, a country that revels in its revolutionary heritage as a secular republic. In a nation where the principle of laïcité is ingrained as an ultimate expression of French culture, freedom of religion will always be defined from within this framework. Partially inspired by the Enlightenment philosophy of glorified Reason doing battle against the corrupt influence of religion, France abides by a secular tradition which sees national republican identity as taking precedence over individual identity, with ethnic belonging and religious differences relegated to the private sphere.

II.   COMPARATIVE LAW

A.   CONSTITUTIONAL TEXTS

1.   *United States*

First Amendment

Congress shall make no law respecting an establishment of religion, or prohibiting the free exercise thereof

Article VI

The Senators and Representatives before mentioned, and the Members of the several State Legislatures, and all executive and judicial Officers, both of the United States and of the several States, shall be bound by Oath or Affirmation, to support this Constitution; but no religious Test shall ever be required as a Qualification to any Office or public Trust under the United States.

2.   *Turkey*

Article 2 Characteristics of the Republic

The Republic of Turkey is a democratic, secular and social state governed by the rule of law; bearing in mind the concepts of public peace, national solidarity and justice; respecting human rights; loyal to the nationalism of Atatürk, and based on the fundamental tenets set forth in the Preamble.

Article 24 Freedom of Religion and Conscience

Everyone has the right to freedom of conscience, religious belief and conviction.

Acts of worship, religious services, and ceremonies shall be conducted freely, provided that they do not violate the provisions of Article 14 [a provision setting limits on the exercise of fundamental rights to prevent their abuse.]

No one shall be compelled to worship, or to participate in religious ceremonies and rites, to reveal religious beliefs and convictions, or be blamed or accused because of his religious beliefs and convictions.

Education and instruction in religion and ethics shall be conducted under state supervision and control. Instruction in religious culture and moral education shall be compulsory in the curricula of primary and secondary schools. Other religious education and instruction shall be subject to the individual's own desire, and in the case of minors, to the request of their legal representatives.

No one shall be allowed to exploit or abuse religion or religious feelings, or things held sacred by religion, in any manner whatsoever, for the purpose of personal or political influence, or for even partially basing the fundamental, social, economic, political, and legal order of the state on religious tenets

3. *Ireland*

Article 44

1. The State acknowledges that the homage of public worship is due to Almighty God. It shall hold His Name in reverence, and shall respect and honor religion.

2.1. Freedom of conscience and the free profession and practice of religion are, subject to public order and morality, guaranteed to every citizen.

2.2. The State guarantees not to endow any religion.

2.3. The State shall not impose any disabilities or make any discrimination on the ground of religious profession, belief or status.

2.4. Legislation providing State aid for schools shall not discriminate between schools under the management of different religious denominations, nor be such as to affect prejudicially the right of any child to attend a school receiving public money without attending religious instruction at that school.

2.5   Every religious denomination shall have the right to manage its own affairs, own, acquire and administer property, movable and immovable, and maintain institutions for religious or charitable purposes.

2.6   The property of any religious denomination or any educational institution shall not be diverted save for necessary works of public utility and on payment of compensation.

4. Egypt

Art. 2.   Islam is the Religion of the State. Arabic is its official language, and the principal source of legislation is Islamic Jurisprudence (Sharia).

Art. 19.   Religious education shall be a principal subject in the courses of general education.

Art. 40.   All citizens are equal before the law. They have equal public rights and duties without discrimination due to sex, ethnic origin, language, religion or creed.

Art. 46.   The State shall guarantee the freedom of belief and the freedom of practicing religious rights.

5. South Africa

15. Freedom of religion, belief and opinion

1.   Everyone has the right to freedom of conscience, religion, thought, belief and opinion.

2.   Religious observances may be conducted at state or state-aided institutions, provided that

   a.   those observances follow rules made by the appropriate public authorities;

   b.   they are conducted on an equitable basis; and

   c.   attendance at them is free and voluntary.

3.

   a.   This section does not prevent legislation recognizing

      i.   marriages concluded under any tradition, or a system of religious, personal or family law; or

      ii.   systems of personal and family law under any tradition, or adhered to by persons professing a particular religion.

    b.   Recognition in terms of paragraph (a) must be consistent with this section and the other provisions of the Constitution.

31. Cultural, religious and linguistic communities

1. Persons belonging to a cultural, religious or linguistic community may not be denied the right, with other members of that community

    a.   to enjoy their culture, practice their religion and use their language; and

    b.   to form, join and maintain cultural, religious and linguistic associations and other organs of civil society.

2. The rights in subsection (1) may not be exercised in a manner inconsistent with any provision of the Bill of Rights.

36. Limitation of Rights

1. The rights in the Bill of Rights may be limited only in terms of law of general application to the extent that the limitation is reasonable and justifiable in an open and democratic society based on human dignity, equality and freedom, taking into account all relevant factors, including

    a.   the nature of the right;

    b.   the importance of the purpose of the limitation;

    c.   the nature and extent of the limitation;

    d.   the relation between the limitation and its purpose; and

    e.   less restrictive means to achieve the purpose.

6. Canada

Constitutional Act of 1982

1. Guarantee of Rights and Freedoms

The *Canadian Charter of Rights and Freedoms* guarantees the rights and freedoms set out in it subject only to such reasonable limits prescribed by law as can be demonstrably justified in a free and democratic society.

2. Fundamental Freedoms

2. Everyone has the following fundamental freedoms:

    (a) freedom of conscience and religion

15. Equality Rights

1. Every individual is equal before and under the law and has the right to the equal protection and equal benefit of the law

without discrimination and, in particular, without discrimination based on race, national or ethnic origin, color, religion, sex, age or mental or physical disability.

2. Subsection (1) does not preclude any law, program or activity that has as its object the amelioration of conditions of disadvantaged individuals or groups including those that are disadvantaged because of race, national or ethnic origin, color, religion, sex, age or mental or physical disability.

27. Multicultural heritage

This Charter shall be interpreted in a manner consistent with the preservation and enhancement of the multicultural heritage of Canadians.

7. *Germany*

Article 4 (Freedom of faith, of conscience and of creed).

1. Freedom of faith and of conscience, and freedom of creed religious or ideological, are inviolable.

2. The undisturbed practice of religion is guaranteed.

3. No one may be compelled against his conscience to render war service as an armed combatant. Details will be regulated by a Federal law.

Article 7 (School Education).

1. The entire education system is under the supervision of the state.

2. The persons entitled to bring up a child have the right to decide whether they shall receive religious instruction.

3. Religious instruction forms part of the ordinary curriculum in state and municipal schools, excepting secular schools. Without prejudice to the state's right of supervision, religious instruction is given in accordance with the tenets of the religious communities. No teacher may be obliged against his will to give religious instruction.

4. The right to establish private schools is guaranteed. Private schools as a substitute for state or municipal schools, require the approval of the state and are subject to the laws of the Laender. This approval must be given if private schools are not inferior to the state or municipal schools in their educational aims, their facilities and the professional training of their teaching staff, and if a segregation of the pupils according to the means of the parents is not promoted. This approval must be withheld if the economic and legal position of the teaching staff is not sufficiently assured.

5. A private elementary school shall be admitted only if the educational authority finds that it serves a special pedagogic interest or if, on the application of persons entitled to bring up children, it is to be established as an interdenominational or denominational or ideological school and a state or municipal elementary school of this type does not exist in the community

8. *Australia*

Chapter 5.   The States

116.   The Commonwealth shall not make any law for establishing any religion, or for imposing any religious observance, or for prohibiting the free exercise of any religion, and no religious test shall be required as a qualification for any office or public trust under the Commonwealth.

9.   *Japan*

Article 20.

Freedom of religion is guaranteed to all. No religious organization shall receive any privileges from the State, nor exercise any political authority. No person shall be compelled to take part in any religious act, celebration, rite or practice. The State and its organs shall refrain from religious education or any other religious activity.

Article 89.

No public money or other property shall be expended or appropriated for the use, benefit or maintenance of any religious institution or association, or for any charitable, educational or benevolent enterprises not under the control of public authority.

B.   CONSTITUTIONAL FRAMEWORKS

W. Cole Durham, Jr.
Perspectives on Religious Liberty:
A Comparative Framework

in HUMAN RIGHTS IN GLOBAL PERSPECTIVES: LEGAL PERSPECTIVES 1, 20–23
(Johan d. van der Vyver & John Witte, Jr. eds., Martinus Nijhoff Publishers 1996)

[The church-state regimes of different countries can be categorized along a religious-liberty continuum. At one end of the continuum] one first encounters *absolute theocracies* of the type one associates with stereotypical views of Islamic fundamentalism. In fact, a range of regimes is possible in Muslim theory, depending on the scope given to internal Muslim beliefs about toleration and also depending on the extent to which flexible interpretation of Shari'a law creates normative space for modernization. [Other church-state arrangements along the continuum vary substantially.]

Established Churches. The notion of an "established church" is vague, and can in fact cover a range of possible church-state configurations with very different implications for the religious freedom of minority groups. At one extreme, a regime with an established church that is granted a strictly enforced monopoly in religious affairs is closely related to one with theocratic rule. Spain or Italy at some periods are classical exemplars. The next position is held by countries that have an established religion that tolerates a restricted set of divergent belief. An Islamic country that tolerates "people of the Book" (but not others) would be one example; a country with an established Christian church that tolerates a number of major faiths, but disparages others would be another. The next position is a country that maintains an established church, but guarantees equal treatment for all other religious beliefs. Great Britain would be a fitting example.

Endorsed Churches. The next category consists of regimes that fall just short of formally affirming that one particular church is the official church of a nation, but acknowledge that one particular church has a special place in the country's traditions. This is quite typical in countries where Roman Catholicism is predominant and a new constitution has been adopted relatively recently (at least since Vatican II). The endorsed church is specially acknowledged, but the country's constitution asserts that other groups are entitled to equal protection. Sometimes the endorsement is relatively innocuous, and remains strictly limited to recognition that a particular religious tradition has played an important role in a country's history and culture. In other cases, endorsement operates in fact as a thinly disguised method of preserving the prerogatives of establishment while maintain[ing] the formal appearance of a more liberal regime.

Cooperationist Regimes. The next category of regime grants no special status to dominant churches, but the state continues to cooperate closely with churches in a variety of ways. Germany provides the prototypical example of this type of regime, though it is certainly not alone in this regard. Most notably, the cooperationist state may provide significant funding to various church-related activities, such as religious education or maintenance of churches, payment of clergy, and so forth. Very often in such regimes, relations with churches are managed through special agreements, concordats, and the like. Spain, Italy and Poland as well as several Latin American countries follow this pattern. The state may also cooperate in helping with the gathering of contributions (e.g., the withholding of "church tax" in Germany). Cooperationist countries frequently have patterns of aid or assistance that benefit larger denominations in particular. However, they do not specifically endorse any religion, and they are committed to affording equal treatment to all religious organizations. Since different religious communities have different needs, cooperationist programs can raise more complex interdenominational problems of equal treatment. It is all too easy to slip from cooperation into patterns of state preference. Also, vis-à-vis more separationist regimes, more complex questions of protecting the self-determination and internal autonomy of religious organizations arise.

Note that in some cases, a cooperationist approach may be necessary for a transition period. For example, because of the devastated condition of churches after communism in East Central Europe and the former U.S.S.R., corrective justice seems to require return of extensive properties wrongfully taken from various churches. This process of restoration will necessarily entail heavy cooperation on the part of the state with churches, but it is not completely clear whether this process should be handled in a way that will aim at restoration of patterns of cooperation, or whether the required cooperation will be merely transitional, while the long term policy is to establish a more voluntarist regime.

Accommodationist Regimes. A regime may insist on separation of church and state, yet retain a posture of benevolent neutrality toward religion. Accommodationism might be thought of as cooperationism without the provision of any direct financial subsidies to religion or religious education. An accommodationist regime would have no qualms about recognizing the importance of religion as part of national or local culture, accommodating religious symbols in public settings, allowing tax, dietary, holiday, Sabbath, and other kinds of exemptions, and so forth. . . .

Separationist Regimes. [T]he slogan "separation of church and state" can be used to cover a fairly broad and diverse range of regimes. At the benign end, separationism differs relatively little from accommodationism. The major difference is that separationism, as it[s] name suggests, insists on more rigid separation of church and state. Any suggestion of public support for religion is deemed inappropriate. Religious symbols in public displays such as Christmas crèches are not allowed. Even indirect subsidies to religion through tax deductions or tax exemptions are either suspect or proscribed. Granting religiously-based exemptions from general public laws is viewed as impermissible favoritism for religion. No religious teaching or indoctrination of any kind is permitted in public schools (although some teaching about religion from an objective standpoint may be permitted). The mere reliance on religious premises in public argument is deemed to run afoul of the church-state separation principle. Members of the clergy are not permitted to hold public office.

More extreme forms of separationism make stronger attempts to cordon off religion from public life. One form this can take is through tightening the state monopoly on certain forms of educational or social services. In the educational realm, the state can ban home schooling altogether, can proscribe private schools, or can submit either of the foregoing to such extensive accreditation requirements that it is virtually impossible for independent religious education to function. Different regimes make differing judgments about the extent to which religious marriages will be recognized. A range of social or charitable services (including health care) may be regulated in ways that make it difficult for religious organizations to carry out their perceived ministries in this area. "Separation" [may require] that religion retreat from any domain that the state desires to occupy, but [be] untroubled by intrusive state regulation and intervention in religious affairs.

Inadvertent Insensitivity. Overlapping with some forms of separationism is a recurrent pattern of legislative or bureaucratic insensitivity to distinctive religious needs. Bureaucrats often fail to distinguish between conduct regulated in secular settings (e.g., regulating land use planning, labor discrimination, taxation with respect to secular business activities) and regulating similar conduct in religious settings. In many cases, fairly simple accommodations can satisfactorily solve religious concerns. Regulations as initially formulated often lack any anti-religious animus; those drafting the regulations were simply unaware of the religious implications of their regulations. At some point, those afflicted by the unintended burden bring the problem to the attention of government officials. At this point, a reasonable accommodation can be worked out, or inadvertent insensitivity shades into conscious persecution. The flip side of inadvertent insensitivity is subtle or not-so-subtle privileging of main-line or dominant groups. . . .

Hostility and Overt Persecution. The test in this area is how smaller religious groups are treated. Government officials seldom persecute larger religious groups (though this was certainly not unheard of in communist lands). Persecution can take the form of imprisonment of those who insists on acting in accordance with divergent religious beliefs. In its most egregious forms, it involves "ethnic cleansing" or most extreme, genocide. More typical problems involve less dramatic forms of bureaucratic roadblocks which cumulatively have the effect of significantly impairing religious liberty. These can take the form of denying or delaying registration (granting entity status) and obstructing land use approvals.

Notes and Questions

1. As can be seen in the excerpts from constitutional texts presented on pp. 120–25, the provisions relating to religion and the relationship between church and state in the constitutions of many countries are much more detailed and comprehensive than the relatively sparse language of the religion clauses of the First Amendment. Part of that textual detail may be a result of the far greater involvement between church and state which is permitted in those constitutional systems. Yet these countries also recognized that church-state relationships were too sensitive to be left to the discretion of the political branches of government. Accordingly, they adopted extensive constitutional requirements to structure and control the cooperative arrangements between government and religion.

2. As should be clear from Professor Durham's approach to classifying countries in terms of their church-state systems, there is considerable variation within each category that he describes in his article. Other scholars might employ other classification frameworks to describe the range of church-state relations that have developed throughout the world. Given this diversity, do you think it is possible to identify any universal principles relating to religion that should apply today in every nation?

3. In comparing the separation of church and state in the U.S. and France, Joan Wallach Scott explains:

In America, home to religious minorities who fled persecution at the hands of European rulers, the separation between church and state was meant to protect religions from unwarranted government intervention. . . . This was designed to prevent any single religion from dominating the affairs of state, and it was soon extended to keep religiosity as such out of government. In France, separation was intended to secure the allegiance of individuals to the republic and so break the political power of the Catholic Church. There the state claimed the undivided loyalty of citizens to the nation, and that meant relegating to a private sphere the claims of religious communities. This was expressed as state protection of individuals from the claims of religion. In France, the state protects individuals from religion; in America, religions are protected from the state and the state from religion.

JOAN WALLACH SCOTT, POLITICS OF THE VEIL 91–92 (Princeton Univ. Press 2007).

III. INTERNATIONAL AND SUPRANATIONAL LAW

A. GENERAL PRINCIPLES OF INTERNATION-AL LAW

1. *Universal Declaration of Human Rights*

(Adopted by the UN General Assembly 10 December 1948)

Article 18.

Everyone has the right to freedom of thought, conscience and religion; this right includes freedom to change his religion or belief, and freedom, either alone or in community with others and in public or private, to manifest his religion or belief in teaching, practice, worship and observance.

2. *International Covenant on Civil and Political Rights*

(Adopted by the UN General Assembly 16 December 1966)

Article 18.

1.   Everyone shall have the right to freedom of thought, conscience and religion. This right shall include freedom to have or to adopt a religion or belief of his choice, and freedom, either individually or in community with others and in public or private, to manifest his religion or belief in worship, observance, practice and teaching.

2.   No one shall be subject to coercion which would impair his freedom to have or to adopt a religion or belief of his choice.

3.   Freedom to manifest one's religion or beliefs may be subject only to such limitations as are prescribed by law and are necessary to protect public safety, order, health, or morals or the fundamental rights and freedoms of others.

4.   The States Parties to the present Covenant undertake to have respect for the liberty of parents and, when applicable, legal guardians to ensure the religious and moral education of their children in conformity with their own convictions.

B. SUPRANATIONAL LAW

1. *European Convention on Human Rights (ECHR)*

(Adopted by the Council of Europe 4 November 1950)

Article 9. Freedom of thought, conscience and religion

1.   Everyone has the right to freedom of thought, conscience and religion; this right includes freedom to change his religion

or belief and freedom, either alone or in community with others and in public or private, to manifest his religion or belief, in worship, teaching, practice and observance.

2 Freedom to manifest one's religion or beliefs shall be subject only to such limitations as are prescribed by law and are necessary in a democratic society in the interests of public safety, for the protection of public order, health or morals, or for the protection of the rights and freedoms of others.

Article 14. Prohibition of discrimination

The enjoyment of the rights and freedoms set forth in this Convention shall be secured without discrimination on any ground such as sex, race, color, language, religion, political or other opinion, national or social origin, association with a national minority, property, birth or other status.

Article 2 of Protocol No. 1 (P1–2). Right to education

No person shall be denied the right to education. In the exercise of any functions which it assumes in relation to education and to teaching, the State shall respect the right of parents to ensure such education and teaching in conformity with their own religious and philosophical convictions.

2. The Meaning and Enforcement of Article 9 of the ECHR

Carolyn Evans & Christopher A. Thomas,
Church-State Relations in the European Court of Human Rights

,

2006 BYU L. Rev. 699, 700

The focus of the European Court of Human Rights ("the Court") with regard to religion is summarized in a passage that it used in the case of *Kokkinakis v. Greece*, 20 Eur. Ct. H.R. (1993) and has repeated in every major religious freedom case since:

> [F]reedom of thought, conscience and religion is one of the foundations of a "democratic society." . . . It is, in its religious dimension, one of the most vital elements that go to make up the identity of believers and their conception of life, but it is also a precious asset to atheists, agnostics, skeptics and the unconcerned. The pluralism indissociable from a democratic society, which has been dearly won over the centuries, depends on it.

These words are at the heart of the European approach to religious-freedom cases brought under the ECHR. The passage acknowledges the importance of religious freedom to society but does not deal in any detail with the precise nature of the relationship between church and state except to say that religious freedom, rather than religion itself, is a "foundation" of a democratic society and indissociable from pluralism. The state itself, therefore, must be democratic and pluralistic in order to fit within the requirements of the ECHR, and it must respect religious freedom, but within those boundaries, there is no requirement or prohibition of establishment between church and state.

Peter G. Danchin & Lisa Forman
The Evolving Jurisprudence of the European Court of Human Rights and the Protection of Religious Minorities

in Protecting the Human Rights of Religious Minorities in Eastern Europe 192, 197 (Peter Danchin & Elizabeth A. Cole eds., Columbia Univ. Press 2002)

Article 9(1) provides that everyone has the right to freedom of thought, conscience, and religion. This includes the freedom to change religion or belief, and the freedom to manifest religion or belief in worship, teaching, practice, and observance. The protection in Article 9(1) extends beyond solely religious thought and conscience and protects the rights of conscience of atheists and agnostics. However the *schema* of protection afforded under Article 9(1) does not extend to every act motivated by religious belief. In *Arrowsmith v. United Kingdom* [(No. 8), 123 Eur. Ct. H.R. (1977)], the Court held that the applicant's dissemination of leaflets to troops urging them not to serve in Northern Ireland was not protected under Article 9(1) as religious "practice" of her pacifism because not every part of the leaflet endorsed pacifist philosophy and it did not constitute a general call for all persons to give up violence. The Court has also consistently found that acts of conscientious objection do not fall within the scope of Article 9(1). Such acts include conscientious objection to military service, to alternative service, to paying taxes used for military purposes, and even to making tax payments to churches.

The Court has held that for a belief to be protected under Article 9 it must attain a "certain level of cogency, seriousness, cohesion and importance." Such beliefs include those pertaining both to conventional and less mainstream religious beliefs: Christianity, Judaism, Islam, Hinduism, Sikhism, and Buddhism, as well as beliefs held by members of the Jehovah's Witnesses, the Church of Scientology, and the Unification Church fall under the protection of Article 9. If there are doubts as to a religion's existence, it is for the applicant to demonstrate its existence. For instance, on the basis that the applicant had failed to prove its existence, the Court has disputed the existence of Wicca as a religion.

3. Margin of Appreciation

Javier Martínez-Torrón
*Freedom of Expression versus Freedom of Religion
in the European Court of Human Rights*

in ISSUES IN CONSTITUTIONAL LAW 4. CENSORIAL ACTIVITIES: FREE SPEECH AND RELIGION
IN A FUNDAMENTALIST WORLD 233, 239 n.17
(András Sajó, ed., Eleven Publishing 2007)

The doctrine of the margin of appreciation was adopted by the [European Court of Human Rights] to reconcile the roles of the Court and of national authorities in the interpretation of the 'necessity' of restrictions on fundamental rights within the context of the ECHR. In brief, that doctrine maintains that, when applying the limitations on individual freedoms permitted by different articles of the ECHR (especially Arts. 8–11), the national authorities of every state must be recognized a reasonable margin of appreciation. The reason is that national authorities, being closer to the respective societies, are in a better position to evaluate the necessity of the restrictive measures adopted and can better appraise the needs of the public interest and interpret the relevant domestic law. That power of appreciation, nevertheless, is not unlimited but goes hand in hand with a 'European control' of national authorities' decisions, which are subject to the European Court's supervision. If national authorities are in a better condition to assess the domestic circumstances–factual and legal, the Court is better qualified to interpret the spirit of the Convention and its consequences with respect to the protection of citizens' freedom.

Laura Barnett
*Freedom of Religion and Religious Symbols
in the Public Sphere*
Parliamentary Information and Research Service,
Library of Parliament (Canada), 35–36 (2006)

Under the European Convention, Article 9(1) protects freedom of thought, conscience and religion.... However, subsection (2) permits certain restrictions on the manifestation of belief.... The ECHR accordingly grants the State Parties a "margin of appreciation" to assess those needs, allowing them to balance the religious freedoms of one group against those of others. The court has proven less willing to uphold religious freedoms when the impugned beliefs are expressed through conduct that has an adverse effect on the interests of others. The margin of appreciation means that the ECHR will always play a subsidiary role, as, in principle, national authorities are better placed than an international court to evaluate local needs and conditions. Thus, decisions made by local authorities are granted some leeway, but are ultimately subject to review by the court for conformity requirements of the European Convention.

Where the relationship between religion and the state is at stake, the role of the national decision-making body is given particular importance. Each state's attitude towards religion is, at its core, a political issue, and generally a product of historical tradition and the social circumstances in each country. The ECHR recognizes the need for a fair balance among all of the interests at stake–the rights and freedoms of others, the need to avoid civil unrest, threats to public order, and policies of pluralism. The margin of appreciation is especially important in discussions of religious symbols in the educational system, as policy on this issue varies widely depending on national traditions, and because there is no uniform conception of the requirements of "the protection of the rights and freedoms of others."

Ultimately, the emphasis of Article 9 is on pluralism and tolerance of the views of others, rather than on the protection of individual beliefs which sometimes conflict with the demands of a secular democratic society.

Notes and Questions

1. Some provisions of the European Convention on Human Rights are identified as Articles while others are identified as Protocols. The Articles are part of the original Convention. Each Protocol operates as an amendment to the Convention, but only applies to those countries who are signatories to it. Since the ECHR went into effect, thirteen Protocols have been adopted. Six of them, Protocols Nos. 1, 4, 6, 7, 12, and 13, provide for rights and liberties in addition to those already recognized and guaranteed by the Articles of the Convention. Guaranteeing a right through a Protocol, rather than an Article in the original Convention, does not imply that the right is of lesser importance or value. More likely, it reflects the difficulty experienced in obtaining a consensus on the text of the guarantee.

2. The "margin of appreciation" the ECHR applies is wider for freedom of religion cases than freedom of speech cases. As one international law scholar noted, "whereas an inclination to seek more general (universal) standards may be seen in respect to freedom of expression or to some purely political freedoms, interpretations of the freedom of religion cannot ignore that—as [the Court] observed ... in *Otto-Preminger–Institut* [*v. Austria*, 26 Eur. Ct. H.R. (1994)]—'it is not

possible to discern throughout Europe a uniform conception of significance of religion in society.' " Leszek Lech Garlicki, *Collective Aspects of the Religious Freedoms: Recent Developments in the Case Law of the European Court of Human Rights, in* ISSUES IN CONSTITUTIONAL LAW 4. CENSORIAL SENSITIVITIES: FREE SPEECH AND RELIGION IN A FUNDAMENTALIST WORLD 217, 231 (András Sajó, ed., Eleven Publishing 2007).

Chapter Five

DEFINING RELIGION

I. INTERNATIONAL AND SUPRANATIONAL LAW

Jeremy Gunn
The Complexity of Religion and the Definition of "Religion" in International Law

16 HARV. HUM. RTS. J. 189, 189–91 (2003)

Although many international and regional human rights instruments guarantee rights related to freedom of religion or belief, none attempts to define the term "religion." ... [T]he term "religion" remains undefined as a matter of international law. The absence of a definition of "religion" is not peculiar to international human rights conventions; most national constitutions also include clauses on freedom of religion without defining "religion." Thus we are presented, on the one hand, with important provisions guaranteeing fundamental rights pertaining to religion, but on the other hand the term itself is left undefined. Of course, the absence of a definition of a critical term does not differentiate religion from most other rights identified in human rights instruments and constitutions. However, because religion is much more complex than other guaranteed rights, the difficulty of understanding what is and is not protected is significantly greater.

. . .

While academics have the luxury of debating whether the term "religion" is hopelessly ambiguous, judges and lawyers often do not. Asylum-case adjudicators, for example, may be called upon to decide whether there is a "well-founded fear of being persecuted for reasons of . . . religion" regardless of whether the 1951 Refugee

136

Convention offers a definition. Similarly, judges on the European Court of Human Rights may be required to give meaning to the term "religion" for purposes of interpreting Article 9 of the European Convention. Judicial decisions about what constitutes religion make a very real difference in the lives of persons who may or may not obtain refugee status, or in the economic viability of a group that may or may not be recognized as a tax-exempt religious association.[1]

II. COMPARATIVE LAW

CHURCH OF THE NEW FAITH v. COMMISSIONER OF PAY–ROLL TAX (VICTORIA)

(1983) 154 CLR. 120
High Court of Australia

Mason A.C.J. and Brennan J.

1. The Church of the New Faith Incorporated was incorporated under that name on 31 January 1969.... Subsequently, a change in name to "The Church of Scientology Incorporated" was registered in South Australia.

2. The corporation was assessed to pay-roll tax ... [on] wages ... paid or payable during the period 1 July 1975 to 30 June 1977. The corporation objected to the assessment upon the ground that the wages were exempt under the provisions of s. 10(b) [as wages paid or payable by a religious institution]....

3. [The case has focused on the question] ... "Is Scientology a religion?"

---

1. The British Charity Commissioners must decide, for example, whether an entity is "religious" for the purpose of determining whether it is tax-exempt. In the United States, courts must sometimes consider whether governmental financing of certain institutions constitutes an impermissible "establishment of *religion*" under the U.S. Constitution.... [T]he French Law on the Separation of Church and State of 1905 ... [provides that if] a religious organization is recognized by appropriate administration officials as a "religion," it becomes eligible to receive certain benefits under French law.

Whether or not state institutions are competent to determine what is and is not religion, in the actual world of law, judicial and political institutions are sometimes forced to make such determinations. Other situations where state officials (including judges, administrators, and legislators) are called upon to determine whether something is religious include most notably:

—whether an entity is a "religion" or "religious association" for purposes of granting legal personality, obtaining tax benefits, or limiting the personal liability of the organizers;

—whether someone has "religious" beliefs for the purpose of obtaining conscientious objector status;

—whether someone should be exempted from a law of general applicability on the grounds of religious belief (e.g., a Sikh motorcyclist being exempted from a requirement to wear a helmet or a Muslim or Jewish slaughterhouse being permitted to kill animals in accordance with ritual laws).

. . .

7.   Counsel for the corporation contended for a wide definition of religion in accordance with the indicia of a religion set out by Adams J. in *Malnak v. Yogi*, [592 F.2d 197] (1979), though it is clear that the formulation of those indicia owed much to the tests adopted by the Supreme Court of the United States in construing particular Acts of the Congress. On the other hand, counsel for the Commissioner contended for a narrow definition which accorded with the test of a religion . . . which confines the concept to theistic religions. . . .

8.   An endeavor to define religion for legal purposes gives rise to peculiar difficulties. . . . A definition cannot be adopted merely because it would satisfy the majority of the community or because it corresponds with a concept currently accepted by that majority. The development of the law towards complete religious liberty and religious equality . . . would be subverted and the guarantees in s. 116 of the Constitution would lose their character as a bastion of freedom if religion were so defined as to exclude from its ambit minority religions out of the main streams of religious thought. Though religious freedom and religious equality are beneficial to all true religions, minority religions–not well established and accepted– stand in need of special protection. . . .

. . .

10.   These considerations, tending against the adoption of a narrow definition, may suggest the rejection of any definition which would exclude from the category of religion the beliefs, practices and observances of any group who assert their beliefs, practices and observances to be religious. But such an assertion cannot be adopted as a legal criterion. The mantle of immunity would soon be in tatters if it were wrapped around beliefs, practices and observances of every kind whenever a group of adherents chose to call them a religion. A more objective criterion is required.

. . .

12.   . . . The relevant inquiry is to ascertain what is meant by religion as an area of legal freedom or immunity, and that inquiry looks to those essential indicia of religion which attract that freedom or immunity. . . .

13.   The law seeks to leave man as free as possible in conscience to respond to the abiding and fundamental problems of human existence. In all societies and in all ages man has pondered upon the explanation of the existence of the phenomenological universe, the meaning of his existence and his destiny. . . . Under our law, the State has no prophetic role in relation to religious belief; the State can neither declare supernatural truth nor deter-

mine the paths through which the human mind must search in a quest for supernatural truth. The courts are constrained to accord freedom to faith in the supernatural, for there are no means of finding upon evidence whether a postulated tenet of supernatural truth is erroneous or whether a supernatural revelation of truth has been made. . . .

14. Religious belief is more than a cosmology; it is a belief in a supernatural Being, Thing or Principle. But religious belief is not by itself a religion. Religion is also concerned, at least to some extent, with a relationship between man and the supernatural order and with supernatural influence upon his life and conduct. . . . Thus religion encompasses conduct, no less than belief. . . . What man feels constrained to do or to abstain from doing because of his faith in the supernatural is prima facie within the area of legal immunity, for his freedom to believe would be impaired by restriction upon conduct in which he engages in giving effect to that belief. The canons of conduct which he accepts as valid for himself in order to give effect to his belief in the supernatural are no less a part of his religion than the belief itself. Conversely, unless there be a real connection between a person's belief in the supernatural and particular conduct in which that person engages, that conduct cannot itself be characterized as religious.

. . .

17. We . . . hold that, for the purposes of the law, the criteria of religion are twofold: first, belief in a supernatural Being, Thing or Principle; and second, the acceptance of canons of conduct in order to give effect to that belief, though canons of conduct which offend against the ordinary laws are outside the area of any immunity, privilege or right conferred on the grounds of religion. . . .

. . .

24. . . . [But this test cannot be limited to theistic religions.] To restrict the definition of religion to theistic religions is to exclude Theravada Buddhism, an acknowledged religion, and perhaps other acknowledged religions. It is too narrow a test. We would hold the test of religious belief to be satisfied by belief in supernatural Things or Principles and not to be limited to belief in God or in a supernatural Being. . . .

. . .

47. . . . [T]he state of the evidence in this case requires a finding that the general group of adherents have a religion. The question whether their beliefs, practices and observances are a

religion must, in the state of that evidence, be answered affirmatively....

...

Murphy J.

...

7. Religious freedom is a fundamental theme of our society.... Whenever the legislature prescribes what religion is, or permits or requires the executive or the judiciary to determine what religion is, this poses a threat to religious freedom. Religious discrimination by officials or by courts is unacceptable in a free society. The truth or falsity of religions is not the business of officials or the courts.... There is no religious club with a monopoly of State privileges for its members. The policy of the law is "one in, all in."

...

9. ... The better approach is to state what is sufficient, even if not necessary, to bring a body which claims to be religious within the category. Some claims to be religious are not serious but merely a hoax ... but to reach this conclusion requires an extreme case.... Any body which claims to be religious, and offers a way to find meaning and purpose in life, is religious. The Aboriginal religion of Australia and of other countries must be included. The list is not exhaustive; the categories of religion are not closed.

...

Wilson and Deane JJ.

17. ... There is no single characteristic which can be laid down as constituting a formularized legal criterion, whether of inclusion or exclusion, of whether a particular system of ideas and practices constitutes a religion within a particular State of the Commonwealth. The most that can be done is to formulate the more important of the indicia or guidelines by reference to which that question [may] be answered. Those indicia must ... be derived by empirical observation of accepted religions. They are liable to vary with changing social conditions and the relative importance of any particular one of them will vary from case to case....

18. One of the more important indicia of "a religion" is that the particular collection of ideas and/or practices involves belief in the supernatural, that is to say, belief that reality extends beyond that which is capable of perception by the senses. If that be absent, it is unlikely that one has "a religion." Another is that the ideas relate to man's nature and place in the universe and his relation to things supernatural. A third is that the ideas are accepted by adherents as requiring or encouraging them to observe particular

standards or codes of conduct or to participate in specific practices having supernatural significance. A fourth is that, however loosely knit and varying in beliefs and practices adherents may be, they constitute an identifiable group or identifiable groups. A fifth, and perhaps more controversial, indicium is that the adherents themselves see the collection of ideas and/or practices as constituting a religion.

19. ... [N]o one of the above indicia is necessarily determinative of the question whether a particular collection of ideas and/or practices should be objectively characterized as "a religion." They are no more than aids in determining that question and the assistance to be derived from them will vary according to the context in which the question arises. All of those indicia are, however, satisfied by most or all leading religions. It is unlikely that a collection of ideas and/or practices would properly be characterized as a religion if it lacked all or most of them or that, if all were plainly satisfied, what was claimed to be a religion could properly be denied that description. Ultimately however, that question will fall to be resolved as a matter of judgment on the basis of what the evidence establishes about the claimed religion. Putting to one side the case of the parody or sham, it is important that care be taken, in the exercise of that judgment, to ensure that the question is approached and determined as one of arid characterization not involving any element of assessment of the utility, the intellectual quality, or the essential "truth" or "worth" of tenets of the claimed religion.

* * *

NAPPALLI PETER WILLIAMS v. INSTITUTE OF TECHNICAL EDUCATION

[1999] 2 S.L.R. 569
Singapore Court of Appeal

YONG PUNG HOW CJ

[A teacher at a Singapore public school refused to recite the National Pledge or sing the National Anthem at school assemblies because "[a]s a Jehovah's Witness, he believed that taking the National Pledge or singing the National Anthem were acts of worship which should be reserved exclusively for God and not for country." After he was fired for his refusal, he filed a law suit arguing that his discharge violated Article 16(1) of the Singapore Constitution which prohibits discrimination on the basis of religion and 16(3) which provides that "No person shall be required to receive instruction in or to take part in any ceremony or act of worship of a religion other than his own."

The court ruled that requiring performance of the National Pledge and Anthem did not violate Article 16. The challenged policy did not require participation in a religious ceremony.]

24. ... [The Court explained that,] [f]or example, the policy does not introduce compulsory 'Bible Knowledge' classes for all students including those under 18 years of age whose parents are not of the Christian faith. It simply enforces the pledge and anthem ceremony as part of a student's educational exposure. Clearly, the 'prescribed purpose' of the policy was to encourage and instill a student's allegiance to the nation. It did not seek to establish a religion other than the religion of one's choice.

25. In the same vein, the appellant ... contended that the policy infringed his constitutional right to profess and practice his religion.... [He relied on a Canadian case, *Donald v. Hamilton Board of Education* [1945] O.R. 518, which ruled that children could not be expelled from school for refusing to recite the Canadian pledge and anthem.] This case does not apply to our local context. Firstly, the national anthem in *Donald* consisted of a prayer hymn. This unquestionably reflected some religious character. In contrast, the secular tenet of our [Constitution] ... is reflected in the secular tone of the pledge and national anthem. The respect attributed to country implicit in the pledge-taking cannot be found to bear religious significance.

26. ... The 'religion' referred to in ... the Constitution ... is not about a system of belief in one's own country but about a citizen's faith in a personal God, sometimes described as a belief in a supernatural being.... This acceptance that any belief or thought potentially holds religious value is, in our view, wholly misplaced....

27. ... [T]he protection of freedom of religion under our Constitution is premised on removing restrictions to one's choice of religious belief. This has been described as accommodative secularism. Obviously, not every conviction or belief, including those held with what ironically may best be described as religious fervor, qualifies as a religious belief. Indeed, we were inclined to agree with the view of the lower court in *Thomas v Review Board of the Indiana Employment Security Division* (1981) 450 U.S. 707 that such beliefs would best be philosophical choices rather than religious beliefs. In other words, although the pledge ceremony does not demand worship of the flag as a symbol, if a person held that understanding, that perception was a philosophical choice. It seemed clear to us that the appellant's interpretation of the pledge and anthem ceremony as a religious ceremony was a distortion of secular fact into religious belief. It is not accepted as a religious

belief and is not entitled to protection under the Constitution of Singapore.

29. Indeed, to accept the appellant's interpretation would rob the Constitution of any operative effect. How can the same Constitution guarantee religious freedom if, by asking citizens to pledge their allegiance to country, it is (as the appellant suggests) coercing participation in a religious ceremony? This excruciatingly absurd interpretation cannot have been what was envisaged by the authors of the Constitution. Not only did the plaintiff fail to prove the unconstitutionality of the policy; but the irresistible conclusion for this court was that, in the present case, there was no valid religious belief protected by the Constitution.

Notes and Questions

1. The U.S. Supreme Court has never provided a definition for religion for constitutional purposes. However, some lower court jurists such as Judge Adams, whose opinion in *Malnak* was noted by the Australia High Court, have attempted to provide an operational answer to the question of what constitutes a religion. Should the definition of religion accepted by the Australia High Court be adopted by American courts?

2. Is it necessary for religion to be defined the same way for all purposes? Some countries register particular religions as a basis for developing cooperative arrangements for those faith communities. In Germany, for example, religions must satisfy specific criteria to register as public corporations.

Article 137(5) of the Weimar Constitution (incorporated by Article 140 of the German Basic Law) states:

> Religious societies shall remain corporations under public law insofar as they have enjoyed that status in the past. Other religious societies shall be granted the same rights upon application, if their constitution and the number of their members give assurance of their permanency. If two or more religious societies established under public law unite into a single organization, it too shall be a corporation under public law.

Although the Muslim community in Germany is one of the largest religious communities in the country, it has not been granted the status of a public organization because it lacks a centralized organizational structure. The German authorities maintain that such a structure is necessary if a religious community is going to be able to work cooperatively with the government. "This has led to an impasse, with German authorities ... saying the Muslims need to organize themselves in such a way that they can qualify for public corporation status and many Muslims saying the Germans need to make allowance for their [non-hierarchical, decentralized] organizational structures." STEPHEN V. MONSMA & J. CHRISTOPHER SOPER, THE CHALLENGE OF PLURALISM

CHURCH AND STATE IN FIVE DEMOCRACIES 173 (Rowman & Littlefield, Publishers, Inc. 1997).

3. In *Thomas v. Review Board of the Indiana Employment Security Division*, 450 U.S. 707 (1981) referred to by the Singapore Court of Appeal, the plaintiff, Thomas, a Jehovah's Witness, was denied unemployment compensation by Indiana when he quit his job at a steel foundry and machinery company after being transferred to a department that produced turrets for tanks. Thomas explained that it would violate his religion if he worked on the production of military weapons. He argued that in denying him unemployment compensation because of his decision, Indiana had unconstitutionally burdened his right to exercise his religion.

The Indiana Supreme Court, in an opinion cited with approval by the Singapore Court of Appeal in *Williams*, rejected Thomas's claim because it concluded that his decision was more of a " 'personal philosophical choice' " than " 'a religious choice.' " *Id.* at 713. The Indiana court was influenced in reaching this decision by Thomas's willingness to work to produce steel that would be used for military purposes but not to work to produce the weapons more directly and by the fact that other Jehovah's Witnesses did not feel that working to produce military weapons was a violation of their faith.

The Supreme Court reversed. It noted that, "the guarantee of free exercise is not limited to beliefs which are shared by all the members of a religious sect." To the Court, the only issue to be adjudicated in a free exercise case like this one was whether Thomas had "terminated his work because of an honest conviction that such work was forbidden by his religion." *Id.* at 715–16.

4. The U.S. Supreme Court has held that it is unconstitutional for the state to compel an individual to recite the Pledge of Allegiance, but that decision was based on the Free Speech Clause of the First Amendment, not the Free Exercise Clause. In 2000, Michael Newdow brought suit in federal court arguing that it violated the Establishment Clause for a public school to direct children to recite the Pledge when it included the phrase "under God" in its content. Ultimately, the U.S. Supreme Court rejected Newdow's claim on standing grounds, *Elk Grove Unified School Dist. v. Newdow*, 542 U.S. 1 (2004), but several justices wrote concurring opinions arguing, on the merits, that no violation of the Establishment Clause had occurred.

Chief Justice Rehnquist's opinion resonated to some extent with the argument of the Singapore Court of Appeal in *Williams*. Rehnquist wrote, "Reciting the Pledge, or listening to others recite it, is a patriotic exercise, not a religious one; participants promise fidelity to our flag and our Nation, not to any particular god, faith, or church." *Id.* at 31.

Does the fact that a pledge or anthem is primarily intended to serve nationalistic or patriotic goals preclude the conclusion that they also have religious meaning for Free Exercise or Establishment Clause purposes?

Chapter Six

FREE EXERCISE PRINCIPLES

I. COMPARATIVE LAW

A. THE IMPORTANCE AND MEANING OF RELIGIOUS LIBERTY

R. v. BIG M DRUG MART LTD.
[1985] 1 S.C.R. 295
Supreme Court of Canada

94.   A truly free society is one which can accommodate a wide variety of beliefs, diversity of tastes and pursuits, customs and codes of conduct. A free society is one which aims at equality with respect to the enjoyment of fundamental freedoms.... Freedom must surely be founded in respect for the inherent dignity and the inviolable rights of the human person. The essence of the concept of freedom of religion is the right to entertain such religious beliefs as a person chooses, the right to declare religious beliefs openly and without fear of hindrance or reprisal, and the right to manifest religious belief by worship and practice or by teaching and dissemination. But the concept means more than that.

95.   Freedom can primarily be characterized by the absence of coercion or constraint. If a person is compelled by the state or the will of another to a course of action or inaction which he would not otherwise have chosen, he is not acting of his own volition and he cannot be said to be truly free.... Coercion includes not only such blatant forms of compulsion as direct commands to act or refrain from acting on pain of sanction, coercion includes indirect forms of control which determine or limit alternative courses of conduct available to others. Freedom in a broad sense embraces both the absence of coercion and constraint, and the right to manifest beliefs and practices. Freedom means that, subject to such limitations as

are necessary to protect public safety, order, health, or morals or the fundamental rights and freedoms of others, no one is to be forced to act in a way contrary to his beliefs or his conscience.

. . .

123. ... Religious belief and practice are historically proto-typical and, in many ways, paradigmatic of conscientiously-held beliefs and manifestations and are therefore protected by the [Canadian] Charter. Equally protected, and for the same reasons, are expressions and manifestations of religious non-belief and refusals to participate in religious practice.

B. CASE LAW

PRINCE v. PRESIDENT OF THE LAW SOCIETY

2002 (2) SA 794 (CC)
Constitutional Court of South Africa

[For the constitutional provisions of South Africa relating to religion, see pp. 122–23.]

[The appellant, Garreth Prince, had completed his legal studies, but was prohibited from registering to complete the requirement of community service (a prerequisite to being admitted to the practice of law) because he had been convicted on two occasions for the illegal possession of cannabis (marijuana). Prince stated that he would continue to use cannabis because doing so was a central requirement of his faith, the Rastafari religion.]

Judgment by Ngcobo, dissenting

The issues for decision

[33] ... The constitutional complaint is that the impugned provisions [of the statute] are overbroad in that the proscription is so wide that its unlimited terms also encompass the use or possession of cannabis by Rastafarians for bona fide religious purposes.

. . .

Does the prohibition limit the appellant's Constitutional rights?

[40] That Rastafari is a religion is not in dispute. It is now widely acknowledged that Rastafari is a form of religion. Nor is it in dispute that the appellant is a genuine follower of that religion. Similarly, it is not in dispute that the use of cannabis is central to the Rastafari religion. Although it is also used for culinary and medicinal purposes, these uses are no less sacred in the context of the religion....

. . .

Is the limitation on the appellant's constitutional rights justifiable?

[45]   To pass constitutional muster, the limitation on the constitutional rights must be justifiable in terms of section 36(1) of the Constitution. The limitation analysis [set out in section 36(1)] requires an inquiry into whether the limitation is reasonable and justifiable in an open and democratic society based on human dignity, equality and freedom. In that inquiry, the relevant considerations include the nature of the right and the scope of its limitation, the purpose, importance and the effect of the limitation, and the availability of less restrictive means to achieve that purpose. None of these factors is individually decisive. Nor are they exhaustive of the relevant factors to be considered. These factors together with other relevant factors are to be considered in the overall inquiry. . . .

[46]   Where, as here, the constitutional complaint is based on the failure of the statutory provisions to accommodate the religious use of cannabis by the Rastafari, the weighing-up and evaluation process must measure the three elements of the government interest, namely, the importance of the limitation; the relationship between the limitation and the underlying purpose of the limitation; and the impact that an exemption for religious reasons would have on the overall purpose of the limitation. The government interest must be balanced against the appellant's claim to the right to freedom of religion which also encompasses three elements: the nature and importance of that right in an open and democratic society based on human dignity, equality and freedom; the importance of the use of cannabis in the Rastafari religion; and the impact of the limitation on the right to practice the religion. . . .

. . .

(a) The nature of the right limited and the scope of limitation

[51]   The impugned provisions criminalize all use and possession of cannabis except when used for medicinal, analytical or research purposes. They criminalize the use of cannabis by the Rastafari regardless of where, how and why it is used. It matters not that they use it for sacramental purposes as a central part of the practice of their religion. The impugned provisions do not distinguish between the Rastafari who use cannabis for religious purposes and drug abusers. The effect of the prohibition is to state that in the eyes of the legal system all Rastafari are criminals. The stigma thus attached is manifest. Rastafari are at risk of arrest, prosecution and conviction for the offence of possession or use of cannabis. For the appellant, the consequences have gone beyond the stigma of criminal conviction. He is now prevented from practicing the profession of his choice. There can be no doubt that the

existence of the law which effectively punishes the practice of the Rastafari religion degrades and devalues the followers of the Rastafari religion in our society. It is a palpable invasion of their dignity. It strikes at the very core of their human dignity. It says that their religion is not worthy of protection. The impact of the limitation is profound indeed.

(b) The importance of the limitation

[52]   Yet, there can be little doubt about the importance of the limitation in the war on drugs. That war serves an important pressing social purpose: the prevention of harm caused by the abuse of dependence-producing drugs and the suppression of trafficking in those drugs. The abuse of drugs is harmful to those who abuse them and therefore to society. The government thus has a clear interest in prohibiting the abuse of harmful drugs. Our international obligations ... require us to fight that war subject to our Constitution.

[53]   ... On the evidence of the experts on both sides ... cannabis is a harmful drug. However, such harm is cumulative and dose-related. Uncontrolled use of cannabis may lead to the very harm that the legislation seeks to prevent. Effective prevention of the abuse of cannabis and the suppression of trafficking in cannabis are therefore legitimate government goals.... But does the achievement of these goals require a complete ban on even purely religious uses of cannabis by Rastafari, regardless of how and where it is used?

Could a religious exemption be granted without undermining the purpose of the prohibition?

[54]   The government does not contend that the achievement of its goals requires it to impose an absolute ban on the use or possession of drugs. Nor was it contended that any and all uses of cannabis in any circumstances are harmful. The use and possession of cannabis for research or analytical purposes under the control of the government can hardly be said to be harmful, let alone an abuse of cannabis. Similarly, the use of cannabis for medicinal purpose under the care and supervision of a medical doctor cannot be said to be harmful. This is so because a medical doctor will control the dosage taken and thus ensure that its use does not cause harm. These uses of cannabis are exempted because they do not undermine the purpose of the prohibition. It follows therefore that if the use of cannabis by the Rastafari is not inherently harmful or if its use can effectively be controlled by the government to prevent harm and trafficking in cannabis, refusal to allow for a religious exemption in these circumstances can hardly be said to be reasonable and justifiable....

[55]   Two points need to be made at the outset in this regard. First, it is significant to bear in mind that the Rastafari use cannabis in different circumstances: it may be consumed by smoking it as a cigarette or in a chalice, eating it as part of a meal or drinking it as a tonic, or it may be used in bathing or burnt as an incense at religious ceremonies and gatherings. While it is not obligatory to consume it, it is nevertheless required that it must be used in one form or another. . . .

. . .

[57]   . . . [To justify its decision in this case, the Government has] to demonstrate that all religious uses of cannabis by Rastafari . . . in any circumstance pose a risk of harm regardless of how it is used and that a religious exemption cannot be granted without undermining the objective of the statutes. . . .

[58]   There was no evidence that the use of cannabis in bathing or burning it as incense poses a risk of harm to the user. Indeed there was no suggestion that the burning of cannabis as incense in a carefully circumscribed ritual context poses any risk of harm. . . .

[Judge Ngcobo also noted that the medical evidence is unclear as to just how much cannabis must be consumed for it to pose a risk to the user. It is clear that some level of consumption would not be harmful, but that amount has not been identified.]

. . .

[63]   . . . [T]he government contended that any exemption would be difficult to administer. In contending that it would be difficult to police any exemption the Attorney–General pointed out certain difficulties including the problem of identifying bona fide Rastafari; the source from which cannabis is to be obtained; and how to safeguard against the abuse of the exemption. . . .

. . .

[66]   There is no suggestion that these problems cannot effectively be regulated. . . .

. . .

[69]   The suppression of illicit drugs does not require a blanket ban on the sacramental use of cannabis when such use does not pose a risk of harm. What is required is the regulation of such use in the same manner as the government regulates the exempted uses of drugs, including the more dangerous and addictive drugs, for which there is no doubt a huge illicit market. . . .

. . .

[73]   It is true that the granting of a religious exemption for a limited use of cannabis in circumstances that do not pose a risk of

harm has certain risks. Such risks involve the use of cannabis for purposes other than those allowed by the exemption and the illegal passing of cannabis lawfully acquired to third parties. However, these risks are inherent in any exemption. They did not preclude the government from allowing exemptions for medicinal, research or analytical purposes. To minimize these risks the government subjected the use of drugs for these purposes to strict control such as restricting persons who may acquire drugs; prescribing the source from which they may be obtained; requiring the recording of the date of sale and the quantity of drugs sold; and making possession or use of drugs outside the statutory provisions subject to criminal penalties....

[74] The above analysis illustrates that the prohibition contained in the impugned provisions is too extensive....

. . .

The evaluation of proportionality

[79] In a constitutional democracy like ours that recognizes and tolerates diverse religious faiths, tolerance of diversity must be demonstrated by accommodating the practices of all faiths, if this can be done without undermining the legitimate government interest. Thus when Parliament is faced with a religious practice that involves some conduct that runs counter to its objectives, the proper approach under our Constitution is not to proscribe the entire practice but to target only that conduct that runs counter to its objectives, if this can be done without undermining its objectives....

. . .

Judgment by Chaskalson, majority

Freedom of religion and the criminal law

[111] ... [Unlike Ngcobo, J.] we do not believe that it is incumbent on the State to devise some form of exception to the general prohibition against the possession or use of cannabis in order to cater for the religious rights of Rastafarians.

. . .

[114] ... In substance, the appellant contends that the legislation, though legitimate in its purpose and application to the general public, is overbroad because it has been formulated in a way that brings within its purview the use of cannabis by Rastafari that is legitimate and ought not to be prohibited. A challenge to the constitutionality of legislation on the grounds that it is overbroad is in essence a challenge based on the contention that the legitimate government purpose served by the legislation could be achieved by less restrictive means.

. . .

[116]   The unchallenged general prohibition in the disputed legislation against the possession or use of harmful drugs is directed in the first instance to cutting off the supply of such drugs to potential users. It seeks to address the harm caused by the drug problem by denying all possession of prohibited substances (other than for medical and research purposes) and not by seeking to penalize only the harmful use of such substances. . . .

[117]   The state was not called upon to justify this method of controlling the use of harmful drugs. The validity of the general prohibition against both possession and use was accepted. The case the state was called upon to meet in this Court was that in addition to the medical and research exemptions contained in the legislation, provision should also have been made for the use of cannabis for religious purposes by members of the Rastafari religion.

. . .

[The Court discussed the United States Supreme Court's decision in *Employment Division v. Smith*, 494 U.S. 872 (1990), at some length. It described the balancing analysis employed by the dissenting justices and noted that even the dissenting justices who argued that the religious use of Peyote in Native American religious ceremonies should not be constitutionally prohibited focused on the controlled and limited circumstances in which the drug would be ingested. The dissenting justices had also argued that the fact that numerous states exempted the ceremonial use of Peyote by the Native American Church from their drug laws demonstrated that a religious exemption was feasible and would not unreasonably interfere with the enforcement of state drug laws.]

Section 36 Analysis

[128]   [T]he approach of the minority of the Court in [*Smith*] is more consistent with the requirements of our Constitution and our jurisprudence on the limitation of rights, than the approach of the majority. However, . . . our Constitution in dealing with the limitation of rights does not call for the use of different levels of scrutiny, but "expressly contemplates the use of a nuanced and context-sensitive form of balancing" in the section 36 proportionality analysis [*Christian Education South Africa v Minister of Education*, 2000 (4) S.A. 757 at para. 30 (CC)].

[129]   Cannabis, unlike peyote, is a drug in which there is a substantial illicit trade which exists within South Africa and internationally. Moreover, the use to which cannabis is put by Rastafari is not simply the sacramental or symbolic consumption of a small quantity at a religious ceremony. It is used communally and privately, during religious ceremonies when two or more Rastafari

come together, and at other times and places.... All that distinguishes [appellant's] use of cannabis from the general use that is prohibited, is the purpose for which he uses the drug, and the self-discipline that he asserts in not abusing it.

[130]   There is no objective way in which a law enforcement official could distinguish between the use of cannabis for religious purposes and the use of cannabis for recreation. It would be even more difficult, if not impossible, to distinguish objectively between the possession of cannabis for the one or the other of the above purposes. Nor is there any objective way in which a law enforcement official could determine whether a person found in possession of cannabis, who says that it is possessed for religious purposes, is genuine or not. Indeed, in the absence of a carefully controlled chain of permitted supply, it is difficult to imagine how the island of legitimate acquisition and use by Rastafari for the purpose of practicing their religion could be distinguished from the surrounding ocean of illicit trafficking and use.

   . . .

[132]   ... If an exemption in general terms for the possession and use of harmful drugs by persons who do so for religious purposes were to be permitted, the State's ability to enforce its drug legislation would be substantially impaired.

[133]   The appellant, appreciating this difficulty, suggested that a permit system be introduced allowing bona fide Rastafari to possess cannabis for religious purposes. In support of this contention he sought an analogy in the provisions of the legislation permitting the use of harmful drugs for medical purposes. The analogy is unsound, however. Permitted use of a prohibited substance for medical purposes is dependent upon a written prescription being issued by a medical practitioner which must limit the use of the drug to particular quantities for a limited period of time, and is subject to ongoing control by the doctor....

[134]   There would be practical difficulties in enforcing a permit system.... They include the financial and administrative problems associated with setting up and implementing any such system, and the difficulties in policing that would follow if permits were issued sanctioning the possession of cannabis for religious purposes.

   . . .

[138]   But more importantly, the religious use of cannabis cannot be equated to medical use. It would expose Rastafari to the same harm as others are exposed to by using cannabis, depending only on their self-discipline to use it in ways that avoid such harm. Moreover, to make its use for religious purposes dependent upon a

permit issued by the State to "bona fide Rastafari" would, in the circumstances of the present case, be inconsistent with the freedom of religion. It is the essence of that freedom that individuals have a choice that does not depend in any way upon the permission of the executive.... Quite apart from this objection, such a permit system would not address the law enforcement problems referred to above....

[139] ... The failure to make provision for an exemption in respect of the possession and use of cannabis by Rastafari is thus reasonable and justifiable under our Constitution.

...

[141] ... [T]he disputed legislation ... consistent with the international protocol, is not formulated so as to penalize only the harmful use of cannabis.... It seeks to prohibit the very possession of cannabis, for this is obviously the most effective way of policing the trade in and use of the drug. This method of control was not disputed save for the religious exemption sought. The question is therefore not whether the non-invasive use of cannabis for religious purposes will cause harm to the users, but whether permission given to Rastafari to possess cannabis will undermine the general prohibition against such possession. We hold that it will.

...

Judgment by Sachs, dissenting

The role of the courts in securing reasonable accommodation

[155] Limitations analysis under our Constitution is based not on formal or categorical reasoning but on processes of balancing and proportionality as required by section 36. This Court has accordingly rejected the view of the majority in the United States Supreme Court that it is an inevitable outcome of democracy that in a multi-faith society, minority religions may find themselves without remedy against burdens imposed upon them by formally neutral laws. Equally, on the other hand, it would not accept as an inevitable outcome of constitutionalism that each and every statutory restriction on religious practice must be invalidated. On the contrary, limitations analysis under section 36 is antithetical to extreme positions which end up setting the irresistible force of democracy and general law enforcement, against the immovable object of constitutionalism and protection of fundamental rights. What it requires is the maximum harmonization of all the competing considerations, on a principled yet nuanced and flexible case-by-case basis, located in South African reality yet guided by international experience, articulated with appropriate candor and accomplished without losing sight of the ultimate values highlighted by our Constitution. In achieving this balance, this Court may fre-

quently find itself faced with complex problems as to what properly belongs to the discretionary sphere which the Constitution allocates to the legislature and the executive, and what falls squarely to be determined by the judiciary.

. . .

[158]   The Rastafari are . . . not an established religious group whose interests no legislature would dare ignore. One may compare their position to that of major faiths. Thus, in the period when the racist liquor laws forbade Africans generally to possess liquor, the power of the Christian Church was such that access to communion wine was granted to African congregants (just as in the USA even at the height of prohibition the use of communion wine was exempted). On the other hand, Africans who sought to brew beer as part of traditional religious supplication rites were prosecuted. The difference of treatment lay not in the nature of the activity or exemption, but in the status of the religious groups involved. One must conclude that in the area of claims freely to exercise religion, it is not familiarity, but unfamiliarity, that breeds contempt.

. . .

[160]   One cannot imagine in South Africa today any legislative authority passing or sustaining laws which suppressed central beliefs and practices of Christianity, Islam, Hinduism and Judaism. These are well-organized religions, capable of mounting strong lobbies and in a position materially to affect the outcome of elections. They are not driven to seek constitutional protection from the courts. A threat to the freedom of one would be seen as a threat to the freedom of all. The Rastafari, on the other hand, are not only in conflict with the public authorities, they are isolated from mainstream religious groups.

. . .

Conclusion

[170]   In conclusion I wish to say that this case illustrates why the principle of reasonable accommodation is so important. The appellant has shown himself to be a person of principle, willing to sacrifice his career and material interests in pursuance of his beliefs. An inflexible application of the law that compels him to choose between his conscience and his career threatens to impoverish not only himself but all of South Africa and to dilute its burgeoning vision of an open democracy.

* * *

MULTANI v. COMMISSION SCOLAIRE MARGUERITE–BOURGEOYS

[2006] 1 S.C.R. 256 (Can.)
Supreme Court of Canada

[For the constitutional provisions of Canada relating to religion, see pp. 123–24.]

[The appellant, Gurbaj Singh Multani, a student at a public school, is an orthodox Sikh who believes that he is required by his faith to wear a kirpan, a ceremonial metal dagger, under his clothing at all times. The school board and council of commissions of his school district refused to allow him to wear the metal kirpan in school on the grounds that it violated the school's code of conduct which prohibits students from carrying weapons or dangerous objects to school. They would only permit him to wear a plastic or wooden kirpan. The appellant claimed that this decision violated his rights under section 2(a) of the Canadian Charter. The trial judge ruled that the appellant could wear the kirpan to school under specified conditions including the requirement that it be "placed in [a wooden sheath] and wrapped and sewn securely in a sturdy cloth envelope." The Court of Appeal reversed on the grounds that the council of commissioners' decision was a reasonable one. There was a direct and rational connection between prohibiting a student from wearing a kirpan to school and the goal of providing students a safe learning environment. Further, the conditions imposed by the trial judge could not entirely eliminate the risks associated with bringing the kirpan to school.]

6. Infringement of Freedom of Religion

32. This Court has on numerous occasions stressed the importance of freedom of religion....

. . .

34. ... [I]n order to establish that his or her freedom of religion has been infringed, the claimant must demonstrate (1) that he or she sincerely believes in a practice or belief that has a nexus with religion, and (2) that the impugned conduct of a third party interferes, in a manner that is non-trivial or not insubstantial, with his or her ability to act in accordance with that practice or belief.

. . .

36. In the case at bar, Gurbaj Singh must therefore show that he sincerely believes that his faith requires him at all times to wear a kirpan made of metal. Evidence to this effect was introduced and was not contradicted. No one contests the fact that the orthodox

Sikh religion requires its adherents to wear a kirpan at all times. . . .

. . .

39. . . . Gurbaj Singh's refusal to wear a replica made of a material other than metal is not capricious. He genuinely believes that he would not be complying with the requirements of his religion were he to wear a plastic or wooden kirpan. The fact that other Sikhs accept such a compromise is not relevant, since as [the Court of Appeal recognized] "people who profess the same religion may adhere to the dogma and practices of that religion to varying degrees of rigor."

40. Finally, the interference with Gurbaj Singh's freedom of religion is neither trivial nor insignificant. Forced to choose between leaving his kirpan at home and leaving the public school system, Gurbaj Singh decided to follow his religious convictions and is now attending a private school. . . .

41. Thus, there can be no doubt that the council of commissioners' decision prohibiting Gurbaj Singh from wearing his kirpan to . . . school infringes his freedom of religion. This limit must therefore be justified under s. 1 of the *Canadian Charter*.

7. Section 1 of the *Canadian Charter*

. . .

43. [Under s. 1 of the *Charter*] [t]he onus is on the respondents to prove that, on a balance of probabilities, the infringement is reasonable and can be demonstrably justified in a free and democratic society. To this end, two requirements must be met. First, the legislative objective being pursued must be sufficiently important to warrant limiting a constitutional right. Next, the means chosen by the state authority must be proportional to the objective in question.

7.1 Importance of the Objective

. . .

45. Clearly, the objective of ensuring safety in schools is sufficiently important to warrant overriding a constitutionally protected right or freedom. It remains to be determined what level of safety the governing board was seeking to achieve by prohibiting the carrying of weapons and dangerous objects, and what degree of risk would accordingly be tolerated. . . .

46. Although the parties did not present argument on the level of safety sought by the governing board, the issue was addressed by the intervener Canadian Human Rights Commission, which correctly stated that the standard that seems to be applied in schools is reasonable safety, not absolute safety. The application of

a standard of absolute safety could result in the installation of metal detectors in schools, the prohibition of all potentially dangerous objects (such as scissors, compasses, baseball bats and table knives in the cafeteria) and permanent expulsion from the public school system of any student exhibiting violent behavior. Apart from the fact that such a standard would be impossible to attain, it would compromise the objective of providing universal access to the public school system.

47. On the other hand, the governing board ... was not seeking to establish a minimum standard of safety ... [V]iolence and weapons are not tolerated in schools, and students exhibiting violent or dangerous behavior are punished. Such measures show that the objective is to attain a certain level of safety beyond a minimum threshold.

48. I therefore conclude that the level of safety chosen by the governing council and confirmed by the council of commissioners was reasonable safety. The objective of ensuring a reasonable level of safety in schools is without question a pressing and substantial one.

7.2 Proportionality

7.2.1 Rational Connection

49. The first stage of the proportionality analysis consists in determining whether the council of commissioners' decision was rendered in furtherance of the objective. The decision must have a rational connection with the objective. In the instant case, prohibiting Gurbaj Singh from wearing his kirpan to school was intended to further this objective. Despite the profound religious significance of the kirpan for Gurbaj Singh, it also has the characteristics of a bladed weapon and could therefore cause injury. The council of commissioners' decision [to prohibit Gurbaj Singh from wearing his kirpan to school] therefore has a rational connection with the objective of ensuring a reasonable level of safety in schools....

7.2.2 Minimal Impairment

50. The second stage of the proportionality analysis is often central to the debate as to whether the infringement of a right protected by the *Canadian Charter* can be justified. The limit, which must minimally impair the right or freedom that has been infringed, need not necessarily be the least intrusive solution. In *RJR-MacDonald Inc. v. Canada (Attorney General)*, [1995] 3 S.C.R. 199, ¶ 160, this Court defined the test as follows:

The impairment must be "minimal," that is, the law must be carefully tailored so that rights are impaired no more than necessary. The tailoring process seldom admits of perfection and the courts must accord some leeway to the legislator. If the law falls within a range of reasonable alternatives, the courts will not find it overbroad merely because they can conceive of an alternative which might better tailor objective to infringement.

51. ... Thus, it must be determined whether the decision to establish an absolute prohibition against wearing a kirpan "falls within a range of reasonable alternatives."

. . .

53. ... [There is a logical relationship between the duty to accommodate and the principle of minimal impairment.] ... In relation to discrimination, the courts have held that there is a duty to make reasonable accommodation for individuals who are adversely affected by a policy or rule that is neutral on its face, and that this duty extends only to the point at which it causes undue hardship to the party who must perform it.... [T]he analogy with the duty of reasonable accommodation seems to me to be helpful to explain the burden resulting from the minimal impairment test with respect to a particular individual, as in the case at bar....

54. The council of commissioners' decision establishes an absolute prohibition against Gurbaj Singh wearing his kirpan to school.... It is important to note that Gurbaj Singh has never claimed a right to wear his kirpan to school without restrictions. Rather, he says that he is prepared to wear his kirpan under the ... conditions imposed by [the trial judge] of the Superior Court. Thus, the issue is whether the respondents have succeeded in demonstrating that an absolute prohibition is justified.

7.2.2.1 Safety in Schools

56. According to the respondents, the presence of kirpans in schools, even under certain conditions, creates a risk that they will be used for violent purposes, either by those who wear them or by other students who might take hold of them by force.

57. The evidence shows that Gurbaj Singh does not have behavioral problems and has never resorted to violence at school. The risk that this particular student would use his kirpan for violent purposes seems highly unlikely to me. In fact, the [school authorities] never argued that there was a risk of his doing so.

58. As for the risk of another student taking his kirpan away from him, it also seems to me to be quite low, especially if the kirpan is worn under conditions such as were imposed by [the trial judge]. [I]f the kirpan were worn in accordance with those conditions, any student wanting to take it away from Gurbaj Singh would first have to physically restrain him, then search through his clothes, remove the sheath ... and try to unstitch or tear open the cloth enclosing the sheath in order to get to the kirpan. There is no

question that a student who wanted to commit an act of violence could find another way to obtain a weapon, such as bringing one in from outside the school. Furthermore, there are many objects in schools that could be used to commit violent acts and that are much more easily obtained by students, such as scissors, pencils and baseball bats.

59. [The trial judge] explained that her decision was based in part on the fact that "the evidence revealed no instances of violent incidents involving kirpans in schools in Quebec." ... In fact, the evidence in the record suggests that, over the 100 years since Sikhs have been attending schools in Canada, not a single violent incident related to the presence of kirpans in schools has been reported....

60. The lack of evidence of risks related to the wearing of kirpans was also noted in 1990 by a board of inquiry of the Ontario Human Rights Commission, which considered the presence of kirpans in schools in great depth.... The board of inquiry allowed kirpans to be worn in Ontario schools under conditions similar to the ones imposed by ... the Quebec Superior Court.... The decision was affirmed by the Ontario Divisional Court.... While noting the lack of kirpan-related incidents in schools, the Divisional Court [noted that there had been a few instances of a kirpan being used in an act of violence, but none of these instances had occurred at a school. It also noted that Sikh students were permitted to wear a kirpan to school in many Canadian jurisdictions]....

61. The parties introduced into evidence several newspaper articles confirming the lack of incidents involving kirpans....

62. The respondents maintain that freedom of religion can be limited even in the absence of evidence of a real risk of significant harm, since it is not necessary to wait for the harm to occur before correcting the situation. [They point to decisions where Sikhs were prohibited from wearing kirpans on an airplane or a court room during a criminal proceeding.] ...

63. There can be no doubt that safety is just as important in schools as it is on airplanes and in courts. However, it is important to remember that the specific context must always be borne in mind in resolving the issue.

. . .

65. ... [There are important differences that distinguish the school environment from that of an airplane or courtroom. For example, t]he school environment is a unique one that permits relationships to develop among students and staff. These relationships make it possible to better control the different types of situations that arise in schools....

66.   ... [E]ach environment is a special case with its own unique characteristics that justify a different level of safety, depending on the circumstances.

67.   ... I agree that it is not necessary to wait for harm to be done before acting, but the existence of concerns relating to safety must be unequivocally established for the infringement of a constitutional right to be justified. Given the evidence in the record, it is my opinion that the respondents' argument in support of an absolute prohibition–namely that kirpans are inherently dangerous–must fail.

. . .

7.2.2.3   *Negative Impact on the School Environment*

70.   The respondents submit that the presence of kirpans in schools will contribute to a poisoning of the school environment. They maintain that the kirpan is a symbol of violence and that it sends the message that using force is the way to assert rights and resolve conflict, compromises the perception of safety in schools and establishes a double standard.

71.   The argument that the wearing of kirpans should be prohibited because the kirpan is a symbol of violence and because it sends the message that using force is necessary to assert rights and resolve conflict must fail. Not only is this assertion contradicted by the evidence regarding the symbolic nature of the kirpan, it is also disrespectful to believers in the Sikh religion and does not take into account Canadian values based on multiculturalism.

. . .

77.   In my opinion, the respondents have failed to demonstrate that it would be reasonable to conclude that an absolute prohibition against wearing a kirpan minimally impairs Gurbaj Singh's rights.

7.2.3   Effects of the Measure

78.   Since we have found that the council of commissioners' decision is not a reasonable limit on religious freedom, it is not strictly necessary to weigh the deleterious effects of this measure against its salutary effects. I do believe, however, like the intervener Canadian Civil Liberties Association, that it is important to consider some effects that could result from an absolute prohibition. An absolute prohibition would stifle the promotion of values such as multiculturalism, diversity, and the development of an educational culture respectful of the rights of others. . . .

79.   A total prohibition against wearing a kirpan to school undermines the value of this religious symbol and sends students the message that some religious practices do not merit the same protection as others. On the other hand, accommodating Gurbaj

Singh and allowing him to wear his kirpan under certain conditions demonstrates the importance that our society attaches to protecting freedom of religion and to showing respect for its minorities. The deleterious effects of a total prohibition thus outweigh its salutary effects.

Notes and Questions

1. The foundation of free exercise jurisprudence in the United States is the rule set out by the United States Supreme Court in *Employment Division v. Smith* that denies free exercise protection to individuals whose religious practices are burdened by neutral laws of general applicability. Many countries reject this limited understanding of religious liberty as the principal cases in this chapter demonstrate. Additional cases from Germany and Ireland that also reject the *Smith* analysis are described in notes 2 and 3 below.

One of the key arguments offered by Justice Scalia to defend the majority position in *Smith* challenged the legitimacy of courts engaging in a detailed balancing analysis to determine whether the government's refusal to grant an exemption from a general law for religious practices could be justified. In reading the principal cases in this chapter, think about the way the Canadian and South African Supreme Courts evaluate the government's justification for its regulations. Are courts incompetent to engage in this kind of searching review of the decisions of the other branches of government? Does this kind of analysis usurp the legislature's responsibilities? Is it unacceptably intrusive into legislative prerogatives? Or do these cases suggest that Justice Scalia was wrong when he argued that courts should not engage in this kind of balancing analysis?

2. In *Quinn's Supermarket Ltd. v. Attorney General*, [1972] 1 I.R. 1, 11, 24–25 (Ir.), plaintiffs argued that an exemption provided to kosher butcher shops from a statute regulating the hours when butcher shops could be open for business constituted religious discrimination in violation of the Ireland Constitution. In rejecting the plaintiffs' argument, the Court stated:

> If ... the implementation of the guarantee of free profession and practice of religion requires that a distinction should be made to make possible for the persons professing or practicing a particular religion their guaranteed right to do so, then such a distinction is not invalid having regard to the provisions of the Constitution. It would be completely contrary to the spirit and intendment of the provisions ... to permit the guarantee against discrimination on the ground of religious profession or belief to be made the very means of restricting or preventing the free profession or practice of religion. The primary purpose of the guarantee against discrimination is to ensure the freedom of practice of religion. Any law which by virtue of the generality of its application would by its effect restrict or prevent the free profession and practice of religion by

any person or persons would be invalid having regard to the provisions of the Constitution, unless it contained provisions which saved from such restriction or prevention the practice of religion of the person or persons who would otherwise be so restricted or prevented.

3.   In the *German Ritual Slaughter Case*, [BVerfG] [Federal Constitutional Court] Jan. 15, 2002, 1 BvR 1783/99 (F.R.G.), the Constitutional Court evaluated a statute which prohibited the slaughtering of warm-blooded animals unless they were stunned before blood was drained from their bodies. An exemption from the statute to accommodate religious groups had been interpreted to only provide exemptions where it had been "objectively established that a religious group had mandatory provisions about the ban on stunning animals before slaughtering them." In rejecting this interpretation on constitutional grounds, the Court offered several arguments. First, an exemption must be offered to members of a particular faith even if some members or groups within the religion hold different views about the slaughtering of animals. The existence of conflicting positions on this issue cannot be held to mean that religious obligations are not "mandatory" for those persons who adhere to them. Second, the State cannot justify the refusal to grant an exemption on the grounds that religious individuals can avoid violating their faith by foregoing the consumption of meat or eating meat that is imported from abroad that has been slaughtered in the manner required by their faith. Having to renounce the consumption of meat imposes an unreasonable burden on the practice of the believer's faith and believers can rely more fully on the satisfaction of ritual requirements by dealing with local slaughterers rather than importers. Third, the Court noted that exceptions to the stunning requirement were permitted for a variety of activities including hunting and pest control. Since exemptions were provided for secular reasons of expediency, tradition and social acceptance, exemptions based on religious obligations could not be reasonably denied.

4.   In thinking about *Multani v. Commission scolaire Marguerite–Bourgeoys*, note that the India Constitution has an explicit provision allowing Sikhs to wear kirpans (Article 25, Constitution of India).

5.   In *Adelaide Co. of Jehovah's Witnesses v. The Commonwealth*, (1943) 67 CLR 116 Latham C.J. offered this analogy to explain the scope of free exercise protection.

Latham C.J.

8.   Section 116 does not merely protect the exercise of religion, it protects the free exercise of religion. The word 'free' is vague and ambiguous, as is shown by the many decisions in this Court and in the Privy Council upon the meaning of the word 'free' in another place when it appears in the Constitution.... Freedom of speech is a highly valued element in our society. But freedom of speech does not mean ... free speech; it means speech hedged in by all the laws against defamation, blasphemy, sedition and so forth; it means freedom governed by law....

Is this a useful analogy? Does it reflect the relationship between free exercise rights and free speech rights in American First Amendment jurisprudence?

6. The language of Section 116 of the Australia Constitution parallels the text of the First Amendment far more than the constitution of other countries, but there are important differences in the two documents. Moreover, the meaning of the religion clauses of the First Amendment has varied considerably over time. Thus, if the Australia courts looked to United States case law for guidance in interpreting their religious-liberty provision, should they focus on what the First Amendment had been interpreted to mean at the time the Australia Constitution was adopted in 1900? The Jehovah's Witnesses case mentioned in note 5 answers that question this way:

Latham C.J.

9. ... [B]efore the Constitution of the Commonwealth was adopted in 1900 decisions of the Supreme Court of the United States had dealt with the subject of the constitutional protection of religious freedom. These cases quite clearly determined that such protection was not absolute and that it did not involve a dispensation from obedience to a general law of the land which was not directed against religion.

The Court then went on to discuss *Reynolds v. United States*, 98 U.S. 145 (1878), and *Davis v. Beason*, 133 U.S. 333 (1890). It concluded:

9. ... [These cases] show that in 1900 it had been thoroughly established in the United States that the provision preventing the making of any law prohibiting the free exercise of religion was not understood to mean that the criminal law dealing with the conduct of citizens generally was to be subject to exceptions in favor of persons who believed and practiced a religion which was inconsistent with the provisions of the law....

10. There is, therefore, full legal justification for adopting in Australia an interpretation of s. 116 which had, before the enactment of the Commonwealth Constitution, already been given to similar words in the United States.

7. It is recognized at the national and international level that religious liberty has both an individual and a communal dimension. Thus, Section 31 of the South Africa Constitution (see pp. 122–23 supra) guarantees the right of members of a religious community to join with co-believers to organize associations for the collective practice of their faith. This provision is described as paralleling article 27 of the ICCPR which states, "In those States in which ethnic, religious or linguistic minorities exist, persons belonging to such minorities shall not be denied the right, in community with the other members of their group, to enjoy their own culture, to profess and practice their own religion, or to use their own language."

In *Christian Education South Africa v. Minister of Education*, 2000 (10) BCLR 1051 (CC) (2000), the South Africa Constitutional Court explained that these provisions "affirm the right of people to be who they are without being forced to subordinate themselves to the cultural and religious norms of others, and highlight the importance of individuals and communities being able to enjoy what has been called the 'right to be different'. In each case, space has been found for members of communities to depart from a general norm."

Compare these provisions with the U.S Supreme Court's opinion in *Wisconsin v. Yoder*, 406 U.S. 205 (1972), which holds that Amish parents must be granted an exemption from state compulsory education laws so they may remove their children from public school at the age of 14. Do these provisions help to justify the Court's analysis in *Yoder*?

II. INTERNATIONAL AND SUPRANATIONAL LAW

A. THE ECHR FRAMEWORK FOR PROTECTING RELIGIOUS LIBERTY

LEYLA SAHIN v. TURKEY

Application No. 44774/98, (2005)
European Court of Human Rights

[For the text of Article 9, see pp. 130–31.]

[The European Court of Human Rights typically sets out the general principles that have evolved in interpreting Article 9 before it begins the substantive analysis in each case. These principles are described below.]

104. The court reiterates that as enshrined in Art. 9, freedom of thought, conscience and religion is one of the foundations of a 'democratic society' within the meaning of the convention. This freedom is, in its religious dimension, one of the most vital elements that go to make up the identity of believers and their conception of life, but it is also a precious asset for atheists, agnostics, skeptics and the unconcerned. The pluralism indissociable from a democratic society, which has been dearly won over the centuries, depends on it. That freedom entails, inter alia, freedom to hold or not to hold religious beliefs and to practice or not to practice a religion.

105. While religious freedom is primarily a matter of individual conscience, it also implies, inter alia, freedom to manifest one's religion, alone and in private, or in community with others, in public and within the circle of those whose faith one shares. Article 9 lists the various forms which manifestation of one's religion or belief may take, namely worship, teaching, practice and observ-

ance.... Article 9 does not protect every act motivated or inspired by a religion or belief.

106.   In democratic societies, in which several religions coexist within one and the same population, it may be necessary to place restrictions on freedom to manifest one's religion or belief in order to reconcile the interests of the various groups and ensure that everyone's beliefs are respected. This follows both from paragraph 2 of Art. 9 and the state's positive obligation under Art. 1 of the convention to secure to everyone within its jurisdiction the rights and freedoms defined in the convention.

107.   The court has frequently emphasized the state's role as the neutral and impartial organizer of the exercise of various religions, faiths and beliefs, and stated that this role is conducive to public order, religious harmony and tolerance in a democratic society. It also considers that the state's duty of neutrality and impartiality is incompatible with any power on the state's part to assess the legitimacy of religious beliefs or the ways in which those beliefs are expressed ... and that it requires the state to ensure mutual tolerance between opposing groups. Accordingly, the role of the authorities in such circumstances is not to remove the cause of tension by eliminating pluralism, but to ensure that the competing groups tolerate each other.

108.   Pluralism, tolerance and broadmindedness are hallmarks of a 'democratic society.' Although individual interests must on occasion be subordinated to those of a group, democracy does not simply mean that the views of a majority must always prevail: a balance must be achieved which ensures the fair and proper treatment of people from minorities and avoids any abuse of a dominant position. Pluralism and democracy must also be based on dialogue and a spirit of compromise necessarily entailing various concessions on the part of individuals or groups of individuals which are justified in order to maintain and promote the ideals and values of a democratic society. Where these 'rights and freedoms' are themselves among those guaranteed by the convention or its protocols, it must be accepted that the need to protect them may lead states to restrict other rights or freedoms likewise set forth in the convention. It is precisely this constant search for a balance between the fundamental rights of each individual which constitutes the foundation of a 'democratic society.'

109.   Where questions concerning the relationship between state and religions are at stake, on which opinion in a democratic society may reasonably differ widely, the role of the national decision-making body must be given special importance.... It is not possible to discern throughout Europe a uniform conception of the significance of religion in society, and the meaning or impact of

the public expression of a religious belief will differ according to time and context. Rules in this sphere will consequently vary from one country to another according to national traditions and the requirements imposed by the need to protect the rights and freedoms of others and to maintain public order. Accordingly, the choice of the extent and form such regulations should take must inevitably be left up to a point to the state concerned, as it will depend on the domestic context.

B. JUSTIFIED LIMITATIONS ON RELIGIOUS LIBERTY

Peter G. Danchin & Lisa Forman
The Evolving Jurisprudence of the European Court of Human Rights and the Protection of Religious Minorities

in Protecting the Human Rights of Religious Minorities in Eastern Europe 192, 198–99, 210–12 (Peter G. Danchin & Elizabeth A. Cole eds., Columbia Univ. Press 2002)

Article 9(2) states that manifestations of religion or belief may be limited if the restrictions are prescribed by law and are necessary in a democratic society. Permissible grounds of limitation include those of public safety, public order, health, or morals, and the protection of the rights and freedoms of others. These limitations relate only to *manifestations* of thought, conscience, and religion. The right to entertain any thoughts or views is guaranteed absolutely and without limitation. The Court has expressed the distinction in terms of the well-acknowledged difference between the *forum internum* (the sphere of personal beliefs and religious creeds) and the *forum externum* (the sphere where such personal beliefs and religious creeds are physically manifested). The scope of religious liberty is therefore determined in part by the line the Court has drawn between these two spheres.

. . .

Article 9(2) also provides the framework within which the margin of appreciation doctrine usually arises. It is legitimate in terms of Article 9(2) for states to limit manifestations of religion or belief in the interests of public safety and order, health or morals, and to protect the rights and freedoms of others. The determination of what constitutes a legitimate limitation on this basis appears *ex facie* the wording of Article 9(2) itself, namely conduct prescribed by law and necessary in a democratic society. The court's determination of whether conduct violates Article 9 therefore follows a two-stage inquiry. The court's first task is to determine whether challenged governmental action interferes with a right protected under Article 9(1). If there is no state interference with protected rights, then the application is dismissed. If the Court finds interference, then it proceeds to the second level of determining whether the interference is permissible according to the limitations in Article 9(2). This is determined according to a three part test by which the Court assesses whether the action was (1) prescribed by law, (2) had a legitimate aim, and (3) was necessary in a democratic society. According to the Court's jurisprudence, conduct is prescribed by law if the relevant rule or prohibition is adequately accessible and foreseeable, and formulated with sufficient precision to enable the individual to regulate his or her conduct. To be considered necessary in a democratic society, impugned conduct must correspond to a "pressing social need" and must be proportionate to the legitimate aim pursued.

Finally, the limitations in Article 9(2) are similar (but not identical) to those contained in the second parts of Articles 8, 10, and 11. All these provisions delineate acceptable limitations of the respective rights. The Court's determination of limitations under Article 9(2) in this way constitutes part of a larger jurisprudential tradition whereby the Court is called on to decide whether state interference with rights protected under the Convention falls within the margin of appreciation that member states have to determine the legitimate limits on fundamental freedoms necessary in a democratic society.

. . .

Objective Versus Subjective Assessment of the Impact of "Neutral" Laws of General Application

[A] discernible trend in Article 9 cases . . . is that the Court has tended to substitute the actual experience of affected minorities with its own objective assessment of the impact of state action. In a series of recent decisions, the Court has rejected an applicant's claim on the basis that the impugned conduct did not constitute an interference with religious freedom, in spite of the applicant's clear subjective experience to the contrary. For example, in the twin cases of *Efstratiou v. Greece* [1996–VI, Eur. Ct. H.R. 2347] and *Valsamis v. Greece* [1996–VI, Eur. Ct. H.R. 2312], the Court held that requiring students to take part in school parades commemorating the outbreak of war between Greece and Italy in 1940 was not an interference with their or their parent's pacifist convictions as Jehovah's Witnesses. The Court also held that suspending pupils for refusing to march in such parades did not violate their freedom of religion in that the disciplinary rules applied generally and in a neutral manner. Important to the Court's reasoning was the finding that such measures had a limited duration and therefore a limited impact.

The result of these decisions was that, in accordance with what the Court deemed to be "objective criteria," the legitimate societal objective of achieving national unity was held to outweigh the deeply held religious convictions of the Witness children and their parents against participation in the parade. The majority judgment justified its finding of the limited impact of requiring the applicant's attendance by reiterating that the parade served the "dominant public interest." This was because the commemoration of national events served both pacifist and public interests, and because the presence of military representatives at the parade did not alter its nature as an expression of national values and unity. Furthermore, the majority suggested that the applicant's religious interests were being adequately addressed by other means such as exemption from religious-education lessons and the Orthodox mass.

. . .

Neutral laws of general application will usually conform to the dominant ethical values in a given society at a given point of time. Thus, they will not often conflict with majority religious values or morality. They will, however, cause conflicts with minority religious values and practices that are socially atypical. The fact that the Court has fashioned an approach whereby "neutral" laws will automatically prevail, and whereby the state is under no obligation to justify that its refusal to grant exemptions from the application of such laws is a measure that is "necessary in a democratic society," constitutes a significant risk for the rights of minorities.

* * *

REFAH PARTISI (THE WELFARE PARTY) AND OTHERS v. TURKEY

2003–II Eur. Ct. H.R. 267
European Court of Human Rights

[The facts of this case and the legal analysis are described in Part I, Chapter II, pp. 87–96. The following excerpts from the Court's opinion deal exclusively with Turkey's commitment to secularism and the Court's rejection of Islamic fundamentalism and Sharia law as inconsistent with the principles of pluralism and democracy on which the ECHR is based.]

23. On 16 January 1998 the Constitutional Court dissolved Refah on the ground that it had become a "centre of activities contrary to the principle of secularism." . . .

. . .

25. . . . The Constitutional Court referred to the provisions of the Constitution which imposed respect for secularism on the

various organs of political power. It also cited the numerous provisions of domestic legislation requiring political parties to apply the principle of secularism in a number of fields of political and social life. The Constitutional Court observed that secularism was one of the indispensable conditions of democracy. In Turkey the principle of secularism was safeguarded by the Constitution, on account of the country's historical experience and the specific features of Islam. The rules of sharia were incompatible with the democratic regime. The principle of secularism prevented the State from manifesting a preference for a particular religion or belief and constituted the foundation of freedom of conscience and equality between citizens before the law. Intervention by the State to preserve the secular nature of the political regime had to be considered necessary in a democratic society.

. . .

Democracy and religion in the Convention system

90.   For the purposes of the present case, the Court also refers to its case-law concerning the place of religion in a democratic society and a democratic State. It reiterates that, as protected by Article 9, freedom of thought, conscience and religion is one of the foundations of a "democratic society" within the meaning of the Convention. . . .

91.   Moreover, in democratic societies, in which several religions coexist within one and the same population, it may be necessary to place restrictions on this freedom in order to reconcile the interests of the various groups and ensure that everyone's beliefs are respected. . . . The Court has frequently emphasized the State's role as the neutral and impartial organizer of the exercise of various religions, faiths and beliefs, and stated that this role is conducive to public order, religious harmony and tolerance in a democratic society. . . .

92.   The Court's established case-law confirms this function of the State. It has held that in a democratic society the State may limit the freedom to manifest a religion, for example by wearing an Islamic headscarf, if the exercise of that freedom clashes with the aim of protecting the rights and freedoms of others, public order and public safety.

. . .

93.   In applying the above principles to Turkey, the Convention institutions have expressed the view that the principle of secularism is certainly one of the fundamental principles of the State which are in harmony with the rule of law and respect for human rights and democracy. An attitude which fails to respect that principle will not necessarily be accepted as being covered by

the freedom to manifest one's religion and will not enjoy the protection of Article 9 of the Convention.

94.   In order to perform its role as the neutral and impartial organizer of the exercise of religious beliefs, the State may decide to impose on its serving or future civil servants, who will be required to wield a portion of its sovereign power, the duty to refrain from taking part in the Islamic fundamentalist movement, whose goal and plan of action is to bring about the pre-eminence of religious rules.

95.   In a country like Turkey, where the great majority of the population belong to a particular religion, measures taken in universities to prevent certain fundamentalist religious movements from exerting pressure on students who do not practice that religion or on those who belong to another religion may be justified under Article 9 § 2 of the Convention. In that context, secular universities may regulate manifestation of the rites and symbols of the said religion by imposing restrictions as to the place and manner of such manifestation with the aim of ensuring peaceful coexistence between students of various faiths and thus protecting public order and the beliefs of others.

. . .

The main grounds for dissolution cited by the Constitutional Court

116.   The Court considers on this point that among the arguments for dissolution pleaded by Principal State Counsel at the Court of Cassation those cited by the Constitutional Court as grounds for its finding that Refah had become a centre of anticonstitutional activities can be classified into three main groups: (i) the arguments that Refah intended to set up a plurality of legal systems, leading to discrimination based on religious beliefs; (ii) the arguments that Refah intended to apply sharia to the internal or external relations of the Muslim community within the context of this plurality of legal systems; and (iii) the arguments based on the references made by Refah members to the possibility of recourse to force as a political method. The Court must therefore limit its examination to those three groups of arguments cited by the Constitutional Court.

The plan to set up a plurality of legal systems

. . .

119.   The Court sees no reason to depart from the Chamber's conclusion that a plurality of legal systems, as proposed by Refah, cannot be considered to be compatible with the Convention system. In its judgment, the Chamber gave the following reasoning:

> 70.   . . . The Court considers that Refah's proposal that there should be a plurality of legal systems would introduce

into all legal relationships a distinction between individuals grounded on religion, would categorize everyone according to his religious beliefs and would allow him rights and freedoms not as an individual but according to his allegiance to a religious movement.

The Court takes the view that such a societal model cannot be considered compatible with the Convention system, for two reasons.

Firstly, it would do away with the State's role as the guarantor of individual rights and freedoms and the impartial organizer of the practice of the various beliefs and religions in a democratic society, since it would oblige individuals to obey, not rules laid down by the State in the exercise of its above-mentioned functions, but static rules of law imposed by the religion concerned. But the State has a positive obligation to ensure that everyone within its jurisdiction enjoys in full, and without being able to waive them, the rights and freedoms guaranteed by the Convention.

Secondly, such a system would undeniably infringe the principle of non-discrimination between individuals as regards their enjoyment of public freedoms, which is one of the fundamental principles of democracy. A difference in treatment between individuals in all fields of public and private law according to their religion or beliefs manifestly cannot be justified under the Convention, and more particularly Article 14 thereof, which prohibits discrimination. Such a difference in treatment cannot maintain a fair balance between, on the one hand, the claims of certain religious groups who wish to be governed by their own rules and on the other the interest of society as a whole, which must be based on peace and on tolerance between the various religions and beliefs.

Sharia

120.   The Court observes in the first place that the intention to set up a regime based on sharia was explicitly portended in the ... remarks cited by the Constitutional Court, which had been made by certain members of Refah, all of whom were MPs....

   . . .

123.   The Court concurs in the Chamber's view that sharia is incompatible with the fundamental principles of democracy, as set forth in the Convention:

72.   Like the Constitutional Court, the Court considers that sharia, which faithfully reflects the dogmas and divine rules laid down by religion, is stable and invariable. Principles such as pluralism in the political sphere or the constant evolu-

tion of public freedoms have no place in it. The Court notes that, when read together, the offending statements, which contain explicit references to the introduction of sharia, are difficult to reconcile with the fundamental principles of democracy, as conceived in the Convention taken as a whole. It is difficult to declare one's respect for democracy and human rights while at the same time supporting a regime based on sharia, which clearly diverges from Convention values, particularly with regard to its criminal law and criminal procedure, its rules on the legal status of women and the way it intervenes in all spheres of private and public life in accordance with religious precepts. . . . In the Court's view, a political party whose actions seem to be aimed at introducing sharia in a State party to the Convention can hardly be regarded as an association complying with the democratic ideal that underlies the whole of the Convention.

124.   The Court must not lose sight of the fact that in the past political movements based on religious fundamentalism have been able to seize political power in certain States and have had the opportunity to set up the model of society which they had in mind. It considers that, in accordance with the Convention's provisions, each Contracting State may oppose such political movements in the light of its historical experience.

125.   The Court further observes that there was already an Islamic theocratic regime under Ottoman law. When the former theocratic regime was dismantled and the republican regime was being set up, Turkey opted for a form of secularism which confined Islam and other religions to the sphere of private religious practice. Mindful of the importance for survival of the democratic regime of ensuring respect for the principle of secularism in Turkey, the Court considers that the Constitutional Court was justified in holding that Refah's policy of establishing sharia was incompatible with democracy.

Sharia and its relationship with the plurality of legal systems proposed by Refah

126.   The Court will next examine the applicants' argument that the Chamber contradicted itself in holding that Refah supported introducing both a plurality of legal systems and sharia simultaneously.

It takes note of the Constitutional Court's considerations concerning the part played by a plurality of legal systems in the application of sharia in the history of Islamic law. These showed that sharia is a system of law applicable to relations between Muslims themselves and between Muslims and the adherents of other faiths. In order to enable the communities owing allegiance to other religions to live in a society dominated by sharia, a plurality of legal systems had also been introduced by the Islamic theocratic regime during the Ottoman Empire, before the Republic was founded.

127.   The Court is not required to express an opinion in the abstract on the advantages and disadvantages of a plurality of legal systems. It notes, for the purposes of the present case, that—as the Constitutional Court observed—Refah's policy was to apply some of sharia's private-law rules to a large part of the population in Turkey (namely Muslims), within the framework of a plurality of legal systems. Such a policy goes beyond the freedom of individuals to observe the precepts of their religion, for example by organizing religious wedding ceremonies before or after a civil marriage (a common practice in Turkey) and according religious marriage the effect of a civil marriage. This Refah policy falls outside the private sphere to which Turkish law confines religion and suffers from the same contradictions with the Convention system as the introduction of sharia.

128.   Pursuing that line of reasoning, the Court rejects the applicants' argument that prohibiting a plurality of private-law systems in the name of the special role of secularism in Turkey amounted to establishing discrimination against Muslims who wished to live their private lives in accordance with the precepts of their religion.

It reiterates that freedom of religion, including the freedom to manifest one's religion by worship and observance, is primarily a matter of individual conscience, and stresses that the sphere of individual conscience is quite different from the field of private law, which concerns the organization and functioning of society as a whole.

It has not been disputed before the Court that in Turkey everyone can observe in his private life the requirements of his religion. On the other hand, Turkey, like any other Contracting Party, may legitimately prevent the application within its jurisdiction of private-law rules of religious inspiration prejudicial to public order and the values of democracy for Convention purposes (such as rules permitting discrimination based on the gender of the parties concerned, as in polygamy and privileges for the male sex in matters of divorce and succession). The freedom to enter into contracts cannot encroach upon the State's role as the neutral and impartial organizer of the exercise of religions, faiths and beliefs.

Notes and Questions

1. The ECHR has not protected religious liberty with anything like the rigor displayed by many national constitutional courts including Canada, South Africa, Germany, and Ireland. Does this reflect a substantive commitment to the kind of legal regime suggested in *Employment Division v. Smith* that focuses more on formal discrimination against religious minorities than the practical impact of neutral laws on the ability of individuals to practice their faith? Would it be more accurate to conclude that the lack of rigor displayed in ECHR opinions reflects the intrinsic limitations of a supranational court attempting to apply constitutional rules to a large class of nations with an extraordinarily diverse range of church-state relationships?

2. In *Manoussakis v. Greece*, 23 Eur. Ct. H.R. 387 (1996), the ECHR applied a more rigorous standard of review, analogous to strict scrutiny, to an Article 9 claim than it had employed in previous cases, but the challenge in *Manoussakis* was to a law that singled out religion for distinct regulatory attention. The applicant, a Jehovah's Witness, had been arrested for renting a room to carry out religious meetings under a law which prohibited "establish[ing] and operat[ing] a place of worship for religious meetings and ceremonies" without receiving permission to do so from ecclesiastical authorities of the Greek Orthodox Church as well as government officials.

Chapter Seven

RELIGION IN PUBLIC SCHOOLS

I. COMPARATIVE LAW

A. RELIGIOUS EDUCATION IN SCHOOLS

Leszek Lech Garlicki
Perspectives on Freedom of Conscience and Religion in the Jurisprudence of Constitutional Courts
2001 BYU L. REV. 467, 501–06

The teaching of religion in public schools should be viewed with the background and nature of the state in mind. State-religion neutrality exists in [many European countries]. Thus, public schools in such countries tend to be neutral rather than religious schools. However, just as state neutrality does not imply indifference or disregard for religion but rather guarantees "freedom of religion in pluralistic systems of religions and cultures," the notion of a neutral public school does not obligate a school to be purely secular or require complete separation of religious teaching from a school's curriculum.

. . .

The principle of neutrality in many European countries is not viewed as the obligation to separate public schools from Christian values and traditions. Rather, it allows for the teaching of religion as part of the comprehensive operation of public schools.

European countries have not followed the American model of imposing constitutional bans on the teaching of religion in public schools....

In many countries, the Constitution neither prohibits nor requires the organization of the teaching of religion in public schools. In these countries, this area of lawmaking is left to the

175

legislature. Constitutional courts have recognized that the introduction of religion in public schools does not infringe constitutional rights per se but have also recognized that various requirements and specific guarantees must be met. Although the teaching of religion in public schools does not violate constitutional provisions per se, parents and students do not necessarily have the right to require such teaching.

In other countries, the constitution requires the organization of the teaching of religion in public schools. Article 7, Section 3 of the German Constitution allows for the teaching of religion in all public schools that are not specifically designated as non-religious schools. In Belgium, Article 24, Section 1 of the constitution guarantees public school students the choice between studying a recognized religion or non-religious ethics. In the Czech Republic, the teaching of religion in state schools is provided for by Article 16, Section 3 of the Charter of Fundamental Rights and Freedoms. In Poland, the teaching of religion in public schools must be introduced at the request of parents. Countries such as Spain, Italy, Portugal, and Poland that may have a duty under Concordat provisions to introduce the teaching of religion in public schools, may also have a duty, under principles of equality, to do so for all religions. The organization of religious teaching in such countries is a constitutional task of the state and other public authorities.

In order to prevent public schools from becoming religious schools, the teaching of religion in public schools may not be limited to one religion. However, identical treatment and recognition of all existing religions is not required. The teaching of religion in public schools may be limited to the teaching of recognized churches. Another possibility may be to base the right to teach religious doctrine in public schools on the stage of development and degree of the public approval of such doctrine.

. . .

In [some] countries, religion classes are treated as ordinary subjects. They are taught on equivalent terms as other classes, are totally integrated in the school's curriculum and schedule, and are graded like other subjects. Religion teachers are members of the educational staff, and public authorities bear the costs of their salaries and social security. However, in each country, details regarding these matters differ slightly.

States have set their own standards with regard to the curriculum of religious classes. In Germany, religious lessons do not consist of a neutral comparison of religious doctrines. Rather, the lessons must teach specific beliefs of a given religious community. The given church's ideas on teaching are binding on the school. In Austria, the teaching of religion in schools is considered an internal operation of recognized churches and religious groups. A 1991 Polish Constitutional Court decision indicated that due to the principle of state neutrality, the content of religious teaching should be determined by church authority and not by the state.

. . .

Although the teaching of religion in public schools is obligatory, attendance is optional and depends on the decision of parents and students. The right to choose whether or not to participate in religious classes is an essential element of the principle of religious freedom. Here a question arises, among others, about the appropriate form of declarations submitted: in Portugal and in Poland the Constitutional Courts have indicated that the Constitution guarantee the "right to silence" as regards religious beliefs. Thus only "positive" declarations are permissible, where the request to participate in religion classes is declared.

The teaching of religion must take into account the principle of religious pluralism. Thus, if public schools organize the teaching of one religion, they must ensure comparable conditions for the teaching of other religions. However, as mentioned above, such guarantees of equality are usually limited to recognized or registered religions. Countries differ in the implementation of this principle, especially in countries where one religion is dominant.

The principle of religious pluralism also requires the protection of non-believers or those who, for other reasons, do not fit the school's religious curriculum. The majority of countries provide alternative classes in ethics or moral formation for such students.

B. PRAYER IN SCHOOLS

ZYLBERBERG v. DIRECTOR OF EDUCATION OF THE SUDBURY BOARD OF EDUCATION

[1988] 65 O.R.2d 641 (Can.)
Ontario Court of Appeal

[At issue is the constitutionality of s. 28(1), a provincial law that requires the recitation of the Lord's Prayer and the reading of passages from the Christian Bible in public schools.]

35. On its face, s. 28(1) infringes the freedom of conscience and religion guaranteed by s. 2(a) of the *Charter*. . . . The recitation of the Lord's Prayer, which is a Christian prayer, and the reading of scriptures from the Christian Bible impose Christian observances upon non-Christian pupils and religious observances on nonbelievers.

36. The respondents, however, take the position that s. 28 viewed as a whole did not violate the freedoms of conscience and

religion guaranteed by s. 2(a) of the *Charter*. They contend that the right to claim exemption from Christian religious exercises, conferred by [statute] eliminates any suggestion of pressure or compulsion on non-Christian pupils to participate in those exercises....

. . .

38.   While the majoritarian view may be that s. 28 confers freedom of choice on the minority, the reality is that it imposes on religious minorities a compulsion to conform to the religious practices of the majority. The evidence in this case supports this view. The three appellants chose not to seek an exemption from religious exercises because of their concern about differentiating their children from other pupils. The peer pressure and the classroom norms to which children are acutely sensitive, in our opinion, are real and pervasive and operate to compel members of religious minorities to conform with majority religious practices. We adopt the view on this issue expressed by Brennan, J., in *Abington School District v. Schempp*, 374 U.S. 203, 288 (1963) [with regard to the susceptibility of children to informal pressure to conform]....

39.   We consider that s. 28(1) also infringes freedom of conscience and religion in a broader sense. The requirement that pupils attend religious exercises, unless exempt, compels students and parents to make a religious statement. We [also believe] that the effect of the exemption provisions is to discriminate against religious minorities.

40.   [T]he right to be excused from class, or to be exempted from participating, does not overcome the infringement of the *Charter* freedom of conscience and religion by the mandated religious exercises. On the contrary, the exemption provision imposes a penalty on pupils from religious minorities who utilize it by stigmatizing them as nonconformists and setting them apart from their fellow students who are members of the dominant religion. In our opinion, the conclusion is inescapable that the exemption provision fails to mitigate the infringement of freedom of conscience and religion by s. 28(1).

. . .

42.   The effect of religious exercises cannot be glossed over with the comment that the exercises may be "good" for minority pupils. This view was expressed, as we indicated above, by a psychologist in supporting the Board's case who said that it was salutary for minority pupils to confront "the fact of their difference from the majority". This insensitive approach, in our opinion, not only depreciates the position of religious minorities but also fails to take into account the feelings of young children. It is also inconsistent with the multicultural nature of our society as recognized by s. 27 of the *Charter* . . .

[The court went on to hold that 28(1) could not be justified because it was intended to serve a religious purpose, an objective which violates the Charter.]

Notes and Questions

1. The European Court of Human Rights opinion in *Hasan and Eylim Zengin v. Turkey,* (2008) 46 E.H.R.R. 44 (discussed in more detail on pp. 185–87 *infra*) provides a useful description of the scope and nature of religious education in Europe.

30. In Europe, religious education is closely tied in with secular education. Of the 46 Council of Europe member States which were examined, 43 provide religious education classes in state schools. Only Albania, France (with the exception of the Alsace and Moselle regions) and the former Yugoslav Republic of Macedonia are the exceptions to this rule. In Slovenia, non-confessional teaching is offered in the last years of state education.

31. In 25 of the 46 member States (including Turkey), religious education is a compulsory subject. However, the scope of this obligation varies depending on the State. In five countries, namely Finland, Greece, Norway, Sweden and Turkey, the obligation to attend classes in religious education is absolute. All pupils who belong to the religious faith taught in the classes are obliged to follow them, partially or fully. However, ten States allow for exemptions under certain conditions. This is the case in Austria, Cyprus, Denmark, Ireland, Iceland, Liechtenstein, Malta, Monaco, San Marino and the United Kingdom. In the majority of these countries, religious education is denominational.

32. Ten other countries give pupils the opportunity to choose a substitute lesson in place of compulsory religious education. This is the case in Germany, Belgium, Bosnia and Herzegovina, Lithuania, Luxembourg, the Netherlands, Serbia, Slovakia and Switzerland. In those countries, denominational education is included in the curriculum drawn up by the relevant ministries and pupils are obliged to attend unless they have opted for the substitute lesson proposed.

33. In contrast, 21 member States do not oblige pupils to follow classes in religious education. Religious education is generally authorised in the school system but pupils only attend if they have made a request to that effect. This is what happens in the largest group of States: Andorra, Armenia, Azerbaijan, Bulgaria, Croatia, Spain, Estonia, Georgia, Hungary, Italy, Latvia, Moldova, Poland, Portugal, the Czech Republic, Romania, Russia and Ukraine. Finally, in a third group of States, pupils are obliged to attend a religious education or substitute class, but always have the option of attending a secular lesson.

34. This general overview of religious education in Europe shows that, in spite of the variety of teaching methods, almost all of the

member States offer at least one route by which pupils can opt out of religious education classes (by providing an exemption mechanism or the option of attending a lesson in a substitute subject, or by giving pupils the choice of whether or not to sign up to a religious studies class).

2. Note that the Court of Appeal in *Zylberberg* expresses some concern about a system exempting students from having to listen to or participate in a prayer at school because students would have to "make a religious statement" in registering their unwillingness to participate and seeking an exemption. This issue has been raised in other jurisdictions as well and is sometimes described as an abridgement of the right to religious privacy. Do you think a system that provides exemptions for nonbelievers or members of minority faiths is necessarily inconsistent with a commitment to religious privacy? Consider the free exercise cases discussed in Chapter III. Are the exemptions sought and granted in those cases also inconsistent with a commitment to religious privacy?

II. INTERNATIONAL AND SUPRANATIONAL LAW

A. ARTICLE 9 OF THE ECHR

LENA AND ANNA–NINA ANGELENI v. SWEDEN

51 Eur. Comm'n H.R. Dec. & Rep. 41, 48–49 (1986)

European Court of Human Rights

The Commission is of the opinion that Article 9 of the Convention affords protection against indoctrination of religion by the State, be it in education at school or in any other activity for which the State has assumed responsibility....

. . .

... In principle, teaching which provides information only cannot be regarded as being in conflict with the Convention or its Protocols.

The Commission does not find it established that the ... applicant has been obliged to participate in any form of religious worship or that she has been exposed to any religious indoctrination. The fact that the instruction in religious knowledge focuses on Christianity at junior level at school does not mean that the ... applicant has been under religious indoctrination in breach of Article 9 of the Convention.

B.   ARTICLE 2 OF PROTOCOL NO. 1: RESPECT-ING PARENTS' RELIGIOUS AND PHILOSOPHICAL BELIEFS AT SCHOOL

FOLGER v. NORWAY

Application No. 15472/02, 2007
European Court of Human Rights

[Non–Christian parents lodged a complaint under Article 9 of the Convention and Article 2 of Protocol No. 1 based on the Norwegian government's refusal to grant their children a full exemption from a new compulsory curriculum teaching Christianity, Religion, and Philosophy ("the KRL subject") in the public schools. The KRL subject was alleged to emphasize the teaching of Christian doctrine, prayer and ritual with an emphasis on the Evangelical Lutheran Faith. While exemptions from instruction were permitted, the exemptions were to be limited to activities that were clearly religious in nature such as "material of a confessional character and participation in rituals." The applicant parents, who were required to request that their children be exempted from the parts of the program to which they objected, argued that the partial exemption system was not feasible because religious instruction and non-religious instruction were not sufficiently separated in the curriculum to permit parents to identify in advance when an exemption would be necessary. In response to an earlier complaint under the 1966 International Covenant on Civil and Political Rights, The United Nations Human Rights Committee concluded that the challenged curriculum with its limited opportunity for exemptions violated Article 18 § 4 of the Covenant.

The government responded that emphasis on Christianity in the public-school curriculum did not constitute a violation of Article 9, since Christianity was the majority faith in Norway. Further, as an alternative to the public schools, the applicants could send their children to publicly subsidized, private schools offering a curriculum consistent with their beliefs.]

56.   The issue whether the contested Norwegian primary school subject constituted a violation of the relevant human rights standards on freedom of religion, parental rights, freedom of privacy and prohibition of discrimination ought to be seen in the broader context of a society with an extreme Christian predominance. Norway had a State religion, a State Church, with constitutional prerogatives being afforded to the Christian (Evangelical Lutheran) Faith. There was a Christian object clause for State schools and pre-schools. There were State Church priests in the armed forces, prisons, universities and hospitals. There were daily Christian devotions and services in State broadcasting. No less than 86% of

the population belonged to the State Church, the Church of Norway.

57.   Nevertheless, the right to freedom of religion for non-Christians had been taken care of ... by an exemption arrangement from the previous Christian Knowledge subject in State schools. This right to a general exemption–which had been enjoyed for more than 150 years–had been repealed when the KRL subject was introduced in 1997....

. . .

84.   (a) The two sentences of Article 2 of Protocol No. 1 must be interpreted not only in the light of each other but also, in particular, of Articles 8, 9 and 10 of the Convention.

. . .

(f) Although individual interests must on occasion be subordinated to those of a group, democracy does not simply mean that the views of a majority must always prevail: a balance must be achieved which ensures the fair and proper treatment of minorities and avoids any abuse of a dominant position.

(g) However, the setting and planning of the curriculum fall in principle within the competence of the Contracting States. This mainly involves questions of expediency on which it is not for the Court to rule and whose solution may legitimately vary according to the country and the era.... In particular, the second sentence of Article 2 of Protocol No. 1 does not prevent States from imparting through teaching or education information or knowledge of a directly or indirectly religious or philosophical kind. It does not even permit parents to object to the integration of such teaching or education in the school curriculum, for otherwise all institutionalised teaching would run the risk of proving impracticable

(h) The second sentence of Article 2 of Protocol No. 1 implies on the other hand that the State ... must take care that information or knowledge included in the curriculum is conveyed in an objective, critical and pluralistic manner. The State is forbidden to pursue an aim of indoctrination that might be considered as not respecting parents' religious and philosophical convictions. That is the limit that must not be exceeded.

(i) ... [Also, the state must be aware that] abuses can occur as to the manner in which the provisions in force are applied by a given school or teacher and the competent authorities have a duty to take the utmost care to see to it that parents' religious and philosophical convictions are not disregarded at this level by carelessness, lack of judgment or misplaced proselytism.

85.   In applying the above principles to the case under consideration ... the question to be determined is whether the respon-

dent State ... had taken care that information or knowledge included in the Curriculum for the KRL subject be conveyed in an objective, critical and pluralistic manner or whether it had pursued an aim of indoctrination not respecting the applicant parents' religious and philosophical convictions and thereby had transgressed the limit implied by Article 2 of Protocol No. 1.

. . .

89. ... [T]he second sentence of Article 2 of Protocol No. 1 does not embody any right for parents that their child be kept ignorant about religion and philosophy in their education. That being so, the fact that knowledge about Christianity represented a greater part of the Curriculum for primary and lower secondary schools than knowledge about other religions and philosophies cannot, in the Court's opinion, of its own be viewed as a departure from the principles of pluralism and objectivity amounting to indoctrination In view of the place occupied by Christianity in the national history and tradition of the respondent State, this must be regarded as falling within the respondent State's margin of appreciation in planning and setting the curriculum.

90. However, the Court observes that, while stress was laid on the teaching being knowledge-based, [the curriculum] ... provided that the teaching should, subject to the parents' agreement and cooperation, take as a starting point the Christian object clause ... according to which the object of primary and lower secondary education was to help give pupils a Christian and moral upbringing.

91. It is further to be noted that the Christian object clause was compounded by a clear preponderance of Christianity in the composition of the subject.

. . .

94. Moreover, [the curriculum] ... implied that pupils could engage in "religious activities," which would in particular include prayers, psalms, the learning of religious texts by heart and the participation in plays of a religious nature. While it was not foreseen that such activities should relate exclusively to Christianity, but could also concern other religions, for example a visit to a mosque in the case of Islam, the emphasis on Christianity in the Curriculum would naturally also be reflected in the choice of educational activities proposed to pupils in the context of the KRL subject. . . . In the Court's view, it can be assumed that participation in at least some of the activities concerned, especially in the case of young children ... would be capable of affecting pupils' minds in a manner giving rise to an issue under Article 2 of Protocol No. 1.

95. Thus, when seen together with the Christian object clause, the description of the contents and the aims of the KRL subject ... suggest that not only quantitative but even qualitative differences applied to the teaching of Christianity as compared to that of other religions and philosophies. . . .

96. The question then arises whether the imbalance highlighted above could be said to have been brought to a level acceptable under Article 2 of Protocol No. 1 by the possibility for pupils to request partial exemption from the KRL subject. . . .

97. . . . [T]he operation of the partial exemption arrangement presupposed . . . that the parents concerned be adequately informed of the details of the lesson plans to be able to identify and notify to the school in advance those parts of the teaching that would be incompatible with their own convictions and beliefs. This could be a challenging task not only for parents but also for teachers, who often had difficulty in working out and dispatching to the parents a detailed lesson plan in advance. . . . [I]t must have been difficult for parents to keep themselves constantly informed about the contents of the teaching that went on in the classroom and to single out incompatible parts. To do so must have been even more difficult where it was the general Christian leaning of the KRL subject that posed a problem.

98. Secondly, . . . save in instances where the exemption request concerned clearly religious activities–where no grounds had to be given, it was a condition for obtaining partial exemption that the parents give reasonable grounds for their request. . . . [Since] information about personal religious and philosophical conviction concerns some of the most intimate aspects of private life . . . imposing an obligation on parents to disclose detailed information to the school authorities about their religions and philosophical convictions may constitute a violation of Article 8 of the Convention and, possibly also, of Article 9. . . . [While] there was no obligation as such for parents to disclose their own conviction . . . [t]he Court finds, nonetheless, that inherent in the condition to give reasonable grounds was a risk that the parents might feel compelled to disclose to the school authorities intimate aspects of their own religious and philosophical convictions. . . .

99. Thirdly, the Court observes that even in the event that a parental note requesting partial exemption was deemed reasonable, this did not necessarily mean that the pupil concerned would be exempted from the part of the curriculum in question. . . . The Court notes in particular that for a number of activities, for instance prayers, the singing of hymns, church services and school plays, it was proposed that observation by attendance could suitably replace involvement through participation, the basic idea being that

... the exemption relate to the activity as such, not to the knowledge to be transmitted through the activity.... However, in the Court's view, this distinction between activity and knowledge must not only have been complicated to operate in practice but also seems likely to have substantially diminished the effectiveness of the right to a partial exemption as such....

100.   In light of the above, the Court finds that the system of partial exemption was capable of subjecting the parents concerned to a heavy burden with a risk of undue exposure of their private life and that the potential for conflict was likely to deter them from making such requests. In certain instances, notably with regard to activities of a religious character, the scope of a partial exemption might even be substantially reduced by differentiated teaching. This could hardly be considered consonant with the parents' right to respect for their convictions for the purposes of Article 2 of Protocol No. 1, as interpreted in the light of Articles 8 and 9 of the Convention....

101.   According to the Government, it would have been possible for the applicant parents to seek alternative education for their children in private schools, which were heavily subsidised by the respondent State.... However, the Court considers that ... the existence of such a possibility could not dispense the State from its obligation to safeguard pluralism in State schools which are open to everyone.

102.   Against this background, notwithstanding the many laudable legislative purposes stated in connection with the introduction of the KRL subject in the ordinary primary and lower secondary schools, it does not appear that the respondent State took sufficient care that information and knowledge included in the curriculum be conveyed in an objective, critical and pluralistic manner for the purposes of Article 2 of Protocol No. 1.

Accordingly, the Court finds that the refusal to grant the applicant parents full exemption from the KRL subject for their children gave rise to a violation of Article 2 of Protocol No. 1.

* * *

HASAN AND EYLEM ZENGIN v. TURKEY
(2008) 46 E.H.R.R. 44
The European Court of Human Rights

[Parents who are members of the Alevi faith, a branch of Islam that is distinct in important respects from the Sunni or Shia branches of Islam, challenged religious teaching in public schools on the grounds that it constituted indoctrination and failed to provide adequate teaching regarding their religion.]

53. In order to examine the disputed legislation under Art.2 of the Protocol ... one must, while avoiding any evaluation of the legislation's expediency, have regard to the material situation that it sought and still seeks to meet. Although, in the past, the Convention organs have not found education providing information on religions to be contrary to the Convention, they have carefully scrutinized whether pupils were obliged to take part in a form of religious worship or were exposed to any form of religious indoctrination. . . .

. . .

57. In the light of the principles set out above, the Court must determine, first, if the content-matter of this subject is taught in an objective, critical and pluralist manner, in order to ensure that it is compatible with the principles which emerge from the case law concerning the second sentence of Art.2 of Protocol No.1. Secondly, it will examine whether appropriate provisions have been introduced in the Turkish educational system to ensure that parents' convictions are respected.

. . .

61. As to the textbooks used in the context of these classes, examination shows that they are not limited to transmitting information on religions in general; they also contain texts which appear to provide instruction in the major principles of the Muslim faith and provide a general overview of its cultural rites, such as the profession of faith, the five daily prayers, Ramadan, pilgrimage, the concepts of angels and invisible creatures, belief in the other world, etc.

62. Equally, pupils must learn several suras from the Koran by heart and study, with the support of illustrations, the daily prayer s and sit written tests for the purpose of assessment. . . .

63. Thus, the syllabus for teaching in primary schools and the first cycle of secondary school, and all of the textbooks ... give greater priority to knowledge of Islam than they do to that of other religions and philosophies. In the Court's view, this itself cannot be viewed as a departure from the principles of pluralism and objectivity which would amount to indoctrination, ... having regard to the fact that, notwithstanding the State's secular nature, Islam is the majority religion practiced in Turkey.

. . .

65. In this regard, the applicant alleged that no teaching was provided on the Alevi faith or its rituals in the compulsory "religious culture and ethics" lessons, although this religious movement differed in numerous areas from the conception of religion presented in school. According to the Government, this resulted from the

fact that, in this syllabus, the vision of members of a branch of Islam or of a religious order represented in the country was not taken into consideration.

. . .

67. [Thus] in the "religious culture and morals" lessons, the religious diversity which prevails in Turkish society is not taken into account. In particular, pupils receive no teaching on the confessional or ritual specificities of the Alevi faith, although the proportion of the Turkish population belonging to it is very large. As to the Government's argument that certain information about the Alevis was taught in the ninth grade, the Court, like the applicants, . . . considers that, in the absence of instruction in the basic elements of this faith in primary and secondary school, the fact that the life and philosophy of two individuals who had a major impact on its emergence are taught in the ninth grade is insufficient to compensate for the shortcomings in this teaching.

68. Admittedly, parents may always enlighten and advise their children, exercise with regard to their children natural parental functions as educators, or guide their children on a path in line with the parents' own religious or philosophical convictions. . . . Nonetheless, where the contracting states include the study of religion in the subjects on school curricula, and irrespective of the arrangements for exemption, pupils' parents may legitimately expect that the subject will be taught in such a way as to meet the criteria of objectivity and pluralism, and with respect for their religious or philosophical convictions.

. . .

70. In the light of the above, the Court concludes that the instruction provided in the school subject "religious culture and ethics" cannot be considered to meet the criteria of objectivity and pluralism and, more particularly in the applicants' specific case, to respect the religious and philosophical convictions of ;9832;9832 . . . a follower of the Alevi faith, on the subject of which the syllabus is clearly lacking.

. . .

[The court also found the mechanisms for an exemption from religious teachings that parents found objectionable was inadequate.]

Notes and Questions

1. The European Court of Human Rights maintains that Article 9 of the Convention and Article 2 of Protocol No. 1 only protect students against the indoctrination of religion in the public schools. Further, the

Court concludes that religious instruction which overwhelmingly emphasizes the majority faith in a country does not constitute indoctrination as long as adequate provision for exempting students who do not want to participate in such lessons is provided. Does this understanding of the Convention ignore concerns about religious equality? What message does a state school deliver to students when its educational programs emphasize the beliefs and practice of only one faith?

2.   Given the discretionary authority that can be exercised by teachers in public schools over their students, does a formal right to an exemption provide adequate protection to religious and secular minorities against coercion and indoctrination? The Court acknowledges that "abuses can occur" when a state's provisions providing for religious instruction are implemented. How can the Court guarantee that the exercise of the right to an exemption does not have negative repercussions for students?

Chapter Eight

HEADSCARVES

I. THE HEADSCARF IN EUROPE

LEYLA SAHIN v. TURKEY

App. No. 44774/98 Eur. Ct. H.R. (2005)
European Court of Human Rights

[At issue are regulations prohibiting a woman at a university in Turkey from wearing an Islamic headscarf.]

55.   For more than 20 years the place of the Islamic headscarf in state education has been the subject of debate across Europe. In most European countries, the debate has focused mainly on primary and secondary schools. However, in Turkey, Azerbaijan and Albania it has concerned not just the question of individual liberty, but also the political meaning of the Islamic headscarf. These are the only member states to have introduced regulations on wearing the Islamic headscarf in universities.

56.   In France, where secularism is regarded as one of the cornerstones of republican values, legislation was passed on 15 March 2004 regulating, in accordance with the principle of secularism, the wearing of signs or dress manifesting a religious affiliation in state primary and secondary schools. The legislation inserted ... in the Education Code ... provides: "In state primary and secondary schools, the wearing of signs or dress by which pupils overtly manifest a religious affiliation is prohibited. The school rules shall state that the institution of disciplinary proceedings shall be preceded by dialogue with the pupil."

The Act applies to all state schools and educational institutions, including post-baccalaureate courses ... [but not] to state universities. In addition ... it only concerns "signs, such as the Islamic headscarf, however named, the kippa or a cross that is manifestly oversized, which make the wearer's religious affiliation immediately identifiable."

57. In Belgium there is no general ban on wearing religious signs at school. In the French community ... [p]upils are in principle allowed to wear religious signs. However, they may do so only if human rights, the reputation of others, national security, public order, and public health and morals are protected and internal rules complied with. Further, teachers must not permit religious or philosophical proselytism under their authority or the organization of political militancy by or on behalf of pupils.... In the Flemish community, there is no uniform policy among schools on whether to allow religious or philosophical signs to be worn. Some do, others do not....

58. In other countries (Austria, Germany, the Netherlands, Spain, Sweden, Switzerland and the United Kingdom), in some cases following a protracted legal debate, the state education authorities permit Muslim pupils and students to wear the Islamic headscarf.

59. In Germany, where the debate focused on whether teachers should be allowed to wear the Islamic headscarf, the Constitutional Court stated on 24 September 2003 in a case between a teacher and the Land of Baden–Wurttemberg that the lack of any express statutory prohibition meant that teachers were entitled to wear the headscarf. Consequently, it imposed a duty on the Lander to lay down rules on dress if they wished to prohibit the wearing of the Islamic headscarf in state schools.

60. In Austria there is no special legislation governing the wearing of the headscarf, turban or kippa....

61. In the United Kingdom a tolerant attitude is shown to pupils who wear religious signs. Difficulties with respect to the Islamic headscarf are rare. The issue has also been debated in the context of the elimination of racial discrimination in schools in order to preserve their multicultural character.... The Commission for Racial Equality, whose opinions have recommendation status only, also considered the issue of the Islamic headscarf in 1988 in the Altrincham Grammar School case, which ended in a compromise between a private school and members of the family of two sisters who wished to be allowed to wear the Islamic headscarf at the school. The school agreed to allow them to wear the headscarf provided it was navy blue (the colour of the school uniform), kept fastened at the neck and not decorated.

In the case of R (On the application of Begum) v. Headteacher and Governors of Denbigh High School, [2004] EWHC 1389 (Admin.), the High Court had to decide a dispute between the school and a Muslim pupil wishing to wear the jilbab (a full-length gown).

The school required pupils to wear a uniform, one of the possible options being the headscarf and a *shalwar kameeze* (long traditional garments from the Indian subcontinent). In June 2004 the High Court dismissed the pupil's application, holding that there had been no violation of her freedom of religion. However, that judgment was reversed in March 2005 by the Court of Appeal *R (on the application of SB) v. Governors of Denbigh High School*, [2005] EWCA Civ 199, which accepted that there had been interference with the pupil's freedom of religion, as a minority of Muslims in the United Kingdom considered that a religious duty to wear the *jilbab* from the age of puberty existed and the pupil was genuinely of that opinion. No justification for the interference had been provided by the school authorities, as the decision-making process was not compatible with freedom of religion.

62.   In Spain, there is no express statutory prohibition on pupils' wearing religious head coverings in state schools. . . . Generally speaking, state schools allow the headscarf to be worn.

63.   In Finland and Sweden the veil can be worn at school. However, a distinction is made between the *burka* (the term used to describe the full veil covering the whole of the body and the face) and the *niqab* (a veil covering all the upper body with the exception of the eyes). In Sweden mandatory directives were issued in 2003 by the National Education Agency. These allow schools to prohibit the *burka* and *niqab*, provided they do so in a spirit of dialogue on the common values of equality of the sexes and respect for the democratic principle on which the education system is based.

64.   In the Netherlands, where the question of the Islamic headscarf is considered from the standpoint of discrimination rather than of freedom of religion, it is generally tolerated. In 2003 a non-binding directive was issued. Schools may require pupils to wear a uniform provided that the rules are not discriminatory and are included in the school prospectus and that the punishment for transgressions is not disproportionate. A ban on the *burka* is regarded as justified by the need to be able to identify and communicate with pupils. In addition, the Equal Treatment Commission ruled in 1997 that a ban on wearing the veil during general lessons for safety reasons was not discriminatory.

65.   In a number of other countries (Russia, Romania, Hungary, Greece, the Czech Republic, Slovakia and Poland), the issue of the Islamic headscarf does not yet appear to have given rise to any detailed legal debate.

. . .

(b) The Court's assessment

109. Where questions concerning the relationship between state and religions are at stake, on which opinion in a democratic society may reasonably differ widely, the role of the national decision-making body must be given special importance.... This will notably be the case when it comes to regulating the wearing of religious symbols in educational institutions, especially ... in view of the diversity of the approaches taken by national authorities on the issue.

. . .

(ii) Application of [Article 9] principles to the present case

112. The interference [with religious conduct] caused by the circular ... imposing restrictions as to place and manner on the rights of students such as Ms Sahin to wear the Islamic headscarf on university premises was, according to the Turkish courts ... based in particular on the two principles of secularism and equality.

113. In its judgment ... the Constitutional Court stated that secularism, as the guarantor of democratic values, was the meeting point of liberty and equality. The principle prevented the state from manifesting a preference for a particular religion or belief; it thereby guided the state in its role of impartial arbiter, and necessarily entailed freedom of religion and conscience. It also served to protect the individual not only against arbitrary interference by the state but from external pressure from extremist movements. The Constitutional Court added that freedom to manifest one's religion could be restricted in order to defend those values and principles....

114. [T]he [ECtHR] considers this notion of secularism to be consistent with the values underpinning the convention. It finds that upholding that principle, which is undoubtedly one of the fundamental principles of the Turkish state which are in harmony with the rule of law and respect for human rights, may be considered necessary to protect the democratic system in Turkey. An attitude which fails to respect that principle will not necessarily be accepted as being covered by the freedom to manifest one's religion and will not enjoy the protection of art 9 of the convention....

[The Court accepted the analysis of the Chamber which focused on three points: the importance that both the Turkish constitutional system and the ECHR assign to gender equality, the impact that permitting some women to wear a headscarf may have on other women who decide not to do so, and the power of extremist Islamic political movements in Turkey.]

116. Having regard to the above background, it is the principle of secularism, as elucidated by the Constitutional Court ... which is the paramount consideration underlying the ban on the

wearing of religious symbols in universities. In such a context, where the values of pluralism, respect for the rights of others and, in particular, equality before the law of men and women are being taught and applied in practice, it is understandable that the relevant authorities should wish to preserve the secular nature of the institution concerned and so consider it contrary to such values to allow religious attire, including, as in the present case, the Islamic headscarf, to be worn.

117.   The court must now determine whether in the instant case there was a reasonable relationship of proportionality between the means employed and the legitimate objectives pursued by the interference.

118.   Like the Chamber ... the Grand Chamber notes at the outset that it is common ground that practicing Muslim students in Turkish universities are free, within the limits imposed by educational organizational constraints, to manifest their religion in accordance with habitual forms of Muslim observance. In addition, the resolution adopted by Istanbul University ... shows that various other forms of religious attire are also forbidden on the university premises.

. . .

120.   Furthermore, the process [leading to the implementation of the regulations] took several years and was accompanied by a wide debate within Turkish society and the teaching profession.... It is quite clear that throughout that decision-making process the university authorities sought to adapt to the evolving situation in a way that would not bar access to the university to students wearing the veil, through continued dialogue with those concerned, while at the same time ensuring that order was maintained and in particular that the requirements imposed by the nature of the course in question were complied with.

. . .

122.   In the light of the foregoing and having regard to the contracting states' margin of appreciation in this sphere, the court finds that the interference in issue was justified in principle and proportionate to the aim pursued.

123.   Consequently, there has been no breach of art 9 of the convention.

Notes and Questions

1.   Courts in other Moslem countries have also upheld the power of educational institutions to regulate the religious garb of students. The Supreme Constitutional Court of Egypt, for example, upheld the

policies of a secondary school which prohibited female students from wearing the *niqab,* a veil which covers most of a woman's face and only leaves her eyes uncovered. The Court concluded that Islamic law, the *shari'a,* does not require women to be totally veiled. Accordingly, the political branches of government have the discretion to make decisions in this area. The limitations on a student's attire were found to serve a legitimate state interest and not to violate a student's ability to practice their faith. Nathan J. Brown & Clark B. Lombard, *The Supreme Constitutional Court of Egypt on Islamic Law, Veiling and Civil Rights: An Annotated Translation of Supreme Constitutional Court of Egypt: Case No. 8 of Judicial Year 17 (May 18, 1996),* 21 Am. U. Int'l L. Rev. 437 (2006).

2. Ruti Teitel, *Militating Constitutional Democracy: Comparative Perspectives, in* Issues in Constitutional Law 4. Censorial Sensitivities: Free Speech and Religion in a Fundamentalist World 71, 75–76 (Andras Sajo ed., Eleven Publishing, 2007).

> In the United States, religion rights, as the constitutional language reflects, are seen as a matter to be exercised by the individual of constitutionally protected "free exercise." Accordingly, in the US, there would be no limit to the wearing of religious garb of any faith, as such a limitation would violate the First Amendment, subject to possible conflict with a compelling competing state law or another constitutional right. But, in Europe generally and in France, more particularly, issues of religious freedom are seen again in terms of a balance of individual and community rights.
>
> Consider an area of rapidly escalating controversy involving religious garb in the public sphere. Religious garb bans, in Europe, have been justified by the ideal of keeping the public sphere secular. The view is that no one should feel overtly proselytized. Therefore, the banning of such garb is seen as a protection against proselytizing, despite its disproportionate impact upon Muslims. Along these lines, France ended up banning overt religious symbols on this basis, prohibiting headscarves, together with skullcaps, or outsize crosses from being worn in state primary and secondary schools. While ultimately including other garb, tellingly, the ban's original draft singled out the hijab for exclusion from public life.

While it would clearly violate the First Amendment for a school district to prohibit students from wearing the religious garb of a particular faith, would it be unconstitutional for a school district to impose a uniform clothing requirement on its students or its employees–even if those requirements conflicted with a student or teacher's religious obligations?

3. Joan Wallach Scott, Politics of the Veil 94 (Princeton Univ. Press, 2007).

> [We can compare the controversies surrounding] [k]eeping creationism out of the public school curriculum in the United

States or banning Islamic headscarves in French public schools. In order to distinguish between these two instances, we have to look at concrete outcomes; in the first case, it's what all children are taught that's at issue; in the second, it's the right of a small group of children to be taught what everybody else is learning despite the personal religious identification their clothing proclaims. Of course, secularism figures in both cases: in the first, it rules out claims of religious truth in public school curriculum; in the second, it requires that there be no sign of student religious affiliation in a public school. But there's something about the democratic result of the process that's important too: in the first case, a minority is prevented from dictating its religious belief to a majority; in the second, a minority is denied access, on the grounds of its religious belief, to what the majority enjoys.

Do you agree with Scott's analogy? Religious families that believe in creationism might argue that their situation is similar to that of Moslem children in France. In both cases, they would argue, students are forced to surrender their religious commitments as the price for attending public school. Should it matter that families that believe in evolution are a minority in many communities in the United States? Isn't the real difference between the creationism controversy and the head scarf controversy that there is an obvious solution that respects religious pluralism to the head scarf controversy (allow children to wear whatever garb their religion requires), but there is no way to be respectful of religious diversity and teach the Christian biblical account of the creation of the world as scientific truth?

Chapter Nine

ESTABLISHMENT CLAUSE

I. COMPARATIVE LAW

A. RELIGIOUS LIBERTY AND EQUALITY WITHOUT AN ESTABLISHMENT CLAUSE

Most countries do not have a formal Establishment Clause in their constitutions (Australia is one notable exception, but as the case law in Chapter 10, pp. 213–19, *infra*, demonstrates, it has been given a very narrow interpretation). In some cases, however, the same constitutional principles that are debated and enforced under the Establishment Clause in United States constitutional jurisprudence are debated and enforced in other countries under different constitutional provisions.

For example, under U.S. case law, the Establishment Clause prohibits the government from discriminating among religions and treating some faiths more favorably than others. This anti-preferentialism principle is stated explicitly in cases like *Larson v. Valente*, 456 U.S. 228 (1982). It also underlies the "endorsement test," first suggested by Justice O'Connor in *Lynch v. Donnelly*, 465 U.S. 668 (1984), that has been employed in many Establishment Clause cases. The endorsement test prohibits government action that "sends a message to non-adherents that they are outsiders, not full members of the political community, and an accompanying message to adherents that they are insiders, favored members of the political community." *Id.* at 688.

In other constitutional systems, this same concern about discrimination and religious favoritism is reflected in cases grounded on specific constitutional provisions guaranteeing religious liberty and equality, notwithstanding the absence of a formal Establishment Clause.

R. v. BIG M DRUG MART LTD.

[1985] 1 S.C.R. 295

Supreme Court of Canada

In *Big M*, the Canadian Supreme Court evaluated the constitutionality of the Lord's Day Act, a law that prohibited any person to carry on or transact any business on Sunday. The defenders of the law argued that "unlike the American Bill of Rights, the Canadian Charter of Rights and Freedoms does not include an 'establishment clause.' [Accordingly] the protection of freedom of conscience and religion extends only to the 'free exercise' of religion.... [In light of the absence of an anti-establishment] principle in the Charter ... the Lord's Day Act does not in any way affect the guarantee [of religious liberty] in s. 2(a)." 1 S.C.R. 295, ¶ 104.

In response, Chief Justice Dickson acknowledged the distinction between the two constitutional texts, but explained that "recourse to categories from the American jurisprudence is not particularly helpful in defining the meaning of freedom of conscience and religion under the Charter. The adoption in the United States of the categories 'establishment' and 'free exercise' is perhaps an inevitable consequence of the wording of the First Amendment. The cases illustrate, however, that these are not two totally separate and distinct categories, but rather, as the Supreme Court of the United States has frequently recognized, in specific instances 'the two clauses may overlap'." *Id.* ¶ 105.

In striking down the Lord's Day Act as unconstitutional, Dickson's opinion included two arguments that resonate with Establishment Clause doctrine. First, he emphasized the issue of religious equality and the endorsement of majoritarian faiths:

> What may appear good and true to a majoritarian religious group, or to the state acting at their behest, may not, for religious reasons, be imposed upon citizens who take a contrary view. The Charter safeguards religious minorities from the threat of 'the tyranny of the majority'. To the extent that it binds all to a sectarian Christian ideal, the Lord's Day Act works a form of coercion inimical to the spirit of the Charter and the dignity of all non-Christians. In proclaiming the standards of the Christian faith, the Act creates a climate hostile to, and gives the appearance of discrimination against, non-Christian Canadians. It takes religious values rooted in Christian morality and, using the force of the state, translates them into a positive law binding on believers and non-believers alike. The theological content of the legislation remains as a subtle and constant reminder to religious minorities within the coun-

try of their differences with, and alienation from, the dominant religious culture.

Non–Christians are prohibited for religious reasons from carrying out activities which are otherwise lawful, moral and normal. The arm of the state requires all to remember the Lord's day of the Christians and to keep it holy. The protection of one religion and the concomitant non-protection of others imports disparate impact destructive of the religious freedom of the collectivity. *Id.* ¶ ¶ 95–98.

In an earlier time, when people believed in the collective responsibility of the community toward some deity, the enforcement of religious conformity may have been a legitimate object of government, but since the Charter, it is no longer legitimate. With the Charter, it has become the right of every Canadian to work out for himself or herself what his or her religious obligations, if any, should be and it is not for the state to dictate otherwise. The state shall not use the criminal sanctions at its disposal to achieve a religious purpose, namely, the uniform observance of the day chosen by the Christian religion as its day of rest. *Id.* ¶ 136.

Second, Dickson focused on the religious purpose of the Lord's Day Act in an analysis that parallels American doctrine requiring a "secular purpose" for legislation:

A finding that the Lord's Day Act has a secular purpose is . . . simply not possible. Its religious purpose, in compelling sabbatical observance, has been long-established and consistently maintained by the courts of this country. The Attorney–General for Alberta concedes that the Act is characterized by this religious purpose, [but he argues] . . . that it is effects alone which must be assessed in determining whether legislation violates a constitutional guarantee of freedom of religion. I cannot agree. In my view, both purpose and effect are relevant in determining constitutionality; either an unconstitutional purpose or an unconstitutional effect can invalidate legislation. . . . Purpose and effect respectively, in the sense of the legislation's object and its ultimate impact, are clearly linked, if not indivisible. Intended and actual effects have often been looked to for guidance in assessing the legislation's object and thus, its validity.

. . .

Moreover, consideration of the object of legislation is vital if rights are to be fully protected. The assessment by the courts of legislative purposes focuses scrutiny upon the aims and objectives of the legislature and ensures they are consonant with the guarantees enshrined in the Charter. The declaration that certain objects lie outside the legislature's power checks governmental action at the first stage of unconstitutional conduct. Further, it will provide more ready and more vigorous protection of constitutional rights by obviating the individual litigant's need to prove effects violative of Charter rights. It will also allow courts to dispose of cases where the object is clearly improper, without inquiring into the legislation's actual impact. *Id.* ¶ ¶ 79–82.

. . .

In my view, the guarantee of freedom of conscience and religion prevents the government from compelling individuals to perform or abstain from performing otherwise harmless acts because of the religious significance of those acts to others. The element of religious compulsion is perhaps somewhat more difficult to perceive (especially for those whose beliefs are being enforced) when, as here, it is non-action rather than action that is being decreed, but in my view compulsion is nevertheless what it amounts to.... [T]he Charter ... mandates that the legislative preservation of a Sunday day of rest should be secular, the diversity of belief and non-belief, the diverse sociocultural backgrounds of Canadians make it constitutionally incompetent for the federal Parliament to provide legislative preference for any one religion at the expense of those of another religious persuasion. *Id.* ¶ ¶ 134–135.

S v. LAWRENCE

1997 (4) Sa 1176 (Cc)
Constitutional Court of South Africa

In *S v. Lawrence*, justices on the South Africa Constitutional Court debated the extent to which their constitution protected religious equality, notwithstanding the lack of an Establishment Clause in its text. The appellant argued that a law prohibiting the sale of wine by grocers on "closed days" was intended to serve a religious purpose since all of the days designated, Sunday, Good Friday and Christmas Day, had special religious significance for Christians. In rejecting the claim that the law unconstitutionally favored the Christian faith, Chaskalson, writing for the majority explained:

93. I am not unmindful of the fact that constraints on the exercise of freedom of religion can be imposed in subtle ways and that the choice of Christian holy days for particular legislative purposes may be perceived to elevate Christian beliefs above others; and that as a result adherents of other religions may be made to feel that the State accords less value to their beliefs than it does to Christianity.

. . .

95.   [But] in South Africa, Sundays have acquired a secular as well as a religious character. . . . Patterns established over the years by legislation have resulted in Sundays being the most common day of the week on which people do not work.

96.   Amongst those who observe Sundays as rest days, are many who do so because it has become the most convenient day for such purpose, and not because of any wish to observe the Christian Sabbath. The secular nature of Sundays is evidenced by the ways in which many people spend their Sundays, engaging in sport and recreation rather than in worship.

. . .

100.   The primary purpose of the "establishment clause" in the United States constitution is to prevent the advancement or inhibition of religion by the State. The primary purpose of the "free exercise" clause is to permit adherents of different faiths to pursue their religious beliefs without being impeded from doing so by State coercion. Our Constitution deals with issues of religion differently to the United States constitution. It does so under the equality provisions of section 8, the freedom of religion, belief and opinion provisions of section 14, and [other provisions not related to this case].

101.   The only provision relied on by the appellant in the present case is section 14. Section 14 does not include an "establishment clause" and in my view we ought not to read into its provisions principles pertaining to the advancement or inhibition of religion by the State. To do so would have far reaching implications beyond the apparent scope and purpose of section 14. If such obligations on the part of the State are to be read into section 14 does this mean that Christmas Day and Easter Friday can no longer be public holidays, that "Family Day" is suspect because it falls on Easter Monday, that the SABC as public broadcaster cannot broadcast church services (as it does regularly on Sunday mornings, though it does not regularly broadcast Muslim services on Fridays or Jewish services on Saturdays or Hindu services on any particular day of the week), that its daily religious programs must be cancelled, and that State subsidies to denominational schools are prohibited? These examples can be multiplied by reference to the extremely complex United States law which has developed around the "establishment clause".

102.   I should add that I can see nothing in the text of section 14(1) or in the historical background to a constitution which made no provision for an establishment clause, which would require such a principle to be read into its provisions. The

Constitution deals with unequal treatment and discrimination under section 8. Unequal treatment of religions may well give rise to issues under section 8(2), but that section was not relied upon by the appellant in the present case. To read "equitable considerations" relating to State action into section 14(1) would give rise to any number of problems not only in relation to freedom of religion but also in relation to freedom of conscience, thought, belief and opinion, which would go far beyond the difficulties raised by the "establishment clause" of the United States constitution.

. . .

104. There may be circumstances in which endorsement of a religion or a religious belief by the State would contravene the "freedom of religion" provisions of section 14. This would be the case if such endorsement has the effect of coercing persons to observe the practices of a particular religion, or of placing constraints on them in relation to the observance of their own different religion. The coercion may be direct or indirect, but it must be established to give rise to an infringement of the freedom of religion. It is for the person who alleges that section 14 has been infringed to show that there has been such coercion or constraint. In my view this has not been established in the present case.

Justice O'Regan dissented. She cited Justice Brennan's opinion in *Larson v. Valente*, 456 U.S. 228, 245 (1982), which stated that the "constitutional prohibition of denominational preferences is inextricably connected with the continuing vitality of the Free Exercise Clause."

O'Regan argued:

123. The requirement of equity in the conception of freedom of religion as expressed in the interim Constitution is a rejection of our history, in which Christianity was given favored status by government in many areas of life regardless of the wide range of religions observed in our society.... The explicit endorsement of one religion over others would not be permitted in our new constitutional order. It would not be permitted, first, because it would result in the indirect coercion that [Justice] Black adverted to in *Engel v. Vitale*, 370 U.S. 421 (1962). And secondly because such public endorsement of one religion over another is in itself a threat to the free exercise of religion, particularly in a society in which there is a wide diversity of religions.

She concluded:

123. In my view, it is not possible to read the inclusion of Sundays in the definition of "closed day" in the abstract. The inclusion of Sundays is accompanied, and ineluctably colored, by the inclusion of Good Friday and Christmas Day. Good Friday and Christmas Day are, without doubt, important days in the Christian calendar. In addition, many Christian denominations consider, as a central tenet of their religion, that Sundays should be observed as a day of rest and religious observance.... The inevitable effect of choosing these days was to give a legislative endorsement to Christianity, but not to other religions.

. . .

129. In this case, the legislation results in a breach of section 14 of the interim Constitution in that it results in the favoring of one religion over others.

Leszek Lech Garlicki
Perspectives on Freedom of Conscience and Religion in the Jurisprudence of Constitutional Courts
2001 BYU L. Rev. 467, 489–493

A. The Principle of Equality of Individuals in the Religious Liberty Context

[M]any constitutions make special reference to the principle of equality as it specifically pertains to religion. Many constitutions clearly prohibit discrimination based on religion.... This understanding of equality of individuals resulted in the development of case law in many countries, which treats the ban of discrimination as one of the premises of freedom of religion.

B. The Principle of Equality of Groups in the Religious Liberty Context

In contrast to its application to individuals, the application of the principle of equality to churches and religious groups is far more complex. Some constitutions explicitly provide for equality before the law for churches or religious groups.

. . .

However, at the constitutional level, the differentiation of churches is often implied or allowed. Clearly, it is seen in all countries where there is an official state church. Even where there is not a state church, constitutions may refer to a particular church. Such is the case with the Constitutions of Spain and Poland, which refer specifically to the Catholic Church. Similarly, the Orthodox Church is referenced in the 1991 Constitution of Macedonia and in the 1991 Constitution of Bulgaria. In Portugal, the 1940 Concordat requires that the state recognize "the principles of Christian doctrine and morality, traditional for the country." The 1997 Russian Law on Freedom of Conscience and Religious Associations recognizes "a particular role of Orthodox religion in the history of Russia, for the future and the development of spirituality and culture" and expresses respect for Christianity, Islam, Buddhism, Judaism and other religions.

. . .

The scope of privileges granted to "main churches" depends on many factors but primarily on the religious structure of society. Privileges for traditional churches will be found in particular in those countries where one religion dominates. These privileges manifest themselves in different ways, including procedures for recognizing and establishing churches, regulation of relations between particular churches, religious teaching and education, direct and indirect financing or state support, and various other forms of state cooperation and assistance.

C. Differential Treatment of Religious Groups

[Many constitutional courts do not require strict equality among faith communities.] The German Constitutional Court stated in a 1965 opinion: "The Constitution does not require the State to treat equally religious communities in a schematic way." Similarly, the Belgian Council of State held in a 1996 case: "[r]eligious equality does not mean that the same regime must be applied to all religions." The Austrian Constitutional Court in a 1972 decision stated: "[d]ifferentiation between religious communities which are recognized by statute and other religions does not infringe the principle of equality." Finally, "the legislature is not prohibited by anything to include the specificity of religion and churches when establishing legal regulations implementing the fundamental right to the freedom of religion."

Thus, differentiation may be allowed provided that it is justified. The justification for differentiation must be substantial. Because "the general constitutional principle of equality also applies to churches and religious organizations . . . the differentiation before law requires a substantial justification which may be attributed to specific features of a given church or religious organization." . . . Switzerland [recognizes differences among faiths] "as regards their strength and history" [and the] "public and charity tasks [they perform]". The German Federal Constitutional Court indicated that the premises of providing public and legal status to a given church are "a conviction of the State that such churches are particularly effective when provided with the status of public institution, that they enjoy a very important position in the society, and that there is a guarantee of durability resulting from it."

Notes and Questions

1. In *Edwards Books and Art Ltd. v. R.R. v. Nortown Foods Ltd.*, [1986] 2 S.C.R. 713 (Can.), the Canada Supreme Court upheld an Ontario statute, the Retail Business Holidays Act, which required most businesses in the province to be closed on Sundays. The statute contained many exceptions, including one that exempted from its requirements any small business that was closed on the previous Saturday. Distinguishing *Big M* on its facts, the Court held that the Ontario law was enacted to serve the secular purpose of providing a uniform day of rest for retail employees. The Court recognized that the law burdened the free exercise of some business owners who observed Saturday as their Sabbath, but it concluded, on balance, that the limited exemptions in the statute were sufficient for the law to survive constitutional scrutiny.

Big M and *Edwards Books* may be compared to two U. S. Supreme Court cases upholding Sunday closing laws against constitutional challenge. In *McGowan v. Maryland*, 366 U.S. 420 (1961), the Court rejected the argument that a Sunday closing law violated the Establishment Clause on the grounds that the original religious purpose of the statute has shifted over time to the secular objective of providing a uniform day of rest for the entire community. The Canada Supreme Court explicitly rejected this "shifting purpose" analysis in *Big M*. In *Braunfeld v. Brown*, 366 U.S. 599 (1961), the Court rejected a free exercise claim challenging a Sunday closing law that provided no exemptions for business owners who observed Saturday as their Sabbath. The Court held that the burden on religious exercise imposed by the law was too indirect to warrant serious constitutional review. Once again, the Canada Supreme Court explicitly repudiated the analysis of its American counterpart. In *Edward Books,* the Court explained that it would clearly be unconstitutional for the legislature to enact a Sunday closing law without making any effort "to accommodate the interests of Saturday-observing retailers." 2 S.C.R. 713, ¶ 143.

2. As Chief Justice Dickson recognized in *Big M,* there is clearly some overlap between a constitutional provision prohibiting the establishment of religion and a provision protecting the free exercise of religion. But these two constitutional provisions also serve distinct goals and on some occasions may be in tension with each other. Can you identify the different principles and values served by the Establishment Clause and the Free Exercise Clause? Is the primary difference that the former provision emphasizes religious equality concerns as well as religious liberty concerns? Do you think that countries that do not prohibit the establishment of religion in their constitutions can adequately guarantee religious liberty and equality in their societies?

II. INTERNATIONAL AND SUPRANATIONAL LAW

Carolyn Evans & Christopher A. Thomas
Church-State Relations in the European Court of Human Rights

2006 BYU L. Rev. 699, 706–707

The European Commission has held that establishment is not in itself a breach of the ECHR. Establishment is only prohibited to the extent that it implicates one of the other ECHR rights. There are a number of reasons for this. The first is textual–the text of the ECHR does not mention establishment and takes no explicit position on whether it should be permitted. The ECHR was drafted well after other constitutions that required separation of church and state, and the absence of such a provision cannot therefore be attributed to mere oversight. The second reason is historical. At the time that the ECHR was drafted, a number of member states had established churches, including the United Kingdom, Sweden, and Norway. If the ECHR had prohibited establishment, then it is quite possible that significant states would not have ratified the ECHR or would have included substantial reservations to their acceptance. These states included important supporters of the ECHR, such as the United Kingdom, which maintains its established church to this day and would likely oppose any attempts to include establishment as a rights violation. While the number of states with established churches in Europe is decreasing over time, a number of states still maintain elements of establishment. The fact that establishment existed in many member states at the time of the drafting of the ECHR is good evidence that Article 9 should not be interpreted as an absolute prohibition on establishment.

The final reason for holding that Article 9 does not prohibit establishment is that the Court is not convinced that all forms of establishment are necessarily incompatible with the rights set out in the ECHR. A country such as the United Kingdom, it might be argued, has a great deal of religious freedom and religious tolerance—more than many secular countries—despite its established church. While establishment certainly presents some dangers to religious freedom, and many states with an established religion have very poor protection of religious freedom, it does not follow that establishment will necessarily lead to the oppression of religious freedom for those who do not belong to the established church.

Notes and Questions

1. Having an established church may not lead to oppression, but is it consistent with religious equality. In England, "the 26 most senior bishops of the Church of England have by right a seat and a vote in the House of Lords as Lords Spiritual." The King or Queen of England heads the Church of England and is prohibited from marrying a Catholic. England's blasphemy law only applies to speech that expresses contempt for the Church of England. No other religion receives the protection of these laws. SAMANTHA KNIGHTS, FREEDOM OF RELIGION, MINORITIES, AND THE LAW 15–16 (Oxford Univ. Press USA 2007). What message do these special privileges communicate to the members of other faiths who live in England? Can these privileges by reconciled with principles of religious equality?

Chapter Ten

SCHOOL FUNDING

I. COMPARATIVE LAW

A. FUNDING RELIGIOUS SCHOOLS: AN OVER-VIEW

Leszek Lech Garlicki,
*Perspectives on Freedom of Conscience and Religion
in the Jurisprudence of Constitutional Courts,*
2001 BYU L. Rev. 467, 498

Subsidy by public authority of private education is one of the most delicate issues in education. None of the countries discussed herein have adopted the U.S. concept of a complete separation that prohibits direct state financial support for religiously-affiliated schools. Consequently, there is no constitutional ban against subsidizing private schools, regardless of their religious affiliation. In practice, many countries finance almost entirely the operation of private schools (including personnel costs and schoolbooks) where the schools have been granted the status of a public school or have entered into agreements with public authorities providing for this subsidy.

Notwithstanding this practice, it is unclear if subsidizing private schools with public funds is merely allowed under the Constitution or whether such subsidizing is constitutionally required. In Switzerland, it is accepted that there is no "claim" by private schools to public funds. In several countries, however, a requirement to subsidize private schools has been interpreted as constitutionally required. The rationale suggests that the equality principle requires state subsidy so that parental choice for the education of their children in religiously-affiliated schools would not be inhibited.

B. CASE LAW

CAMPAIGN TO SEPARATE CHURCH AND STATE IN IRELAND v. THE MINISTER FOR EDUCATION

[1998] 3 I.R. 321, 345–358, 358–59 (Ir.)
Supreme Court of Ireland

[For the constitutional provisions of Ireland relating to religion, see pp. 121–22]

[There are three kinds of secondary schools in Ireland funded by the State. There are denominational schools (controlled by religious authorities), comprehensive schools (affiliated with a religious denomination, but sharing governance with state authorities) and community schools that are operated by the state. Chaplains paid by the State provide educational, spiritual, and counseling services in comprehensive and community schools. Plaintiffs argue that State payment of the salaries of chaplains in community schools constitutes an "endowment" of religion prohibited by Article 44.2.2 of the Constitution.]

Barrington J.

"Establishment" and "Endowment" of religion
Historical background to Article 44

Before analyzing [plaintiffs' claims] in greater detail it may be helpful to say something concerning the historical background to Article 44 of the Constitution and to the concepts of the "establishment" and the "endowment" of religion.

During the period of the Reformation it was common for the kings of Europe to select one religion (be it Roman Catholicism or Protestantism in one of its forms) to be the State religion. The church which practiced the "State religion" was placed in a favored position in law. It was frequently "endowed" by the gifts of lands or by provision for the payment of tithes for the support of its clergy. Those who opposed the State religion were often regarded as disloyal and placed under civil disabilities. Ireland was no exception in this respect. Henry VIII attempted to establish Protestantism in its Anglo–Catholic form as the religion of State. His laws were repealed under Mary Tudor who was a Roman Catholic but her laws were again repealed under Elizabeth I and, finally, by an Act of the Irish Parliament of 1580, the Church of Ireland was restored to the position which it held under Henry VIII.

The Church of Ireland remained the established church until the Act of Union, 1800, which amalgamated it with the Church of England in "The United Church of England and Ireland." ... The Church of Ireland, and at a later stage, the United Church of

England and Ireland were both established and endowed. But Ireland also presented cases of churches which were endowed without being established. By an Act of 1795 ... Parliament provided for a grant for the establishment of a seminary for the education of Roman Catholics. While it was not stated in the Act everyone knew that the purpose of the seminary was to educate young men for the Catholic priesthood the purpose being to discourage them from going to the continent for their education lest they come under the influence of the principles of the French revolution.... The Roman Catholic Church was therefore receiving an endowment from the British Parliament even before the passing of the Catholic Emancipation Act in 1829.

. . .

[Thus] the distinction between an "established" religion and an "endowed" religion would have been well known to parliamentarians at the end of the nineteenth and the beginning of the twentieth century.

. . .

[In the early 1900s, home rule acts prohibited both the establishment and the endowment of religion in Ireland.] The Anglo–Irish Treaty of 1921 [however] did not contain any prohibition on the establishment of a religion.... Why the express prohibition on the establishment of any religion was dropped is not quite clear. But presumably it was because the combined effect of the ban on the endowment of any religion and the prohibition of the granting of any preference on the grounds of religious belief or status was to make an express ban on establishment unnecessary.

. . .

By the time the present Constitution came to be drafted in 1936/1937 many things had changed. Partition [between Northern Ireland, which had a Protestant majority and remained affiliated with Great Britain, and Ireland] was now an established fact and the population of the 26–county area [of Ireland] was now 95% Roman Catholic. [The 1936/1937 constitution included a provision recognizing "the special position of the Holy Catholic Apostolic and Roman Church as the guardian of the Faith professed by the great majority of citizens," but this language was removed in 1972.]

. . .

Conclusion

The result of [this amendment to the Constitution] was to leave us with a Constitution under which the State is obliged to respect and honor religion but is prohibited from endowing any religion or from imposing any disabilities or making any discrimination on the ground of religious profession, belief or status. The history of Ireland shows that, in the absence of constitutional prohibition the State could endow more than one religion. It is difficult, however to see how a church could be "established" (in the traditional sense of that word) without also being endowed. In any event the effect of Article 44.2 of the Constitution is to outlaw either the establishment or the endowment of any religion.

. . .

However . . . the system of denominational education was well known to the framers of the Constitution. We know this because they refer to it. Article 44.2.4 prescribes that legislation providing State aid for schools shall not discriminate between schools under the management of different religious denominations nor be such as to affect prejudicially the right of any child to attend a school receiving public money without attending religious instruction at that school.

These references appear to me to establish two facts. First, the Constitution does not contemplate that the payment of monies to a denominational school for educational purposes is an "endowment" of religion within the meaning of Article 44.2.2 of the Constitution. Secondly, the Constitution contemplated that if a school was in receipt of public funds any child, no matter what his religion, would be entitled to attend it. But such a child was to have the right not to attend any course of religious instruction at the school. . . . [E]ach denominational school has its own ethos. Teachers of a particular religious persuasion do not convey their ideas merely through formal instruction but tend to organize the schools in such a way as best to promote the religious values which they themselves embrace. The framers of the Constitution were clearly aware of this when they contemplated the provision of funds for denominational education. They cannot therefore have regarded such provision as an "endowment" of any religion or religions. The archbishops admit to an indirect benefit received by the churches through the payment of the salaries of school chaplains in the sense that they admit that if the State did not pay the salaries of school chaplains the churches would feel obliged to raise the monies themselves and would thereby be at a loss. I do not think, however, that this argument can be decisive because the exact same argument could be advanced concerning the payment of the salaries of teachers in denominational schools. No doubt had the State refused to subsidize the payment of the salaries of teachers in denominational schools, the churches would have been at a very significant loss. Notwithstanding this fact clearly the framers of the Constitution did not consider such payments an endowment of religion or religions.

But the matter does not end there. Article 42 of the Constitution acknowledges that the primary and natural educator of the child is the family and guarantees to respect the inalienable right and duty of the parents to provide for the religious and moral, intellectual, physical and social education of their children. Article 42.2 prescribes that the parents shall be free to provide "this education" (i.e., religious, moral, intellectual, physical and social education) in their homes or in private schools or "in schools recognized or established by the State". In other words the Constitution contemplates children receiving religious education in schools recognized or established by the State but in accordance with the wishes of the parents.

It is in this context that one must read Article 44.2.4 which prescribes that:

> Legislation providing State aid for schools shall not discriminate between schools under the management of different religious denominations, nor be such as to affect prejudicially the right of any child to attend a school receiving public money without attending religious instruction at that school.

The Constitution therefore distinguishes between religious "education" and religious "instruction"—the former being the much wider term. A child who attends a school run by a religious denomination different from his own may have a constitutional right not to attend religious instruction at that school but the Constitution cannot protect him from being influenced, to some degree, by the religious "ethos" of the school. A religious denomination is not obliged to change the general atmosphere of its school merely to accommodate a child of a different religious persuasion who wishes to attend that school.

The community and the comprehensive schools are an attempt to make post-primary education available to all the children of Ireland irrespective of their means. They involve a vast increase in the number of children receiving post-primary education and a corresponding increase in the number of post-primary teachers most of whom are lay people. In community schools it is no longer practicable to combine religious and academic education in the way that a religious order might have done in the past. Nevertheless parents have the same right to have religious education provided in the schools which their children attend. They are not obliged to settle merely for religious "instruction". The role of the chaplain is to help to provide this extra dimension to the religious education of the children. The evidence establishes that, besides looking after the pastoral needs of the children, the chaplain helps them with counsel and advice about their day to day problems. It therefore appears to me that the present system whereby the salaries of chaplains in community schools are paid by the State is merely a manifestation, under modern conditions, of principles which are recognized and approved by Articles 44 and 42 of the Constitution.

The evidence goes to establish that the work of the chaplains is highly valued by parents. Nevertheless it may be worthwhile entering two caveats. First, this judgment proceeds upon the basis that the system of salaried chaplains is available to all community schools of whatever denomination on an equal basis in accordance with their needs. Secondly, while it is obviously right and proper that a chaplain should counsel and advise any child who may consult him about its problems it would be constitutionally impermissible for a chaplain to instruct a child in a religion other than its own without the knowledge and consent of its parents.

In these circumstances I would dismiss the appeal and affirm the order of the High Court.

Keane J.

As in many other countries throughout the world, religion plays an important part in Irish life and has done so for many centuries. That unquestionable fact is reflected in the provisions of Article 44 of the Constitution. Even were such provisions absent from the Constitution, however, courts could not disregard, at least in a context where it becomes relevant, the fact that religious beliefs and practices are interwoven through the fabric of Irish society.

It is for that reason that our law of charities, for example, deriving from the statute law and common law of a former era, continues to treat trusts established for the advancement of religion as entitled to charitable status without any proof that they are for the public benefit: it is presumed that such trusts are for the public benefit. The same public policy underlies the exemption as of right of ministers of religion and others from the obligation of jury service. . . . Even had Article 44.1 requiring the State to "respect and honor religion" never been enacted—and it had no counterpart in the Constitution of the Irish Free State—there is little reason to doubt that Irish jurisprudence would have acknowledged, as it should in a democratic society, the importance of the part played by religion in the lives of so many people.

Accordingly, if one leaves to one side for the moment the question of the "endowment" of religion, there is no reason in principle why the State, through its different organs, should not confer benefits on religious denominations, provided–and it is, of course, a crucial proviso–that in doing so it remains neutral and does not discriminate in favor of particular religions.

* * *

ATTORNEY–GENERAL (VIC); EX REL
BLACK v. COMMONWEALTH

(1981) 146 CLR 559
High Court of Australia

Barwick C.J.

2. [Plaintiffs claim that certain federal statutes granting funds to state governments for educational purposes violate s. 116 of the Constitution of the Commonwealth which provides that] "the Commonwealth shall not make any law for establishing any religion, or for imposing any religious observance, or for prohibiting the free exercise of any religion, and no religious test shall be required as a qualification for any office or public trust under the Commonwealth."

3. These statutes ... provide for grants to the States on condition that the money so granted is paid by the States to non-government schools to finance their educational programs, including the erection of buildings therefor [sic]. Some of the intended recipients are schools owned and run by religious bodies, as it happens, in large part by the Roman Catholic Church or its agencies.

. . .

12. [With regard to the interpretation of the Constitution] as to the use of the [Constitutional] Convention debates: the settled doctrine of the Court is that they are not available in the construction of the Constitution: and, in my opinion, rightly so. An academic exercise to explain historically why the Constitution was cast in a particular form ... has no place in the task of construing the text of the Constitution except perhaps in the case of an ambiguity in that text which cannot otherwise be resolved.... Indeed, attention to the course of the convention debates might well distract the mind from the proper meaning of unambiguous words in the text.

13. That is not to say, however, that that meaning must be assigned without regard to the sense in which the words of the text were understood in the day of their expression.... [T]he then current meaning of the words used in the text is the meaning, the connotation, they must thereafter bear, though in application in later times they may achieve results not within the contemplation of those who wrote the text.

. . .

16. [With regard to the text of the First Amendment of the American Constitution, which s. 116 parallels to some extent, and judicial decisions interpreting it,] the text of our own Constitution

is always controlling. Even similar or identical language in the American instrument to that in our Constitution can, in my view, rarely, if ever, be controlling. But divergences in the respective texts must inevitably weaken, if indeed they do not destroy, any support which might be sought to be derived from the American text or its construction.

17. Further, in the instant case, not merely is there difference between the Australian text and the language of the relevant provisions of the Bill of Rights, but that language had received an interpretation before the adoption of our Constitution.... It can scarce be said with reason that the use of different, and as I think radically different, language in our Constitution, indicated an intention thereby to achieve what the American courts had decided to be the result of the American text.

. . .

19. The divergence in language to which I have earlier referred is apparent from the use of the word "respecting" in the American text and the word "for" in s. 116. What the former may fairly embrace, quite clearly the latter cannot: and that is so, in my opinion, even without placing critical significance on the purposive nature of the Australian expression and the lack of such an element in the American text.

20. However, in the interpretation and application of s. 116, the establishment of religion must be found to be the object of the making of the law. Further, because the whole expression is "for establishing any religion," the law to satisfy the description must have that objective as its express and, as I think, single purpose. Indeed, a law establishing a religion could scarcely do so as an incident of some other and principal objective. In my opinion, a law which establishes a religion will inevitably do so expressly and directly and not, as it were, constructively.

. . .

30. I find no ambiguity in the language of s.116.... I have considered what was the current significance of "establishing any religion" in 1900 ... [and believe] that there has been no real change in the significance of the words over the years which have intervened.... [W]hat would be involved in establishing a religion has ... remained constant. In my opinion, as used in an instrument brought into existence at the turn of the century, establishing a religion involves the entrenchment of a religion as a feature of and identified with the body politic, in this instance, the Commonwealth. It involves the identification of the religion with the civil authority so as to involve the citizen in a duty to maintain it and the obligation of, in this case, the Commonwealth to patronize, protect and promote the established religion. In other words, estab-

lishing a religion involves its adoption as an institution of the Commonwealth, part of the Commonwealth "establishment".

31. [T]he inclusion in s. 116 of the prohibition of any law imposing any religious observance or for prohibiting the free exercise of any religion and the proscription of any religious test indicate clearly enough the precise limits of the total inhibition of the section. The absence of any prohibition upon the giving of aid to or encouragement of religion from the entire collocation of s. 116 is eloquent. No imposed observance: free exercise of religion: no religious test. No established religion. Otherwise the powers with respect to subject matter and in the nomination of the conditions of a grant to States is plenary and without limitation.

32. Here, the impugned legislation in substance appropriates, and authorizes the disbursement of, part of the consolidated revenue of the Commonwealth for the financial support of the education of Australians by and according to the regiment of non-government schools, including such schools as are owned and conducted by bodies professing and practicing the Christian religion, albeit according to the doctrines of a particular church. The financial aid is expressly limited to the educational activities of such schools.

33. Let it be supposed for the purposes of this discussion . . . that opportunity is taken by those in control of such educational activities to utilize some part of the time set aside for such educational activities to foster the practice of the Christian religion . . . and let it be supposed that buildings to the cost of the construction of which money derived from the legislation has been applied, are on occasions used for some religious activity of the owner of the premises.

34. Can it be said that, therefore, the law made by the Parliament is a law for the establishment of a religion in the sense which I am prepared to give to those words, and thus in breach of the inhibition imposed on the Parliament by the Constitution? Nothing in the laws made by the Parliament expressly authorizes the use of Commonwealth funds for those purposes, though it might justly be said that no provision of that law expressly or adequately prohibits the schools or those conducting them from using the occasion or the buildings assisted or built with money provided for support of educational activities to so use the occasion or the buildings. I cannot think that it can rationally be said that by not preventing such a use of the occasion or buildings which I have assumed, the law providing the funds for the forwarding of the education of Australians by non-government schools is a law for establishing a Christian religion. A law which in operation may indirectly enable a church to further the practice of religion is a

long way away from a law to establish religion as that language properly understood would require it to be if the law were to be in breach of s.116. It would not be enough that the law allowed such activity on the part of the owners of the schools. The law must be a law for it, i.e. intended and designed to set up the religion as an institution of the Commonwealth.

35. [T]he same result might well follow even if it be right and proper to treat the situation I have assumed as authorized by the legislation under attack. But I have no need to decide the question for I have been unable to find any statutory authorization by the Commonwealth of any religious activity on the part of the non-government schools in the course of their educational activities. That there is no statutory prohibition of such religious activities in the course of authorized educational activities is scarce enough to make the appropriation and granting statutes, laws for establishing a religion in the only sense, in my opinion, those words can have in the Constitution. What the Constitution prohibits is the making of a law for establishing a religion. This, it seems to me, does not involve a prohibition of any law which may assist the practice of a religion and, in particular, of the Christian religion. It is the establishment of such a religion which may not be effected by a law of the Commonwealth designed to do so.

Gibbs J.

18. It is strongly argued on behalf of the plaintiffs that since s. 116 was closely modeled on part of the First Amendment to the Constitution of the United States it must be taken to have been intended to have the same meaning as that which had been attributed to the First Amendment in the United States before 1900 when the Constitution was enacted, and further that the United States decisions since that date provide a useful guide to the meaning of the section. [It should be noted, however that there are important differences between s. 116 and the First Amendment and the two countries, Australia and the United States, have very different histories. Accordingly,] the American decisions as to the meaning of the First Amendment do not necessarily provide any safe guide to the meaning of s. 116 of our Constitution.

19. In any case ... it had not been established in the United States by the time Federation occurred in Australia that the First Amendment forbad the Congress to give aid, financial or otherwise, to one or more religious bodies. [Notwithstanding the fact that United States Supreme Court in *Reynolds v. United States*, 98 U.S. 145 (1878), referred to Thomas Jefferson's letter to the Danbury Baptist Association which described the religion clauses of the First Amendment as "building a wall of separation between church and state,"] [i]n that case the court was dealing with the effect of the

free exercise clause, not the establishment clause, and the courts of the United States before 1900 had not had occasion to translate Jefferson's metaphor into terms of specific and practical guidance. The only decision before 1900 in which the Supreme Court considered whether the provision of financial assistance to a body connected with a church violated the establishment clause appears to have been *Bradfield v. Roberts*, 175 U.S. 291 (1899). There, an appropriation for buildings to be constructed on the grounds of a hospital, a private ... corporation, was held valid. The facts that the members of the corporation were members of a Roman Catholic sisterhood, and that the title to its property was vested in the sisters, were said to be "wholly immaterial" [and the Court did not resolve the question of whether the appropriation would have violated the Establishment Clause if the grantee of government funds was a religious corporation].

20. Moreover American commentators, before 1900, had not understood the Establishment Clause to have the effect of forbidding financial aid to church schools.

21. It seems that it was not until 1947 that the Supreme Court first gave extensive consideration to the effect of the establishment clause on the provision of financial aid to church schools [in *Everson v. Board of Education*, 330 U.S. 1 (1947)].

22. Since that time the meaning of the Establishment Clause in the First Amendment has been the subject of [continuing controversy].

23. [F]or a number of reasons, I cannot regard the United States decisions as containing an exposition which should be treated as authoritative in its application to s. 116. In the first place there are the differences, to which I have already referred, between that section and the First Amendment. Secondly, the history of the United States, which provides the background to the Constitution of that country, has been very different from that of Australia. Thirdly ... the courts of the United States, in construing the Constitution, have recourse to material which it is our practice to reject. It would seem paradoxical if we, although forbidden to consider the debates of our own constitutional conventions for the purpose of discovering what the delegates thought was the meaning of a particular provision accepted by the Convention, should nevertheless, in construing s. 116, indirectly give weight to the opinions of Thomas Jefferson as to the meaning of the similar words of the First Amendment. Finally, the course of the decisions in the United States shows that the test which has been adopted in that country, so far from being clear and predictable in its operation, has led, in its application, to continuing controversy. In any case, we should not substitute for the words of s. 116 a test which those words do

not appear to warrant, particularly when it does not commend itself by any obvious considerations of justice or convenience.

. . .

25.   For the reasons I have given, I consider that the words "The Commonwealth shall not make any law for establishing any religion," where they appear in s. 116, mean that the Commonwealth Parliament shall not make any law for conferring on a particular religion or religious body the position of a state (or national) religion or church.

26.   It may be a question of degree whether a law is one for establishing a religion. However, on no view of the evidence in the present case can it be said that any of the laws in question infringes s. 116, if that section is given the meaning which I have attributed to it. If it be assumed that in some schools religious and secular teachings are so pervasively intermingled that the giving of aid to the school is an aid to the religion, and if it be further assumed that some religions, which conduct more schools than others, will receive more aid than others, it still does not follow that any religion is established by the legislation. If the administration of the Schools Commission Act 1973 requires that officers of the Commonwealth be closely involved with religious authorities, that also does not mean that the Act establishes any religion. The primary purpose of the challenged legislation is the advancement of education within Australia.

Stephen J.

12.   Australia's colonial history does . . . disclose, first, something at least approaching official recognition of the Church of England; followed, however, by a general recognition of a wide variety of denominations, accompanied by impartial financial assistance to all their churches and schools; then, in the latter part of the nineteenth century, there occurred a move towards complete separation of church and state, with the abolition of all financial aid to churches and to church schools. It is with this last development that the plaintiffs would seek to associate s. 116, contending that it represents a continuation of the policy of colonial legislatures of the late nineteenth century.

13.   Perhaps the first thing to be observed in examining this proposition is the marked contrast which exists between the language of the colonial Acts which abolished financial aid to churches and church schools and the words of s. 116. It is in terms of "the abolition of state aid to religion" (Victoria), of the prohibition of "future grants of public money in aid of public worship" (New South Wales), of the discontinuance of "grants from the revenue in aid of religion" (Queensland), of the "termination of the parliamen-

tary ecclesiastical grant" (Western Australia) that colonial legislatures ended their financial support of denominations. Likewise, the termination of state financial aid to church schools was also expressed in precise terms which made no reference to the concept of the establishment or disestablishment of religion.

14. The language of the first restriction in s. 116 stands in marked contrast to the precise terms in which these colonial measures were expressed. These measures nowhere refer either to "establishing" or "establishment" nor, for that matter, to "disestablishment," a phrase then much in vogue in connection with the current disestablishment debate in the United Kingdom. The colonial Acts had no need to deal in such concepts because there existed in Australia no established church capable of being disestablished. Section 116, on the other hand, specifically speaks in terms of a prohibition against laws for "establishing any religion." Its language is singularly ill-adapted to ensuring that the spirit of the colonial measures should persist in the new polity which emerged from federation. It is, however, entirely apt if concerned with the quite different subject of the creation of a state church in Australia; something which had come close to occurring in the early colonial period but which s. 116 would prevent for the future. So understood, it is natural that the first restriction in s. 116 should speak in terms quite different from the language of the previous colonial legislation.

Murphy J.

38. The United States' decisions on the establishment clause should be followed. The arguments for departing from them (based on the trifles of differences in wording between the United States and the Australian establishment clauses) are hair-splitting, and not consistent with the broad approach which should be taken to constitutional guarantees of freedom.

39. The purpose of our establishment clause is the same as that in the United States' Constitution. There does not seem to be any real doubt that if the establishment clause is construed in Australia as it is in the United States . . . then the challenged laws are unconstitutional. Section 116 of the Constitution does not assert or deny the value of religion (including religious teaching). It secures its free exercise, but denies that the Commonwealth can support religion in any way whatsoever. The Commonwealth cannot be concerned with religious teaching–that is entirely private. Section 116 recognizes that an essential condition of religious liberty is that religion be unaided by the Commonwealth.

C. SCHOOL FUNDING: AN AFFIRMATIVE OBLI-GATION

1. *South Africa*

IN RE: THE SCHOOL EDUCATION BILL OF 1995 (GAUTENG)

1996 (3) SA 165 (CC) (S. Afr.)
Constitutional Court of South Africa

[At issue is the constitutionality of a statute which empowers the government to set the religious policies of public schools and imposes certain requirements on public schools and private schools which receive a public subsidy. In particular, public schools are prohibited from subjecting their students to religious indoctrination and in both public and subsidized private schools, students cannot be compelled to attend religious education classes and religious practices or discouraged from declining to attend such classes or activities. The government contends that the statute does not abridge any person or group's constitutional rights since the statute does not apply to private schools that do not receive government support. Petitioners and others are free to create a private school that need not comply with the challenged statute's requirements.]

Mahomed, D.P.

[5] [Petitioners argue] that section 32(c) of the Constitution creates a positive obligation on the State to accord to every person the right to require the State to establish, where practicable, educational institutions based on a common culture, language or religion as long as there is no discrimination on the grounds of race. It is contended that on this interpretation of section 32(c), the government is not entitled to ... direct what religious policy should be developed or who should or should not attend religious classes at schools so established ...

[6] Section 32 reads as follows:

Education

32. Every person shall have the right

1. to basic education and to equal access to educational institutions;

2. to instruction in the language of his or her choice where this is reasonably practicable; and

3. to establish, where practicable, educational institutions based on a common culture, language or religion, provided that there shall be no discrimination on the ground of race.

[7] The submission that every person can demand from the State the right to have established schools based on a common culture, language or religion is not supported by the language of section 32(c). The section does not say that every person has the right to have established by the State educational institutions based on such a common culture, language or religion. What it provides is that every person shall have the right to establish such educational institutions.

Linguistically and grammatically it provides a defensive right to a person who seeks to establish such educational institutions and it protects that right from invasion by the State, without conferring on the State an obligation to establish such educational institutions.

[8] Considered in context, there is no logical force in the construction favored by the petitioners. If a person has the right to basic education at public expense in terms of sub-paragraph (a) and if he or she has the right is to be instructed in the language of his or her choice in terms of sub-paragraph (b), why would there be any need to repeat in sub-paragraph (c) the right to education at public expense through a common language? The object of sub-section (c) is to make clear that while every person has a right to basic education through instruction in the language of his or her choice, those persons who want more than that and wish to have educational institutions based on a special culture, language or religion which is common, have the freedom to set up such institutions based on that commonality, unless it is not practicable. Thus interpreted, section 32(c) ... preserves an important freedom. The constitutional entrenchment of that freedom is particularly important because of our special history initiated during the fifties, in terms of the system of Bantu education. From that period the State actively discouraged and effectively prohibited private educational institutions from establishing or continuing private schools and insisted that such schools had to be established and administered subject to the control of the State. The execution of those policies constituted an invasion on the right of individuals in association with one another to establish and continue, at their own expense, their own educational institutions based on their own values. Such invasions would now be constitutionally impermissible in terms of section 32(c).

Notes and Questions

1. Note the difference between Ireland and South Africa with regard to the State's positive obligation to provide religious education to children at the State's expense. Ireland seems to derive the right of parents "to have religious education provided in the schools which

their children attend" from the right of parents to control the education of their children. South Africa denies the existence of such an entitlement to public support.

Many countries wrestle with the problem of reconciling "negative" and "positive" religious freedom—the positive freedom of parents to send their children to a school where they will receive a religious education at state expense and the negative freedom of parents to send their children to a school where they will not be exposed to religious instruction practices that run counter to their beliefs. German courts, for example, resolve this problem by upholding the local government's decision to allow religious instruction and prayer in schools, but deny that parents have "a claim against the state to have their children educated in the desired ideology [or theology]." Interdenominational School Case (1975), 41 BVerfGE 29 (F.R.G.), *translated in* DONALD P. KOMMERS, THE CONSTITUTIONAL JURISPRUDENCE OF THE FEDERAL REPUBLIC OF GERMANY 467, 469 (Duke Univ. Press 1997).

2.   While the text of s.116 of the Australia Constitution parallels the religion clauses of the First Amendment, the Australia Supreme Court believes that the differences in language in the two provisions are of critical importance. The Court also points to a difference in interpretative methodology. Australia courts do not focus on the original intent of the framers of their constitution. Thus, the continuing debate in the United States as to whether the framers intended the religion clauses to require the separation of church and state would be largely irrelevant to Australia jurists.

3.   One of the arguments offered to justify interpreting the Establishment Clause of the First Amendment to prohibit government funding of religious schools is that it endangers the independence of religious institutions if they become dependent on the government for their financial support. Another argument is that it is problematic for a society committed to religious pluralism and equality if most children go to religiously homogeneous schools where they will not study and interact with students and teachers of other faiths. Why do you think these arguments do not seem relevant or persuasive to other countries?

II. INTERNATIONAL AND SUPRANATIONAL LAW

A. SCHOOL FUNDING AND THE EUROPEAN COURT OF HUMAN RIGHTS

Carolyn Evans & Christopher A. Thomas, *Church-State Relations in the European Court of Human Rights*

2006 BYU L. Rev. 699, 713–15

B. Permissible Scope of State Support for Religion

Given the requirement that the relationship between a particular religion and the state must be such that it does not breach the religious freedom of others, what then can a state do to promote or protect a particular religion or religions without breaching the ECHR?

. . .

2. State-sponsored educational assistance for religions

. . . [A]n area in which support may be given by the state to a particular religion or chosen religions is education. The state is not obliged to fund any religious schools, but may choose to do so. Further, the state is not required to distribute the funding equally to schools representing different religions or beliefs. Most states in Europe not only fund schools from a particular denomination, but some religions receive greater funding from the state than others, and certain types of beliefs are excluded from funding altogether in some states.

Further, religious education may be taught within non-denomination state schools. The Court has put restrictions on such teaching:

The second sentence of Article 2 (P1–2) implies . . . that the State, in fulfilling the functions assumed by it in regard to education and teaching, must take care that information or knowledge included in the curriculum is conveyed in an objective, critical and pluralistic manner. The State is forbidden to pursue an aim of indoctrination that might be considered as not respecting parents' religious and philosophical convictions. That is the limit that must not be exceeded.

However, the Court has accepted that religious education may predominantly, if not exclusively, focus on Christianity and has only given the vaguest warning about the possibility of such classes slipping into proselytizing. The Court has placed great faith in students being excused from religion classes that offend the religious beliefs of the parents or children without considering the pressures that such exclusion can place on children. The Court also refused relief in a case where a Polish student claimed that she faced employment and social discrimination because her school record showed that she had refused to participate in a Catholic education class. Thus, the state has relatively wide discretion when it comes to what religions are to be taught in schools; this has the potential to be used to shore up the dominant religion.

Notes and Questions

1. Why do you think the ECHR allows member states to provide greater financial support to the schools of certain faith communities over others? Isn't that a blatant violation of the principle of religious equality?

Chapter Eleven

FUNDING RELIGION IN NON-SCHOOL SETTINGS

I. COMPARATIVE LAW

A. CASE LAW

JUDGMENT UPON CONSTITUTIONALITY OF THE PREFECTURE'S EXPENDI-
TURE FROM PUBLIC FUNDS TO RELIGIOUS CORPORATIONS WHICH
HELD RITUAL CEREMONIES 1992 (Gyo–Tsu) No.156

ANZAI v. SHIRAISHI

51 Minshu 1673 (Sup. Ct., Apr. 2, 1997)
Supreme Court of Japan
Available in English at:
http://www.courts.go.jp/english/judgments/text/1997.04.02–1992–Gyo-Tsu–No.156.
html

[For the constitutional provisions of Japan relating to religion,
see p. 125.]

[Several government officials contributed public funds as various
kinds of offerings to religious corporations, Yasukuni Shrine and
Gokoku Shrine of Ehime Prefecture, during seasonal ceremonies
and ceremonies memorializing Japan's war dead. Taxpayers
brought suit arguing that these expenditures violated Articles 20(3)
and 89 of the Japan Constitution.]

The decision of this court regarding the illegality of the expendi-
ture

The Constitution has several provisions [including] ... Article
20(3), and Article 89, that refer to what is called the principle of
separation of state and religion.

Generally, the principle of separation of state and religion has
been understood to mean that the state, which includes local

government ... is not to interfere with religion and that it should have a secular nature and religious neutrality.... Previously in our country, Article 28 of the Meiji Constitution guaranteed the freedom of religion. However, it was an imperfect guarantee not only because the Meiji Constitution actually restricted freedom of religion ... but also because State Shinto was virtually made the national religion and sometimes belief therein was demanded and other religious groups were subject to severe persecution. Considering these several negative effects occurring from the close connection between the state and Shinto after the Meiji Restoration, the present Constitution has newly provided for the unconditional freedom of religion and, in order to secure its guarantee further, established the principle of separation of state and religion. Historically, several religions have developed pluralistically in Japan. In these circumstances an unconditional guarantee of religious freedom alone has not been enough to guarantee fully the freedom of religion. So as to eliminate all ties between the state and religion, it has also been necessary to enact rules providing for the separation of state and religion....

However ... the provision of the separation of state and religion is only an institutional and indirect guarantee of the freedom of religion. It does not guarantee freedom of religion directly, but it attempts to guarantee it indirectly by securing a system that separates state and religion. Moreover, the state unavoidably connects with religion when the state regulates social life or implements various policies to promote or subsidize education, social welfare, or culture. Thus, an actual system of government that attempts a total separation of state and religion is virtually almost impossible. Furthermore, to attempt total separation would inevitably lead to unreasonable situations in society. Thus, it follows that there are inevitable and natural limits to the separation of state and religion.... Therefore, under these premises, the remaining question must be to what extent such a relationship will be tolerated under the basic purpose of the principle of guaranteeing freedom of religion. From this perspective, the principle of separation of state and religion ... demands the religious neutrality of the state but does not prohibit all connection with religion. Rather, taking the purposes and effects of the given conduct[] into consideration, it should be interpreted as prohibiting the state's conduct[] that [is] beyond the appropriate limits in light of the social and cultural circumstances of our country.

Accordingly[ly] ... "religious activity" in Article 20(3) should not be interpreted as prohibiting all religious activities that the state or state authority might be involved in. Rather, only the activities exceeding such reasonable limits, the purpose of which have some religious meaning and the effect of which is to support, promote, or, [conversely], oppose or interfere with religion, should be prohibited. And in determining whether a given religious act constitutes a prohibited "religious activity" or not, not only the external aspects of the conduct but also the place of the conduct, the average person's religious understanding [of] the conduct, the existence or extent of the actor's religious intention, purpose, or awareness in holding the ceremony, and the effect or influence on the average person should be considered as factors. . . .

Article 89 of the Constitution stipulates that no public money or other property shall be expended or appropriated for the use, benefit, or maintenance of any religious institution or association. [The Court indicated that Article 89 should be interpreted and applied pursuant to an analysis that is similar to the one applied to Article 20 above.]

. . .

. . . [T]he appellees . . . made offerings from . . . public funds as tamagushiryo, kentoryo, or kumotsuryo [different offerings to the gods] at . . . traditional religious ceremonies held by Yasukuni Shrine or Gokoku Shrine, which are religious corporations and clearly religious groups as stipulated by Article 20(1) of the Constitution, within the precincts of each shrine. Now, it is a judicially noted fact that holding ceremonies are the main religious activities for Shinto, that the main points of the Spring and Autumn Ceremony or Memorial Ceremony are religious rites held according to Shinto tradition, that they are among the most important traditional ceremonies held by each shrine. . . . Moreover, it is clear that each shrine has regarded tamagushiryo, kumotsuryo, and kentoryo as having religious meanings, because tamagushiryo and kumotsuryo are offered to the Shinto god when religious rites are held at the time of the Spring and Autumn Ceremony or memorial ceremony, and because, when kentoryo is offered, lights with the contributors' names are displayed within the precincts of the shrines at the time of the Mitamasai ceremony.

According to these facts, it is clear that the prefecture was involved in important religious ceremonies held by specific religious groups. And generally, making such offerings as tamagushiryo at a time when important traditional ceremonies are held by the shrines within their precincts is much different from holding a groundbreaking ceremony, which is a ceremony to pray for stable foundations and accident-free construction held by an owner within a construction site, since a groundbreaking ceremony can be regarded as only a secular social event whose religious significance has gradually weakened over time. The offerings in this case can hardly be thought of as just a secular social courtesy by an average person. So, more or less, the contributors of such offerings as tamagushiryo usually think that they have some religious meanings, and so do the appellees in this case. And in this case, the fact that the prefecture was intentionally involved in the specific religious groups cannot be denied, since the prefecture had never made offerings to the same kind of religious rites held by other religious groups. According to these analyses, if a local government has a special involvement with a specific religious group as in this case, the average person is impressed that the prefecture especially supports this specific religious group and that this religious group is special and different from other religious groups. As an effect of these impressions, interest in the specific religion will be stimulated.

The appellees contended that this expenditure did not violate the Constitution, because it was just a social custom with a secular purpose to mourn for the war dead and to console the bereaved families and an administrative act intended to support the bereaved families. We find that a great number of persons who are enshrined in Yasukuni Shrine and Gokoku Shrine are the war dead of World War II. We [recognize that] ... local residents [and] ... bereaved families wish the local government to mourn for the war dead enshrined in Yasukuni Shrine or other shrines officially. Some of them wish so because of their desire to mourn for the war dead, not because of their religious beliefs. [Notwithstanding the popular support for these expenditures, this] ... relationship between a local government and a specific religion cannot be allowed.... We consider that it is possible to mourn for the war dead and to console the bereaved families without such a special relationship with a specific religion. [The Court distinguished the offerings in question from other kinds of offerings that had a more secular meaning.]

Based on the above consideration, it is reasonable to assume that these offerings by a local government to Yasukuni Shrine or Gokoku Shrine ... constitute prohibited religious activities under Article 20(3) of the Constitution, because the purpose of the offerings had religious significance and the effect of the offerings led to support or promotion of a specific religion, and the relationship between the local government and Yasukuni Shrine or other shrines caused by these offerings exceeded the reasonable limit under the social and cultural conditions of Japan. Thus, these disbursements were illegal because they were made to religious activities prohibited by the article....

[The expenditures at issue were found to violate Article 89 under a similar analysis.]

. . .

Justice Masao Ono

The effect of the conduct in the present case

[An] appellee ... argues that the offering of tamagushiryo was a small sum of money provided for consolation of the war dead and that it did not especially raise interest in the religion, nor did it support or promote the religion.

It may be possible to argue that the offering in this case did not necessarily support or promote the religion from an economic point of view, as its amount was between 5,000 yen and 10,000 yen a time, though the offering had been continued over considerably many years. However, in considering application of the principle of separation of state and religion, one should not be bound only by the outward and economic aspects of the conduct in question but should see its substance in the light of social and historical conditions, and one should also consider its immaterial or spiritual effect and influence on society. . . .

Various religions have developed and are existing pluralistictly [sic] in this country, and each religious group holds memorial services for the war dead following its own doctrines and ceremonial forms. If a local government supports only memorial services held by Yasukuni Shrine, it is difficult to deny that such a conduct gives an impression to the general public that the local government has selected these rituals, giving them priority over others, and takes their religious value as most important. Thus, it is incontrovertible to say that the local government gives important symbolic advantage to a specific religious group. . . . Generally speaking, a public institution is prohibited from supporting or promoting any religion. In particular, it would be against the religious neutrality of the state, which is the core of the separation of state and religion, to select a particular religious group out of coexisting religious groups and support its religious ceremony.

The secular influence of the expenditure from public funds for tamagushiryo by the local government cannot be ignored either.

... [If] a public institution supports Yasukuni Shrine by providing public funds to its rituals ... those who stand in awe of Yasukuni Shrine and those who regard Yasukuni Shrine as the central institution for consolation of the war dead may feel satisfaction and sympathy with it, but those who belong to a religious group whose doctrines are different from that of Shinto and those who remember that they were compelled to worship Yasukuni Shrine as the central existence of the national religion, or those who think it incongruous that Yasukuni Shrine enshrines mainly soldiers [and] army civilian employees ... but few victims of the war who were ordinary citizens, may feel dissatisfaction and antipathy to it. Such antagonism can occur not only in the area of religion but also in the area of society and politics. If a public institution conducts religious activities and widely exerts such an effect on society, the public institution will [be] involved in religious conflict, and, at the same time, religion will be involved in secular conflicts. It is obvious that this will transcend the permissible limits as social courtesies and customs and that this is likely to do harm to both the public institution and the religious group. Avoiding such a situation will conform to the purpose of the Constitution, which adopts the strict principle of separation of state and religion.

. . .

Justice Toru Miyoshi, dissenting

I conclude that the expenditure in question is not a religious activity prohibited by Article 20(3) of the Constitution, it is not an expense of public money prohibited by Article 89 of the Constitution, and it does not violate the latter part of Article 20(1) of the Constitution, which prohibits the state from giving privilege to any religious organization. Therefore, the claim should be dismissed. . . .

. . .

In a real national government system, it is virtually impossible that we can accomplish the total separation of state and religion. To attempt [to do so would lead to] . . . unreasonable situations in various respects in our society. . . . [T]he separation of state and religion . . . has reasonable limits. . . .

. . .

In view of the meaning of the principle, religious activity stipulated in Article 20(3) of the Constitution does not mean all the state's activities that have contact with religion, but rather [only] those which exceed reasonable limits and which have as their purpose some religious meanings or the effect of which is to promote, subsidize, or, conversely, interfere with or oppose religion. [To determine whether an activity is religious for constitutional purposes] . . . we must consider the average person's reaction to it, the actor's purpose, the existence and extent of religious significance, the effect on the average person, and all other circumstances without being obsessed with its appearance.

[A similar test should apply to our understanding of Article 89.]

. . .

The national sentiment of Yasukuni Shrine and Gokoku Shrines in several prefectures

To honor the memory of those who died in the war to protect our country, their parents, wives and children, and other people is a matter of course for not only bereaved families and fellow soldiers but also the people in general. Such behavior signifies praying for peace and consoling bereaved families who lost their spouses and relatives, and it is natural behavior of people regardless of their religion, religious sect, race, and nationality. It is not only consistent with the natural sentiment and bereaved families' feelings but also is considered courteous that the national or municipal governments or their representatives honor the war dead, and they have an obligation to do so from the moral point of view....

. . .

Yasukuni Shrine enshrines 2.46 million war dead.... Gokoku Shrines in several prefectures enshrine the war dead who have some relationship with those prefectures.... Although some of those who visit Yasukuni Shrine ... believe in Saishin God, more generally they ... visit Yasukuni Shrine ... to remember and honor the war dead, including their fathers, sons, brothers, friends, and acquaintances, [rather] than to act religiously....

From [one] point of view, Yasukuni Shrine and other Gokoku Shrines are nothing but Shinto institutions, and ... they treat visitors as those who act based on religious belief. However, in light of the national sentiment mentioned above, they are principally special institutions to remember and honor the war dead, and the majority of people consider these shrines as ... symbolic institutions for the nation's war dead's souls [rather] than those of a specific religion.

. . .

The facts of payments in this case and examination of them

Offerings to Yasukuni Shrine

The offerings to Yasukuni Shrine were made from 1981 to 1986 ... The total amount was 76,000 yen....

. . .

... In determining whether a certain religious activity violates Article 20(3) of the Constitution or a certain disbursement of public funds violates Article 89 of it, we should consider how a lot of Japanese people regard it. We should not put ourselves in the position of Yasukuni Shrine. This is the two-sidedness of religious rites. A religious rite that is considered as a folk custom, such as the jichinsai or groundbreaking ceremony, also has a two-sidedness. That is, the jichinsai is, from the viewpoint of the Shinto priest, a solemn rite to which the Ootokonushi god and Ubusuna god are invited in the ceremony, and the form of the ceremony is nothing but a religious rite. But people at large, including the orderer of the construction and other attendants, regard it as just a folk custom.

. . .

It is clear that the total amount of the offerings ... was very small considering the scale of Ehime Prefecture and its budget [and] ... from the viewpoint of Yasukuni Shrine. Judging from the amount of the offerings, the connection with religion was at a minimum level. Although some may think that we cannot deem the offerings were within the scope of social courtesy because they were made continually ... every year, we should think that if each amount of [an] offering[] ... is within the boundary of social courtesy to mourn the war dead, continual offerings should be regarded as a ... courtesy, like mourning a dead person on an anniversary of his or her death every year. Thus, we cannot deem that offerings are beyond the boundary of social courtesy because they are made continually....

. . .

The offerings to religious corporation Gokoku Shrine in Ehime Prefecture

The offerings to Ehime Gokoku Shrine were made nine times.... The total amount was 90,000 yen. [Given the small amount of the offerings, Justice Miyoshi suggested that the offerings to this shrine should also fall within the boundary of social courtesy.]

Notes and Questions

1.   Note the focus on the allegedly minimal amount of the expenditures at issue in the principal case. Does this argument sound familiar? James Madison wrote in his famous Memorial and Remonstrance Against Religious Assessments in 1785 that "[t]he same authority which can force a citizen to contribute three pence only of his property for the support of any one establishment may force him to conform to any other establishment in all cases whatsoever." Can constitutional doctrine distinguish between large and small expenditures for religious purposes?

2.   In the principal case, the Court struggles with the reality that the ceremonies in question may serve both religious and secular purposes. They are religious rites, but also serve to remember and honor soldiers who died during World War II. Should that make a difference in the adjudication of this dispute? How should a court decide whether the religious aspect of an activity or the secular aspect of the activity is controlling in a case like this? Note that there is an important equality dimension to this case. Would it be constitutional for local officials in the United States to use public funds to support war memorials dedicated to soldiers of only one faith? In *Trunk v. City of San Diego*, 568 F.Supp.2d 1199 (S.D. Cal 2008), plaintiffs argued that a public war memorial in San Diego that is dominated by a Latin

cross over 40 feet high violated the Establishment Clause. Would this case be resolved the same way in the U.S. and Japan?

3. The constitutional case law regarding government involvement with, and support for, religion in Japan is much more complicated than the principal case suggests. In its reference to groundbreakings ceremonies, the Court is attempting to distinguish an earlier case, Sekiguchi v. Kadonaga, 31 Minsch 533 (Sup. Ct., July 13, 1977). In that case, Shinto priests were invited by a city to conduct a groundbreaking ceremony at a construction project. The city subsidized the ceremony which was attended by local officials. The Court held that there was no constitutional violation because the city's actions did not have the purpose and effect of promoting the Shinto religion.

More recently, in 2002, in Higo v. Tsuchiya [see pp. 245–46 *infra*], the Court confronted a challenge to local officials attending Daijosai, a Shinto ceremony celebrating the ascendancy to the throne of a new emperor. The Court held that the local government's involvement with religion was not unreasonable in light of the history and culture of Japan. To many commentators, the Court seemed to be applying a less rigorous standard of review in this case than it had in Anzai v. Shiraisha. For an excellent discussion of these cases, see Shigenori Matsui, *Japan: the Supreme Court and the separation of church and state*, 2 INT'L J. CONST. L. 534 (2004).

4. In their book, THE CHALLENGE OF PLURALISM, (Rowman & Littlefield Publishers, Inc. 1997), Stephen Monsma and J. Christopher Soper studied the church-state systems in the United States, England, Australia, the Netherlands, and Germany. They concluded that "each of the five countries relies extensively on religious agencies to provide social welfare services ... [and a]ll five countries fund religious agencies and generally give them autonomy to run their organizations as they see fit." But, they note, because of its commitment to the separation of church and state, the autonomy of state-funded religious social service providers may be more limited in the United States than in other countries. *Id.* at 208.

II. INTERNATIONAL AND SUPRANATIONAL LAW

A. TAX EXEMPTIONS AND PUBLIC SUBSIDIES FOR RELIGIOUS INSTITUTIONS AND ACTIVITIES

IGLESIA BAUTISTA "EL SALVADOR" & JOSE AQUILINO ORTEGA MORATILLA v. SPAIN

72 Eur. Ct. H.R. 256 (1992)
European Court of Human Rights

[An Evangelical Protestant Church and its minister requested an exemption from paying property tax because the Catholic Church did not have to pay taxes. This request was refused, on the ground that the Catholic Church was exempted from paying property tax under a *Concordat* between the Holy See and Spain in exchange for, among other things, maintaining certain historical sites, whereas the applicant church did not have such an agreement. Applicants appealed this decision, and the Constitutional Court of Spain upheld the denial.]

[T]he Constitutional Court ... noted ... that under the Freedom of Religion Act ... the State could conclude co-operation agreements providing for tax exemptions, *inter alia,* with churches, according to the number of their adherents, the strength of their roots in Spanish society, and the beliefs of the majority of Spanish citizens. As no agreement of that kind had been concluded with the ... applicant, it had no right to claim the tax exemptions in question.

. . .

The applicants further allege that, as the Catholic Church in Spain enjoys exemptions from property tax in respect of places of worship, the refusal of their request to be treated in the same way for tax purposes infringes Article 14 of the Convention in conjunction with Article 9.

. . .

However, the Commission recalls that this provision does not prohibit all differences in treatment in the exercise of the rights and freedoms recognized, equality of treatment being violated only where the difference in treatment has no objective and reasonable justification.

. . .

Lastly, the applicants allege that the sums they are required to pay in property tax indirectly contribute to the funding of the Catholic Church on account of the allowances the latter receives from the State.

In this connection the Commission recalls that the obligation to pay taxes is a general one which has no specific conscientious implications in itself. Its neutrality in that respect is also illustrated by the fact that no taxpayer can influence or determine the purpose for which his or her contributions are applied, once they are collected. Furthermore, the power of taxation is expressly recognized by the Convention system and is ascribed to the State by Article 1 of Protocol No 1. The Commission further notes that the applicants have by no means established or even alleged that property tax is a tax used for a particular purpose.

It follows that Article 9 does not confer on them any right to refuse . . . to submit to the tax legislation in force.

Notes and Questions

1.   There do not seem to be any clear restrictions enforced by the ECHR that limit a state's ability to use public funds to subsidize religious activities. In *Iglesia Bautista*, the Court seems quite comfortable upholding preferential tax exemptions for majority faiths. In *Everson v. Board of Education*, 330 U.S. 1, 16 (1947), Justice Black wrote that "[n]o tax in any amount, large or small, can be levied to support any religious activities or institutions, whatever they may be called." Do you think that taxpayers have a religious liberty interest they should be able to assert to challenge the use of public funds to subsidize religious activities or institutions?

Chapter Twelve

RELIGIOUS DISPLAYS
IN SCHOOLS

I. INTRODUCTION

Leszek Lech Garlicki
Perspectives on Freedom of Conscience and Religion in the Jurisprudence of Constitutional Courts

2001 BYU L. REV. 467, 507–508

PROBLEMS ARISING FROM THE TEACHING OF RELIGION IN PUBLIC SCHOOLS

Various problems may arise from the presence of religion in public schools. One such problem involves the placement of religious symbols, like crosses and crucifixes, in classrooms or on school premises. In some countries this is not allowed. For example, in Germany and Switzerland, the constitutional courts banned the placement of crosses and crucifixes in public schools. [See II. Case Law below for an edited version of the German Court's decision.] The Swiss decision of 1990 stated that the placement of religious symbols in public schools violated the neutrality of religious teaching, which is constitutionally protected. The decision also referred to the state's obligation to ensure religious peace.... However, in other countries, no objections arise as to the placement of crosses in classrooms. In Austria, under the provisions of the Concordat, a cross must be placed in the classroom if the majority of students are Catholic.

School prayer may also pose problems. In some countries, school prayer is not expressly allowed or prohibited. In other countries, school prayer is allowed as long as participation is voluntary. According to the 1993 decision of the Polish Constitutional Court, states would violate the prohibition on their right to interfere in religious practices by denying students the opportunity to pray.

II. CASE LAW

CLASSROOM CRUCIFIX II CASE

(1995) 93 BVerfGE I
Federal Constitutional Court of Germany

[A constitutional challenge was brought against Bavarian legislation that required elementary schools to attach a crucifix to the wall in classrooms.]

Article 4 (I) of the Basic Law protects freedom of belief. Whether under this provision one is for or against particular beliefs is an affair of the individual, not the state.... Freedom of belief includes not only the freedom to uphold a faith but also the freedom to live and act according to one's own religious convictions.... Article 4 also applies to symbols that incorporate a belief or a religion. It allows individuals to decide for themselves which religious symbols they wish to acknowledge or venerate and which they wish to reject. To be sure, in a society that tolerates a wide variety of faiths commitments, the individual clearly has no right to be spared exposure to quaint religious manifestations, cultish activities, or religious symbols. However, a different situation arises when the state itself exposes an individual to the influence of a given faith, without giving the child a chance to avoid such influence, or to the symbols through which such a faith represents itself....

Article 4 (I) does not simply command the state to refrain from interfering in the faith commitments of the individuals or religious communities. It also obliges the state to secure for them a realm of freedom in which they can realize their personalities within an ideological and religious context. The state is thus committed to protect the individual from attacks or obstructions by adherents of different beliefs or competing religious groups. Article 4 (I), however, grants neither to the individual nor to religious communities the right to have their faith commitments supported by the state. On the contrary, freedom of faith as guaranteed by Article 4 (I) of the Basic Law requires the state to remain neutral in matters of faith and religion.... The numerical strength or social importance [of a religious community] has no relevance. Rather, the state is obligated to treat various religious and ideological communities with an even hand. And when the state supports or works together with [these religious communities], it must take care not to identify itself with a particular community.

. . .

Given the context of compulsory education, the presence of crosses in classrooms amounts to state-enforced "learning under the cross," with no possibility to avoid seeing it. This constitutes the crucial difference between the display of the cross in a classroom and the religious symbols people frequently encounter in their daily lives. Encounters of the latter type are not the result of any state action but are merely a consequence of the pervasive presence of various faith commitments and religious communities in society. In addition, the latter situation does not admit to the same degree of compulsion. Admittedly, persons who walk the streets, use public transportation, or enter buildings have no control over such encounters with religious symbols and manifestations. But as a rule, these encounters are fleeting, and even if they are not, they are still not the result of any state preference backed by sanctions....

The cross is the symbol of a particular religious conviction, and not merely an expression of cultural values that have been influenced by Christianity.

Admittedly, numerous Christian traditions have found their way into the general culture of our society over the centuries, and these traditions cannot be denied even by the adversaries of Christianity and its historical heritage. However, these traditions must be distinguished from the particular tenets of the Christian religion, and especially from a particular Christian faith together with its ritual and symbolic representation. Any support of these faith tenets by the state would undermine freedom of religion, a matter already determined by the federal constitutional court in [cases adjudicating the constitutionality of Christian public elementary schools]. In affirming the Christian character of these schools, the court ruled that the state may legitimately recognize Christianity's imprint on culture and education over the course of Western history, but not the particular tenets of the Christian religion. Only if the parameters of its continued historical impact are delineated can the affirmation of Christianity be legally justified in the eyes of non-Christians.

The cross now as before represents a specific tenet of Christianity; it constitutes its most significant faith symbol. It symbolizes man's redemption form original sin through Christ's sacrifice just as it represents Christ's victory over Satan and death and his power over the world. For believing Christians, it is the object of veneration and practiced piety.... On the other hand, because of the significance Christianity attributes to the cross, non-Christians and atheists perceive it to be the symbolic expression of certain faith convictions and a symbol of missionary zeal. To see the cross as nothing more than a cultural artifact of the Western Tradition without any particular religious meaning would amount to a profanation contrary to the self-understanding of Christians and the Christian church....

. . .

Needless to say, the presence of the cross in classrooms does not force children to identify with or to venerate the cross, or to conduct themselves in certain ways.... But the cross does exert influence in other ways.... Its presence constitutes a deeply moving appeal; it underscores the faith commitment it symbolizes, thus making that faith exemplary and worthy of being followed. This is particularly true with young and impressionable people who are still learning to develop their critical capacities and principles of right conduct.

. . .

[When the state's interest in providing public education conflicts with the religious beliefs of students and parents, some compromise of competing values will be necessary.] In working out such a compromise, the state need not abandon all references to religion or ideology. No state, even one that universally guarantees freedom of religion and is committed to religious and ideological neutrality, is in a position completely to divest itself of the cultural and historical values on which social cohesion and the attainment of public goals depend. The Christian religion and the Christian churches have always exerted tremendous influence in our society, regardless of how this influence is evaluated today....

. . .

The Federal Constitutional Court has concluded [in prior cases] that the state legislature is not forbidden to introduce Christian values into the organization of public elementary schools, even if parents who cannot avoid sending their children to this type of school reject all forms of religious education. This presupposes, however, that coercion is to be reduced to an indispensable minimum. In particular, the school must not proselytize on behalf of a particular religious doctrine or actively promote the tenets of the Christian faith. Christianity's influence on culture and education may be affirmed and recognized, but not particular articles of faith.... Confrontation with a Christian worldview will not lead to discrimination or devaluation of a non-Christian ideology so long as the state does not impose the values of the Christian faith on non-Christians; indeed, the state must foster the autonomous thinking that Article 4 of the Basic Law secures within the religious and ideological realms. . . .

The display of crosses in classrooms, however, exceeds [these guidelines and constitutional limits]. As noted earlier, the cross cannot be separated from its reference to particular tenets of Christianity; far from being a mere symbol of western culture, it symbolizes the core of the Christian faith, one that has admittedly shaped the Western world in multiple ways but which is not commonly shared by all members of society. . . . The display of the cross in public compulsory school thus violates Article 4 (I) of the Basic Law. . . .

Parents and pupils who adhere to the Christian faith cannot justify the display of the cross by invoking their positive freedom of religious liberty. All parents and pupils are equally entitled to the positive freedom of faith, not just Christian parents and pupils. The resulting conflict cannot be resolved on the basis of majority rule since the constitutional right to freedom of faith is particularly designed to protect the rights of religious minorities. Moreover Article 4 (I) does not provide the holders of the constitutional right with an unrestricted right to affirm their faith commitments within the framework of public institutions. Inasmuch as schools heed the Constitution, leaving room for religious instruction, school prayer, and other religious events, all of these activities must be conducted on a voluntary basis and the school must ensure that students who do not wish to participate in these activities are excused from them and suffer no discrimination because of their decision not to participate. The situation is different with respect to the display of the cross. Students who do not share the same faith are unable to remove themselves from its presence and message. . . .

. . .

Dissent

The state has a constitutional mandate to remain neutral in religious and ideological matters. But the principle of neutrality must not be construed as indifference toward such matters. . . .

In its decisions regarding the constitutional admissibility of Christian community schools, the Federal Constitutional Court, following the constitutional command of neutrality . . . declared that . . . a public school must not be missionary in nature, nor is the school permitted to demand the obligatory acceptance of Christian faith commitments. . . .

. . .

In evaluating and assessing the concerns of the parties to this case, the . . . majority has mistakenly identified the cross with a

Christian theological view. What matters instead is the effect that the sight of the cross has on individual pupils. Admittedly, the Christian pupil may see the cross in the religious light suggested by the majority. The nonbelieving pupil, however, cannot be assumed to share the same view. From his or her point of view, the cross is less a symbol of the Christian faith than of the values reflected in the Christian community school, namely, those values associated with a Western culture deeply rooted in Christian ideas....

In view of the cross's symbolic character, non-Christian pupils and their parents are obligated to accept its presence in the classroom. The principle of tolerance requires as much....

The psychological effect that exposure to the cross has on non-Christian pupils is relatively mild. The mental burden here is minimal, for pupils are not required to behave in a given way or to participate in religious practices before the cross. In contrast to [compulsory] school prayer, pupils are not forced to reveal their ideological or religious convictions though nonparticipation. This precludes any discrimination against them.

(Translated in DONALD P. KOMMERS, THE CONSTITUTIONAL JURISPRU-DENCE OF THE FEDERAL REPUBLIC OF GERMANY 472, 472–82 (Duke Univ. Press 1997).)

III. ADDITIONAL CRUCIFIX CONTROVERSIES

Disputes concerning the display of crucifixes in schools have been litigated in other European countries as well with mixed results. A controversy arose in Italy when a Muslim father challenged the placement of a crucifix in his son's classroom. The display of the crucifix was mandated in schools, hospitals, and courts by a law adopted under Mussolini's government. In the decision of December 13, 2004 Ordinanza N. 389 Anno 2004, the Italian Constitutional Court rejected, on procedural grounds, a lower court decision banning the display of crucifixes in public school classrooms. The Polish Constitutional Tribunal in 1993 saw no constitutional difficulty with crucifixes in public schools (POL–199–2–009 1 ;13599;13599Orzecznictwo Trybunalu Konstytucyjne-go (Official Digest) 12 (1993)). The Swiss Federal Court in *Cadro v. Guido Bernasconi and the Administrative Court of the Canton of Ticino,* Bundesgericht [BGer] [Federal Court] Sept. 9, 1990, 116 Arrêts du Tribunal Fédéral [ATF] I 252 (Switz.), held that the display of a crucifix in public school classrooms was inconsistent with the requirement of state neutrality on religious matters.

IV. OTHER RELIGIOUS DISPLAY CONTROVERSIES

Javier Martínez-Torrón
Freedom of Religion in the Case Law of the Spanish Constitutional Court

2001 BYU L. Rev. 711, 721–723

[A decision involving] the use of religious symbols by public institutions [was] issued by the [Spanish Constitutional Court in 1991], [STC 130/1991, June 6, 1991]. The . . . Court declared that a state university could legitimately remove the image of the Virgin Mary from its official coat of arms if the governing bodies of the university considered such action to be appropriate in light of the state neutrality in religious matters. However, the Court noted that the constitutional principle of neutrality did not obligate the university to remove the image, because respect [for] history and tradition might have persuaded the university authorities to maintain those religious symbols traditionally included in the university's heraldic emblem.

. . .

[Another case involved] the participation of the armed forces in a religious ceremony, [STC 177/1996, Nov. 11, 1996]. Following an old tradition, the military garrison of Valencia had organized a solemn military parade in honor of the Virgin Mary to celebrate the fifth centennial of the local patron saint, the Virgen de los Desamparados, who had received the honorific title of Supreme General of the Army in 1810. A sergeant in the garrison refused to participate in the ceremony for reasons of conscience and . . . requested permission to not attend the event. Although his superiors did not grant his request, the officer left the parade at the moment when the Virgin was honored. His commanders subsequently punished him with thirty days of home arrest and initiated disciplinary proceedings against him with the aim of imposing further sanctions.

In deciding the case, the Constitutional Court reaffirmed that participation in religious ceremonies is voluntary, a principle recognized implicitly in Article 16(2) of the Constitution and explicitly in Article 2 of the 1980 Organic Law of Religious Freedom. However, the Court did not object to the fact that the army organized an official religious ceremony. On the contrary, after recalling its previous doctrine on state neutrality, the Court justified the army's conduct with enigmatic and contradictory reasoning. Thus, after having referred to the military parades as "acts of unequivocal religious content, convoked and organized by the military authorities," the Court added: "therefore [such parades] were not acts of religious nature in which the military participated, but military acts aimed to the celebration of a religious festivity by military personnel." Most surprisingly, the Court further stated that "Article 16(3) of the Spanish Constitution does not prevent the armed forces from celebrating religious festivities or from participating in ceremonies of that nature."

Notes and Questions

1.   Christian Walter describes what he calls a "striking paradox" in the *German Crucifix II Case*. The majority opinion, which holds that placing a crucifix on the walls of public school classrooms is unconstitutional, "heavily emphasizes the religious meaning of the symbol." The dissenting opinion, which would allow the display of the crucifix, "reduces its symbolic meaning to Western civilization in general." Walter sees a similar paradox in United States establishment clause case law. Commonly, those Supreme Court Justices who maintain that the government's promotion of a religious display violates the establishment clause will emphasize the religious nature of the symbol or message while those Justice who reject the establishment clause challenge will emphasize its non-religious meaning. Christian Walter, *From the Acceptance of Interdenominational Christian Schools to the Inadmissibility of Christian Crosses in the Public Schools, in* RELIGION IN THE PUBLIC SPHERE : A COMPARATIVE ANALYSIS OF GERMAN, ISRAELI, AMERICAN AND INTERNATIONAL LAW 165, 167–68 (Winfried Brugger & Michael Karayanni eds., 2007).

2.   There is an even more striking difference between the German cases and United States jurisprudence. The German courts ruled that it was constitutional to permit teacher-directed school prayer in public schools (*School Prayer Case* (1979) 52 BVerGE 223), but the display of a crucifix on the walls of a public school was unconstitutional. In the United States, however, school prayer would be viewed as more coercive and objectionable than the passive display of a religious symbol. Compare Justice Kennedy's majority opinion in *Lee v. Weisman,* 505 U.S. 577 (concluding that the offering of a prayer at a high school graduation was unconstitutionally coercive), with Kennedy's dissenting opinion in *Allegheny County v. ACLU,* 492 U.S. 573 (arguing that the placement of a nativity display at Christmas in the foyer of City Hall is non-coercive and constitutionally permissible).

3.   Religious displays in schools are, obviously, less problematic in countries that have an established church. England, for example, "is not a secular state and religious education and worship is a requirement in state maintained schools. As such, the existence of religious symbols in schools per se is permissible." SAMANTHA KNIGHTS, FREEDOM OF RELIGION, MINORITIES, AND THE LAW 119 (Oxford Univ. Press 2007).

Chapter Thirteen

RELIGIOUS DISPLAYS OUTSIDE OF SCHOOLS

I. COMPARATIVE LAW

A. CASE LAW

IN RE: CERTIFICATION OF CONSTITUTION OF WESTERN CAPE

1998 (1) SA 655 (CC) (S. Afr.)
Constitutional Court of South Africa

[The South Africa Constitution permits provinces to adopt their own constitution as long as the text of the provincial constitution is consistent with the provisions of the national constitution. The Province of the Western Cape adopted a constitution with a preamble that begins, "in humble submission to Almighty God." The question before the Court was whether this language is inconsistent with section 15 of the national constitution which guarantees freedom of religion and conscience.]

28. ... The invocation of a deity in these prefatory words to the preamble of the WCC has no particular constitutional significance and echoes the peroration to the preamble to the ... [national constitution which includes phrases such as "May God protect our people" and "God bless South Africa".] It is a time-honored means of adding solemnity used in many cultures and in a variety of contexts. Thus, in the United States with its explicit Establishment Clause separating church and state, the use of the national motto ("In God we trust") and the reference to God in the Pledge of Allegiance to the flag have been characterized as "ceremonial deism". Such words have no operative constitutional effect nor are they fundamentally hostile to the spirit and objects of the [Constitution.] They could also not be used to interpret the provisions of

[section] 15 restrictively. These words could therefore have no effect on the rights of believers or non-believers. In the circumstances there is no inconsistency between the preamble of the [provincial and national constitution.].

* * *

JUDGMENT UPON THE CASE CONCERNING THE PARTICIPATION OF THE PREFECTURAL GOVERNOR IN THE DAIJO-SAI CEREMONY 1999 (GyoTsu) No. 93

HIGO v. TSUCHIYA

56 Minshü 1204 (Sup. Ct., July 11, 2002)
Supreme Court of Japan (First Petty Bench)
Available in English at:
http://www.courts.go.jp/english/judgments/text/2002.7.11–1999–Gyo-Tsu–No.93.html

[The question for the Court was whether it violated Article 20 of the Constitution for a prefectural governor to participate in the Daijo–Sai religious ceremony celebrating the enthronement of the emperor.]

2. . . . [D]aijo-sai is a ceremony in which the emperor gives thanks to the ancestors and the gods in heaven and the land for peace and the harvest of various crops and, for the state and the populace, prays for peace and the harvest, and was conducted in a Daijo-palace with Shintoist installations in accordance with the Shintoist ritual. Therefore, the participation and the vowing of the . . . appellee who is the governor of the Kagoshima Prefecture [has] an involvement with religion.

However, . . . (1) Daijo–Sai is an important traditional ceremony of the imperial household normally performed at the time of the succession of the throne since the 7th century although there were occasional interruptions, (2) the . . . appellee, invited by the Imperial Household Agency, merely participated in a . . . ceremony together with the heads of the three powers, ministers and the heads of the local public organizations and . . . (3) the participation of the . . . appellee in the Daijo-sai ceremony was intended to celebrate the enthronement of the emperor . . . as a social courtesy of a person who holds a public office as a governor of the local public organization. . . . In the light of the above, the purpose of the participation of the . . . appellee in the Daijo–Sai ceremony was to extend a social courtesy to the emperor who is the symbol of the integration of the nation and the populace on the occasion of the traditional ceremony of the imperial household at the time of the succession to the throne by the emperor, and its effect does not comprise assistance, promotion or enhancement of a specific religion, or suppression of or interference with it. Therefore, the level of involvement with religion of the participation of the . . . appellee in the Daijo–Sai ceremony cannot be regarded to have exceeded the reasonable limit in relation to the basic goal of [the constitution] i.e. the guarantee of the freedom of religion in the light of the social and cultural conditions of Japan and [it] is not against the constitutional doctrine of the separation of the state and religion.

(*Translated by the Sir Ernest Satow Chair of Japanese Law, University of London)

* * *

QUÉBEC v. LAVAL

2006 CanL II 33156 (QC T.D.P.)

Québec Human Rights Tribunal

Legal Background

[The lower courts in Canada have struggled with the question of whether a city council may begin its public session with the recitation of a prayer. In *Freitag v. Penetanguishene (Town)*, (1999) 179 D.L.R. (4th) 150, the Court of Appeal for Ontario held that it violated the Charter for a Town Council to open its meetings with the Lord's Prayer. Since the goal of the practice was "to impose a Christian moral tone on the deliberations of the Council," the prayer was found to serve an impermissible purpose, *id.* ¶ 50. Also, the effect of the practice infringed the rights of religious minorities and nonbelievers. The Court explained that "[s]omeone who chooses to object to government action which is inclusive of the majority but forces the religious minority to conform or to accept exclusion . . . [will be] subjected to further scrutiny of his actions, together with the further pressure and intimidation which that may occasion. . . . 'The subtle and constant reminder' of his difference from the majority is what causes the [minority group member] to feel intimidated and uncomfortable at council meetings." *Id.* ¶ ¶ 36, 39.

In *Allen v. Renfrew (County)* [2004] 69 O.R.(3d) 742, however, an Ontario Superior Court of Justice distinguished *Freitag* in upholding the recitation of a less sectarian prayer that began "Almighty God, we give thanks for the great blessings which have been bestowed on Canada and its citizens. . . ." The Court explained that "I do not accept the proposition that the mere mention of God in a prayer in a governmental meeting, accompanied by the implication that god is the source of the values referred to in the prayer, can be seen as a coercive effort to compel religious observance. The current prayer is broadly inclusive and is non-denominational, even though the reference to God is not consistent with the beliefs of some minority groups. In a pluralistic society religious, moral or cultural values put forward in a public governmental context cannot always be expected to meet universal acceptance." *Id.* ¶ 19.

The court went on to note that "the preamble to the Charter itself specifically refers to the supremacy of God," that the prayer chosen by the city council in the instant case "was very close to the prayer to God recited in the Ontario Legislature and in the house of Commons, two of the country's principal organs of democracy", and that the phrase "God keep our land glorious and free" was part of the Canadian national anthem. *Id.* ¶ 21.]

THE FACTS

[Ms. Payette, a resident of a city in Quebec, Canada attended a city council meeting at which the Chair began the public session by asking everyone in the room to stand while he recited the following prayer, "We beseech you, Lord, to deign to grant us your grace and the wisdom required to conduct our meeting and run our city well." She complained to the Human Rights Tribunal that the public recitation of a prayer at the opening of a city council meeting violated her right to the equal exercise and recognition of her freedom of religion and conscience under sections 3 and 10 of the Quebec *Charter of human rights and freedoms*. The Council defended its actions by explaining that the prayer was intended to remind those assembled "of the solemnity of the moment and the importance of the councilor's work."]

[108] Section 3 of the Québec *Charter of human rights and freedoms* provides that all people are entitled to freedom of religion and freedom of conscience.

[109] The concept of freedom of religion and conscience has been developed mainly by the courts under section 2(a) of the Canadian Charter. Those two provisions are not significantly different in their wording, with the result that the jurisprudence related to freedom of religion and conscience elaborated under section 2(a) of the Canadian Charter is very useful in determining the content and definition of freedom of religion and conscience as provided for in section 3 of the *Charter of human rights and freedoms*.

. . .

[159] In the case at bar, the evidence shows that the practice of reciting the prayer . . . at the opening of the sittings of City Council of Ville de Laval is essentially religious in nature.

. . .

[163] More particularly, the evidence shows that the use of specifically religious words and expressions such as "Lord", "we beseech you", "grant us your grace" and "Amen" mean that the

text of the prayer constitutes a call and supplication to a higher power, aimed at the intervention of a supernatural force.

. . .

[184] The established principles for the state's obligation of religious neutrality can serve to clarify the matter from the standpoint of the right to equality. The state's obligation not to promote one religion over another or belief over non-belief guarantees the preservation of the equality of all citizens and religions.

[185] The City Council of Ville de Laval cannot advance religious precepts in public without running the risk of violating the full and equal recognition and exercise of the fundamental rights and freedoms guaranteed by sections 3 and 10 of the *Charter of human rights and freedoms*.

. . .

[187] In the case at bar, the recitation of the prayer forced Ms. Payette to participate in a religious practice and be subjected to a religious conception that did not respect her convictions as a nonbeliever. She was also singled out from the majority of people present when, contrary to practice and the by-law, she remained seated while the prayer was recited. The recitation of the prayer therefore engendered, in Ms. Payette's regard, a distinction and difference in treatment based on religion.

[188] Being forced to participate against her will and being singled out caused her prejudice in that she found herself stigmatized in terms of the dominant trend and the majority. Ms. Payette clearly indicated that she was uncomfortable with that situation.

. . .

[192] Ultimately, Ms. Payette had no choice but to tolerate that religious practice, leave the room or agree to enter the room once the prayer was said.

. . .

[194] Involved here is a distinction that impairs Ms. Payette's full and equal exercise of freedom of religion and conscience, contrary to sections 3 and 10 of the *Charter of human rights and freedoms*.

. . .

[212] The objective of preserving a religious tradition, such as the recitation of a prayer, cannot be achieved without regard for the *Charter of human rights and freedoms* and the state's obligation of neutrality stemming from it in religious matters. That neutrality is the result of a long historical evolution that, in Canada "made it possible for the ties between church and state to be loosened, if not dissolved".

Notes and Questions

1.   In the cases from South Africa and Japan excerpted above, the Courts attempt to justify religious references in government documents and the participation by government officials in a religious activity as ceremonial or social courtesy. Does either case provide a useful basis for determining when the invocation of religious messages or involvement by government officials with religion exceeds the limits of what is ceremonial or a matter of social courtesy and violates constitutional guarantees? How would these cases be resolved under United States constitutional law?

2.   *Laval* involves a nonsectarian prayer offered at the beginning of a city council meeting. The United States Supreme Court ruled in *Marsh v. Chambers*, 463 U.S. 783 (1983), that it did not violate the Establishment Clause for the state legislature to open its session with a nonsectarian prayer. Are the concerns expressed in *Laval* about coercion and inequality more likely to be an issue when a prayer is offered before a city council meeting as opposed to a state legislative session? Lower courts in the United States have attempted to apply *Marsh* to city council meetings and school board meetings with inconsistent results.

II.   INTERNATIONAL AND SUPRANATIONAL LAW

A.   PROSELYTISM BY GOVERNMENT OFFICIALS

LARISSIS v. GREECE
1998–I Eur. Ct. H.R. 362
European Court of Human Rights

[Three members of the Greek Air Force, followers of the Pentecostal Christian faith, were arrested and convicted for proselytizing their subordinates in the Air Force and civilians. With regard to the former charges, they were prosecuted for discussing religion with their subordinates, reading passages to them from the Bible, interpreting the Bible in a manner that pointed out discrepancies with the Greek Orthodox religion, and asking the subordinates to visit the Pentecostal Church while they were on leave.]

The proselytising of the airmen

47.   The Government contended that the applicants had abused the influence they enjoyed as air force officers and had committed the acts in question in a systematic and repetitive manner. The measures taken against them were justified by the need to protect the prestige and effective operation of the armed forces and to protect individual soldiers from ideological coercion.

48. The applicants submitted that the practice of evangelism within a superior/subordinate relationship could not without more be equated to an abuse of trust. They emphasised that the airmen were adults, able to die for their country, and that there was no evidence that the applicants had used their positions to coerce or override the wills of their subordinates. To interpret Article 9 so as to restrict evangelism to "equals" would be a severe limitation of religious freedom, both within the armed forces and in other contexts.

. . .

50. The Court observes that it is well established that the Convention applies in principle to members of the armed forces as well as to civilians. Nevertheless, when interpreting and applying its rules in cases such as the present, it is necessary to bear in mind the particular characteristics of military life and its effects on the situation of individual members of the armed forces.

51. In this respect, the Court notes that the hierarchical structures which are a feature of life in the armed forces may colour every aspect of the relations between military personnel, making it difficult for a subordinate to rebuff the approaches of an individual of superior rank or to withdraw from a conversation initiated by him. Thus, what would in the civilian world be seen as an innocuous exchange of ideas which the recipient is free to accept or reject, may, within the confines of military life, be viewed as a form of harassment or the application of undue pressure in abuse of power. It must be emphasised that not every discussion about religion or other sensitive matters between individuals of unequal rank will fall within this category. Nonetheless, where the circumstances so require, States may be justified in taking special measures to protect the rights and freedoms of subordinate members of the armed forces.

B.   STATE REGULATION OF PERSONAL RELIGIOUS DISPLAYS BY GOVERNMENT EMPLOYEES

DAHLAB v. SWITZERLAND

2001–V Eur. Ct. H.R. 447
European Court of Human Rights

[A Moslem woman challenged a regulation barring her from wearing a headscarf while working as a teacher in a public school. The Federal Court in Switzerland rejected her claim and held:]

. . .

"[T]here is no doubt that the appellant wears the headscarf and loose-fitting clothes not for aesthetic reasons but in order to obey a religious precept which she derives from . . . passages of the Koran.

. . .

The wearing of a headscarf and loose–fitting clothes consequently indicates allegiance to a particular faith and a desire to behave in accordance with the precepts laid down by that faith. Such garments may even be said to constitute a 'powerful' religious symbol–that is to say, a sign that is immediately visible to others and provides a clear indication that the person concerned belongs to a particular religion.

What is in issue, therefore, is the wearing of a powerful religious symbol by a teacher at a State school in the performance of her professional duties. No restrictions have been imposed on the appellant as regards her clothing when she is not teaching. . . .

In displaying a powerful religious attribute on the school premises–indeed, in the classroom–the appellant may have interfered with the religious beliefs of her pupils, other pupils at the school and the pupils' parents. Admittedly, there have been no complaints from parents or pupils to date. But that does not mean that none of them has been affected. Some may well have decided not to take any direct action so as not to aggravate the situation, in the hope that the education authorities will react of their own motion. . . .

. . .

[The conduct of teachers] may have a considerable influence on their pupils; they set an example to which pupils are particularly receptive on account of their tender age, their daily contact with them–which, in principle, is inescapable–and the hierarchical nature of this relationship. Teachers are both participants in the exercise of educational authority and representatives of the State, which assumes responsibility for their conduct. It is therefore especially important that they should discharge their duties–that is to say, imparting knowledge and developing skills–while remaining denominationally neutral.

. . .

[T]he appellant teaches in a primary school; her pupils are therefore young children who are particularly impressionable. Admittedly, she is not accused of proselytizing or even of talking to her pupils about her beliefs. However, the appellant can scarcely avoid the questions which her pupils have not missed the opportunity to ask. It would seem somewhat awkward for her to reply by citing aesthetic considerations or sensitivity to the cold–the approach she claims to have adopted to date, according to the file–because the children will realize that she is evading the issue. It is therefore difficult for her to reply without stating her beliefs.... [T]he appellant participates in the exercise of educational authority and personifies school in the eyes of her pupils.... Lastly, it should be emphasized that the Canton of Geneva [where this dispute arose] has opted for a clear separation between Church and State, reflected in particular by the distinctly secular nature of the State education system.

　. . .

Furthermore, religious harmony ultimately remains fragile in spite of everything, and the appellant's attitude is likely to provoke reactions, or even conflict, which are to be avoided. When the various interests at stake are weighed up, regard must also be had to the fact that allowing headscarves to be worn would result in the acceptance of garments that are powerful symbols of other faiths, such as soutanes [black cassock traditionally worn by a priest] or kippas [skullcap worn by religious Jews].... Such a consequence might undermine the principle of denominational neutrality in schools. Lastly, it may be observed that it is scarcely conceivable to prohibit crucifixes from being displayed in State schools and yet to allow the teachers themselves to wear powerful religious symbols of whatever denomination."

　. . .

[The ECHR explained that w]hile religious freedom is primarily a matter of individual conscience, it also implies freedom to manifest one's religion. Bearing witness in words and deeds is bound up with the existence of religious convictions.

　. . .

Applying these principles in the instant case, the Court notes that the Federal Court held that the measure by which the applicant was prohibited, purely in the context of her activities as a teacher, from wearing a headscarf was justified by the potential interference with the religious beliefs of her pupils, other pupils at the school and the pupils' parents, and by the breach of the principle of denominational neutrality in schools. In that connection, the Federal Court took into account the very nature of the profession of State school teachers, who were both participants in the exercise of educational authority and representatives of the State, and in doing so weighed the protection of the legitimate aim of ensuring the neutrality of the State education system against the freedom to manifest one's religion. It further noted that the impugned measure had left the applicant with a difficult choice, but considered that State schoolteachers had to tolerate proportionate restrictions on their freedom of religion. In the Federal Court's view, the interference with the applicant's freedom to manifest her religion was justified by the need, in a democratic society, to protect the right of State school pupils to be taught in a context of denominational neutrality. It follows that religious beliefs were fully taken into account in relation to the requirements of protecting the rights and freedoms of others and preserving public order and safety. It is also clear that the decision in issue was based on those requirements and not on any objections to the applicant's religious beliefs.

. . .

The Court accepts that it is very difficult to assess the impact that a powerful external symbol such as the wearing of a headscarf may have on the freedom of conscience and religion of very young children. The applicant's pupils were aged between four and eight, an age at which children wonder about many things and are also more easily influenced than older pupils. In those circumstances, it cannot be denied outright that the wearing of a headscarf might have some kind of proselytizing effect, seeing that it appears to be imposed on women by a precept which is laid down in the Koran and which, as the Federal Court noted, is hard to square with the principle of gender equality. It therefore appears difficult to reconcile the wearing of an Islamic headscarf with the message of tolerance, respect for others and, above all, equality and non-discrimination that all teachers in a democratic society must convey to their pupils.

Accordingly, weighing the right of a teacher to manifest her religion against the need to protect pupils by preserving religious harmony, the Court considers that, in the circumstances of the case and having regard, above all, to the tender age of the children for whom the applicant was responsible as a representative of the State, the Geneva authorities did not exceed their margin of appreciation and that the measure they took was therefore not unreasonable.

Notes and Questions

1.   Alleged proselytizing and religious coercion in the military has recently caused considerable controversy in the United States. *See e.g., Weinstein v. United States Air Force*, 468 F.Supp.2d 1366 (2006); William J. Dobosh, Jr., *Coercion in the Ranks: The Establishment Clause Implications of Chaplain–Led Prayers at Mandatory Army Events,* 2006 WISC. L. REV. 1493.

2.   Note that in *Dahlab*, the Court upholds the State's decision to prohibit teachers from wearing religious garb. Is there an argument that at some point, allowing a public school teacher to wear religious garb or insignia would raise an Establishment Clause issue under United States constitutional law?

3. Lower courts in the United States have upheld neutral-uniform regulations that prohibit government employees from wearing buttons or pins that communicate any kind of message, *see, e.g., I.N.S. v. Federal Labor Relations Authority*, 855 F.2d 1454 (9th Cir. 1988); *Daniels v. City of Arlington, Tex.*, 246 F.3d 500 (5th Cir. 2001). In some cases, restrictions limiting the religious garb that public school teachers may wear have also been upheld, *see, e.g., Webb v. City of Philadelphia*, 2007 WL 1866763 (E.D. Pa.) Cases involving specific restrictions on public employees having Bibles or religious posters in their offices or engaging in prayer at the workplace have proven more difficult to resolve since they require courts to reconcile free speech, free exercise, and establishment clause concerns, *see, e.g., Berry v. Department of Social Services*, 447 F.3d 642 (9th Cir. 2006); *Brown v. Polk County, Iowa*, 61 F.3d 650 (8th Cir.1995).

PART III

RECONCILING RIGHTS OF FREEDOM OF SPEECH AND RELIGION

Chapter Fourteen

THE COMPLEX INTERPLAY OF RELIGION AND SPEECH

I. INTRODUCTION AND OVERVIEW: INTERNATIONAL AND SUPRA-NATIONAL LAW

Javier Martínez-Torrón

Freedom of Expression versus Freedom of Religion in the European Court of Human Rights

in Issues in Constitutional Law 4. Censorial Sensitivities: Free Speech and Religion in a Fundamentalist World 233, 260–62, 267, 269 (András Sajó ed., Eleven Publishing 2007)

When attempting to find the logic inherent in the principles that orientate the ECtHR's decisions on conflicts between freedom of expression and freedom of religion, we should begin by trying to identify the *raison d'être* of these two fundamental freedoms within the context of the European Convention on Human Rights, as interpreted by the Court.

The essential purpose of freedom of thought, conscience, and religion seems to be the protection of individual autonomy to provide a personal answer (freedom to believe) to the crucial questions that all human beings face—who are we, where do we come from, where do we go—and to organize one's life accordingly (freedom to act). All answers are considered equally valid from the ECHR's perspective, be they religious or non-religious (agnostic or atheistic). All of them are, in some sense, beliefs—although the term 'believer' is usually applied only to people holding religious beliefs. The implicit assumption is that those crucial questions do not have absolute and indisputable answers—this is why they are 'beliefs'—and therefore every person has the inalienable right to search for his own valid responses. For the same reason, religious or non-religious beliefs are not subject to objective proof, and consequently their validity cannot be assessed in objective terms. The content of beliefs is, as such, irrelevant. All religions or beliefs are accepted as equally valid and worthy of protection, not because they provide 'reasonable' or 'true' answers to vital questions, but because they are the result of a person's legitimate choice, which nobody can substitute. Neutral laws, such as the ECHR, avoid pronouncing any judgment on the value of diverse beliefs or discriminating between them by reason of their mere dogmatic content. The European Court has clearly stated that the protection of this freedom is essential for pluralism, which is in turn inseparable from democracy.... The guarantee of freedom of religion or belief entails the elimination of coercion and discrimination on the ground of religion–including, in my view, indirect discrimination by neutral laws–as well as the prohibition of indoctrination by the state.

Naturally, the exercise of freedom of religion or belief often entails the exercise of other fundamental freedoms protected by the European Convention, especially freedom of association and freedom of expression. This overlapping, however, must not lead us to confuse the types of ideas protected by these freedoms, as the European Court has emphasized. In particular, the term 'beliefs,' be they religious or not, denotes, in the meaning of Article 9 ECHR, 'views that attain a certain level of cogency, seriousness, cohesion and importance,' and 'is not synonymous with the words "opinions" and "ideas", such as are utilized in Article 10 of the Convention, which guarantees freedom of expression.'

If we turn now to freedom of expression, as understood in the ECtHR's case law, its essential purpose seems to be, again, the guarantee of pluralism as an indispensable element of democracy, in particular through the protection of every person's right to freely disseminate information or ideas. The implicit notion is that individuals have not only the right to form their own opinion on any subject, but also the right to contribute to public debates in their respective societies. For this reason, the ECtHR remarks that limitations on freedom of expression must be construed narrowly, even with regard to ideas that 'offend, shock or disturb.' This is especially true when dealing with expressions related to matters of general interest–the higher the significance of the issue under discussion, the wider the protection of freedom of speech and the stricter the interpretation of legitimate limitations on it.

In other words, the protection of freedom of expression is inseparable from a reference to the content of the information or the ideas expressed. What deserves to be protected is not just 'expression' understood as a purely formal concept, but rather the expression of a substantive content: information (facts) or opinions (ideas, judgments). This concept is compatible with the understanding that freedom of expression also comprehends the form in which ideas or facts are articulated. Thus, freedom of speech plays a significant role in the formation of a pluralistic social and intellectual debate on a variety of issues, as well as in the search for historical truth. Even more: free discussion is a necessary condition for progress in society. With regard to the substantive data or opinions conveyed, it must be noted that freedom of expression covers a much broader range of subjects than freedom of religion or belief. In addition, contrary to what occurs in the case of religion or belief, the accuracy of some data or opinions can be scrutinized according to objective criteria, as is implicit in the ECtHR's doctrine on the distinction between statements of fact and value judgment.

. . .

Most of the principles utilized by the European Court to decide cases regarding freedom of expression do not raise particular problems–although their application to the facts has sometimes caused perplexity. There are, however, two interconnected principles that have been more controversial. One is the idea that the protection of religious feelings of the population is an integral part of the right to religious freedom and, therefore, may justify limitations on freedom of expression according to Article 10(2) ECHR (limitations can be justified by the 'protection of the reputation or rights of others'). The other is the notion that the state, in use of its legitimate margin of appreciation, may restrict or penalize 'gratuitous offences' to religious feelings.

. . .

Democracy and pluralism could be more endangered by a possible abuse of the power to restrict free speech than the potential harm that abusive forms of expression cause to religious beliefs.

II. THE FUNDAMENTAL FREEDOMS OF RELIGION AND SPEECH AND THEIR INTERPLAY

A. OFFENSIVE SPEECH

OTTO-PREMINGER–INSTITUT v. AUSTRIA
295 Eur. Ct. H.R. (Ser. A) (1995)
European Court of Human Rights

[At issue is the Austrian government's seizure and confiscation of a film titled, "DAS LIEBESKONZIL," in order to protect the religious sensibilities of those people who would be offended by the movie's content and to prevent disorder.]

22.   The film ... portrays the God of the Jewish religion, the Christian religion and the Islamic religion as an apparently senile old man prostrating himself before the Devil with whom he exchanges a deep kiss and calling the Devil his friend. He is also portrayed as swearing by the Devil. Other scenes show the Virgin Mary permitting an obscene story to be read to her and the manifestation of a degree of erotic tension between the Virgin Mary and the Devil. The adult Jesus Christ is portrayed as a low grade mental defective and in one scene is shown lasciviously attempting to fondle and kiss his mother's breasts, which she is shown as permitting. God, the Virgin Mary and Christ are shown in the film applauding the Devil.

. . .

Whether the interference had a "legitimate aim"

47.   ... Those who choose to exercise the freedom to manifest their religion, irrespective of whether they do so as members of a religious majority or a minority, cannot reasonably expect to be exempt from all criticism. They must tolerate and accept the denial by others of their religious beliefs and even the propagation by others of doctrines hostile to their faith. However, the manner in which religious beliefs and doctrines are opposed or denied is a matter which may engage the responsibility of the State, notably its responsibility to ensure the peaceful enjoyment of the right guaranteed under Article 9 (art. 9) to the holders of those beliefs and doctrines. Indeed, in extreme cases the effect of particular methods of opposing or denying religious beliefs can be such as to inhibit those who hold such beliefs from exercising their freedom to hold and express them.

In ... *Kokkinakis* [*v. Greece*, 260 Eur. Ct. H.R. (1993)] ... the Court held, in the context of Article 9 ... that a State may legitimately consider it necessary to take measures aimed at repressing certain forms of conduct, including the imparting of information and ideas, judged incompatible with the respect for the freedom of thought, conscience and religion of others. The respect for the religious feelings of believers as guaranteed in Article 9 ... can legitimately be thought to have been violated by provocative portrayals of objects of religious veneration; and such portrayals can be regarded as malicious violation of the spirit of tolerance, which must also be a feature of democratic society. The Convention is to be read as a whole and therefore the interpretation and application of Article 10 ... in the present case must be in harmony with the logic of the Convention.

48.   The measures complained of [here] were based on section 188 of the Austrian Penal Code, which is intended to suppress behavior directed against objects of religious veneration that is

likely to cause "justified indignation." It follows that their purpose was to protect the right of citizens not to be insulted in their religious feelings by the public expression of views of other persons. Considering also the terms in which the decisions of the Austrian courts were phrased, the Court accepts that the impugned measures pursued a legitimate aim under Article 10 para. 2 namely "the protection of the rights of others."

Whether the seizure and the forfeiture were "necessary in a democratic society"

1. General principles

49. As the Court has consistently held, freedom of expression constitutes one of the essential foundations of a democratic society, one of the basic conditions for its progress and for the development of everyone. Subject to paragraph 2 of Article 10 ... it is applicable not only to "information" or "ideas" that are favorably received or regarded as inoffensive or as a matter of indifference, but also to those that shock, offend or disturb the State or any sector of the population. Such are the demands of that pluralism, tolerance and broadmindedness without which there is no "democratic society."

However, as is borne out by the wording itself of Article 10 para. 2 whoever exercises the rights and freedoms enshrined in the first paragraph of that Article undertakes "duties and responsibilities." Amongst them–in the context of religious opinions and beliefs–may legitimately be included an obligation to avoid as far as possible expressions that are gratuitously offensive to others and thus an infringement of their rights, and which therefore do not contribute to any form of public debate capable of furthering progress in human affairs.

This being so, as a matter of principle it may be considered necessary in certain democratic societies to sanction or even prevent improper attacks on objects of religious veneration, provided always that any "formality," "condition," "restriction" or "penalty" imposed be proportionate to the legitimate aim pursued.

50. As in the case of "morals" it is not possible to discern throughout Europe a uniform conception of the significance of religion in society; even within a single country such conceptions may vary. For that reason it is not possible to arrive at a comprehensive definition of what constitutes a permissible interference with the exercise of the right to freedom of expression where such expression is directed against the religious feelings of others. A certain margin of appreciation is therefore to be left to the national authorities in assessing the existence and extent of the necessity of such interference.

The authorities' margin of appreciation, however, is not unlimited. It goes hand in hand with Convention supervision, the scope of which will vary according to the circumstances. In cases such as the present one, where there has been an interference with the exercise of the freedoms guaranteed in paragraph 1 of Article 10, the supervision must be strict because of the importance of the freedoms in question. The necessity for any restriction must be convincingly established.

. . .

52.   The Government defended the seizure of the film in view of its character as an attack on the Christian religion, especially Roman Catholicism. They maintained that the film . . . ended with a violent and abusive denunciation of what was presented as Catholic morality.

Furthermore, they stressed the role of religion in the everyday life of the people of Tyrol. The proportion of Roman Catholic believers among the Austrian population as a whole was already considerable—78%—but among Tyroleans it was as high as 87%.

Consequently, at the material time at least, there was a pressing social need for the preservation of religious peace; it had been necessary to protect public order against the film and the Innsbruck courts had not overstepped their margin of appreciation in this regard.

. . .

55.   The issue before the Court involves weighing up the conflicting interests of the exercise of two fundamental freedoms guaranteed under the Convention, namely the right of the applicant association to impart to the public controversial views and, by implication, the right of interested persons to take cognizance of such views, on the one hand, and the right of other persons to proper respect for their freedom of thought, conscience and religion, on the other hand. In so doing, regard must be had to the margin of appreciation left to the national authorities, whose duty it is . . . to consider . . . the interests of society as a whole.

56.   The Austrian courts, ordering the seizure and subsequently the forfeiture of the film, held it to be an abusive attack on the Roman Catholic religion according to the conception of the Tyrolean public. Their judgments show that they had due regard to the freedom of artistic expression, which is guaranteed under Article 10 of the Convention and for which Article 17a of the Austrian Basic Law provides specific protection. They did not consider that its merit as a work of art or as a contribution to public debate in Austrian society outweighed those features which made it essentially offensive to the general public within their

jurisdiction. The trial courts, after viewing the film, noted the provocative portrayal of God the Father, the Virgin Mary and Jesus Christ. The content of the film [can support] the conclusions arrived at by the Austrian courts.

The Court cannot disregard the fact that the Roman Catholic religion is the religion of the overwhelming majority of Tyroleans. In seizing the film, the Austrian authorities acted to ensure religious peace in that region and to prevent that some people should feel the object of attacks on their religious beliefs in an unwarranted and offensive manner. It is in the first place for the national authorities, who are better placed than the international judge, to assess the need for such a measure in the light of the situation obtaining locally at a given time. In all the circumstances of the present case, the Court does not consider that the Austrian authorities can be regarded as having overstepped their margin of appreciation in this respect.

No violation of Article 10 can therefore be found as far as the seizure is concerned.

B. BLASPHEMY

WINGROVE v. THE UNITED KINGDOM

1996–V Eur. Ct. H.R. 1937
European Court of Human Rights

[At issue is the British government's refusal to allow the distribution of a film, "Visions of Ecstasy," on the grounds that it was blasphemous. The film depicted "a female character astride the recumbent body of the crucified Christ engaged in an act of an overtly sexual nature."]

27. [The modern law of blasphemy in England is described as follows in the case of *Whitehouse v. Gay News Ltd. and Lemon* [1979]:]

Every publication is said to be blasphemous which contains any contemptuous, reviling, scurrilous or ludicrous matter relating to God, Jesus Christ or the Bible, or the formularies of the Church of England as by law established. It is not blasphemous to speak or publish opinions hostile to the Christian religion, or to deny the existence of God, if the publication is couched in decent and temperate language. The test to be applied is as to the manner in which the doctrines are advocated and not to the substance of the doctrines themselves.

The House of Lords in that case also decided that the mental element in the offence (mens rea) did not depend upon the accused having an intent to blaspheme. It was sufficient for the prosecution to prove that the publication had been intentional and that the matter published was blasphemous.

The *Gay News* case, which had been brought by a private prosecutor, had been the first prosecution for blasphemy since 1922.

. . .

48.   The Court notes at the outset that [the purpose of the law is] to protect against the treatment of a religious subject in such a manner "as to be calculated (that is, bound, not intended) to outrage those who have an understanding of, sympathy towards and support for the Christian story and ethic, because of the contemptuous, reviling, insulting, scurrilous or ludicrous tone, style and spirit in which the subject is presented."

This is an aim which undoubtedly corresponds to that of the protection of "the rights of others" within the meaning of paragraph 2 of Article 10. It is also fully consonant with the aim of the protections afforded by Article 9 to religious freedom.

. . .

50.   It is true that the English law of blasphemy only extends to the Christian faith. . . . However, it is not for the European Court to rule *in abstracto* as to the compatibility of domestic law with the Convention. The extent to which English law protects other beliefs is not in issue before the Court which must confine its attention to the case before it.

The uncontested fact that the law of blasphemy does not treat on an equal footing the different religions practiced in the United Kingdom does not detract from the legitimacy of the aim pursued in the present context.

51.   The refusal to grant a certificate for the distribution of Visions of Ecstasy consequently had a legitimate aim under Article 10 para. 2. . . .

Whether the interference was "necessary in a democratic society"

. . .

54.   According to the applicant, there was no "pressing social need" to ban a video work on the uncertain assumption that it would breach the law of blasphemy; indeed, the overriding social need was to allow it to be distributed. Furthermore, since adequate protection was already provided by a panoply of laws–concerning, inter alia, obscenity, public order and disturbances to places of religious worship–blasphemy laws, which are incompatible with the European idea of freedom of expression, were also superfluous in practice. In any event, the complete prohibition of a video work

that contained no obscenity, no pornography and no element of vilification of Christ was disproportionate to the aim pursued.

56.   The Government contended that the applicant's video work was clearly a provocative and indecent portrayal of an object of religious veneration, that its distribution would have been sufficiently public and widespread to cause offence and that it amounted to an attack on the religious beliefs of Christians which was insulting and offensive. In those circumstances, in refusing to grant a classification certificate for the applicant's video work, the national authorities only acted within their margin of appreciation.

57.   The Court observes that the refusal to grant Visions of Ecstasy a distribution certificate was intended to protect "the rights of others," and more specifically to provide protection against seriously offensive attacks on matters regarded as sacred by Christians. The laws to which the applicant made reference and which pursue related but distinct aims are thus not relevant in this context.

. . . [B]lasphemy legislation is still in force in various European countries. It is true that the application of these laws has become increasingly rare and that several States have recently repealed them altogether. In the United Kingdom only two prosecutions concerning blasphemy have been brought in the last seventy years. Strong arguments have been advanced in favor of the abolition of blasphemy laws, for example, that such laws may discriminate against different faiths or denominations . . . or that legal mechanisms are inadequate to deal with matters of faith or individual belief. . . . However, the fact remains that there is as yet not sufficient common ground in the legal and social orders of the member States of the Council of Europe to conclude that a system whereby a State can impose restrictions on the propagation of material on the basis that it is blasphemous is, in itself, unnecessary in a democratic society and thus incompatible with the Convention.

58.   Whereas there is little scope under Article 10 para. 2 of the Convention for restrictions on political speech or on debate of questions of public interest, a wider margin of appreciation is generally available to the Contracting States when regulating freedom of expression in relation to matters liable to offend intimate personal convictions within the sphere of morals or, especially, religion. . . . What is likely to cause substantial offence to persons of a particular religious persuasion will vary significantly from time to time and from place to place, especially in an era characterized by an ever growing array of faiths and denominations. By reason of their direct and continuous contact with the vital forces of their countries, State authorities are in principle in a better position

than the international judge to give an opinion on the exact content of these requirements with regard to the rights of others as well as on the "necessity" of a "restriction" intended to protect from such material those whose deepest feelings and convictions would be seriously offended.

This does not of course exclude final European supervision. Such supervision is all the more necessary given the breadth and open-endedness of the notion of blasphemy and the risks of arbitrary or excessive interferences with freedom of expression under the guise of action taken against allegedly blasphemous material. In this regard the scope of the offence of blasphemy and the safeguards inherent in the legislation are especially important. Moreover the fact that the present case involves prior restraint calls for special scrutiny by the Court.

. . .

60. As regards the content of the law itself, the Court observes that the English law of blasphemy does not prohibit the expression, in any form, of views hostile to the Christian religion. Nor can it be said that opinions which are offensive to Christians necessarily fall within its ambit. As the English courts have indicated it is the manner in which views are advocated rather than the views themselves which the law seeks to control. The extent of insult to religious feelings must be significant, as is clear from the use by the courts of the adjectives "contemptuous," "reviling," "scurrilous," "ludicrous" to depict material of a sufficient degree of offensiveness.

The high degree of profanation that must be attained constitutes, in itself, a safeguard against arbitrariness. It is against this background that the asserted justification under Article 10 para. 2 in the decisions of the national authorities must be considered.

61. [The national authorities concluded that the film was intended to arouse erotic feelings in its audience.] They further held that since no attempt was made in the film to explore the meaning of [its] imagery beyond engaging the viewer in a "voyeuristic erotic experience," the public distribution of such a video could outrage and insult the feelings of believing Christians and constitute the criminal offence of blasphemy. . . .

Bearing in mind the safeguard of the high threshold of profanation embodied in the definition of the offence of blasphemy under English law as well as the State's margin of appreciation in this area, the reasons given to justify the measures taken can be considered as both relevant and sufficient for the purposes of Article 10 para. 2. Furthermore, having viewed the film for itself, the Court is satisfied that the decisions by the national authorities cannot be said to be arbitrary or excessive.

62. It was submitted . . . that a short experimental video work would reach a smaller audience than a major feature film, such as the one at issue in the *Otto-Preminger–Institut* case. The risk that any Christian would unwittingly view the video was therefore substantially reduced and so was the need to impose restrictions on its distribution. Furthermore, this risk could have been reduced further by restricting the distribution of the film to licensed sex shops. Since the film would have been dispensed in video boxes which would have included a description of its content, only consenting adults would ever have been confronted with it.

63. The Court notes, however, that it is in the nature of video works that once they become available on the market they can, in practice, be copied, lent, rented, sold and viewed in different homes, thereby easily escaping any form of control by the authorities.

In these circumstances, it was not unreasonable for the national authorities . . . to consider that the film could have reached a public to whom it would have caused offence. The use of a box including a warning as to the film's content would have had only limited efficiency given the varied forms of transmission of video works mentioned above. In any event, here too the national authorities are in a better position than the European Court to make an assessment as to the likely impact of such a video, taking into account the difficulties in protecting the public.

C. PROSELYTIZING

[For the relevant provisions of the International Covenant on Civil and Political Rights (ICCPR) and the European Convention of Human Right (ECHR), see pp. 130–31]

Monroe E. Price
Religious Communication and Its Relation to the State: Comparative Perspectives

in ISSUES IN CONSTITUTIONAL LAW 4. CENSORIAL SENSITIVITIES: FREE SPEECH AND RELIGION IN A FUNDAMENTALIST WORLD 85, 96–98 (András Sajó ed., Eleven Publishing 2007)

There are states that regulate conversion practices formally or informally to maintain existing shares, including near monopoly status, in the religious cartel. Informal agreements exist between or among religious entities that tolerate some degree of conversion advocacy but also suggest limits on the practice. Greece, Russia, and the states of Central Asia all provide case studies of regulation of efforts to convert. . . .

. . .

The language of the human rights documents is deceptively simple.

Section 2 [of Article 18 of the ICCPR] seems to limit the right of proselytizers to use "coercion" as a means of inducing conversion or exercise of "choice." This has led to a discourse, including in the decisions of the European Court of Human Rights, of what should be considered coercion. The ICCPR had been amended on this issue differentiating it from the 1948 Universal Declaration of Human Rights. The "religious freedom" in the 1948 version explicitly included the freedom to "change" one's religion, and in the later version ... the word "change" disappeared. Freedom became the "freedom to have or to adopt" a religion or belief. Perhaps this was a subtle effort–under pressure from newly decolonized states to make it clear that *maintaining* religious beliefs was a value equivalent to altering them.

. . .

Note that Article 9 has the "freedom to change" language that was altered in the ICCPR. Note also that both the ICCPR and the European Convention provide (in the usual form) for limitations on the means of "manifesting" one's religion and, likely, activities related to proselytizing are such a manifestation, often a central one. The issue then would be under what circumstances, when all other requirements are met (prescribed by law and necessary in a democratic society), limits on this kind of activity might be justified. Specific attitudes toward conversion appear in Arab states. Article 10 of the Cairo Declaration on Human Rights in Islam of 1990 states that "It is prohibited to exercise any form of compulsion on man or to exploit his poverty or ignorance in order to convert him to another religion or to atheism."

1. Restrictions on Proselytizing

MURPHY v. IRELAND

2003–IX Eur. Ct. H.R. 1
European Court of Human Rights

[This case evaluates a regulation prohibiting religious advertizing in Ireland. It was challenged as violating Article 10, the free speech provision, of the ECHR.]

67.   ... [A] wider margin of appreciation is generally available to the Contracting States when regulating freedom of expression in relation to matters liable to offend intimate personal convictions within the sphere of morals or, especially, religion....

... [That explains why this case can be distinguished from other cases in which] ... the advertisement prohibited concerned a matter of public interest to which a reduced margin of appreciation applied.

68.   It is for the European Court to give a final ruling on the restriction's compatibility with the Convention and it will do so by assessing in the circumstances of a particular case, *inter alia*, whether the interference corresponded to a "pressing social need" and whether it was "proportionate to the legitimate aim pursued."

. . .

. . .

70.   The Court notes at the outset that the nature and purpose of the expression contained in the relevant advertisement accords with it being treated as religious, as opposed to commercial, expression even if the applicant purchased the relevant broadcasting time.

71.   The main factor which the Government considered justified the impugned prohibition was the particular religious sensitivities in Irish society which they submitted were such that the broadcasting of any religious advertising could be considered offensive. The applicant agreed that Article 10 permitted restrictions of religious expression which would offend others' religious sensitivities but submitted that the Convention did not protect an individual from being exposed to a religious view simply because it did not accord with his or her own, noting that his advertisement was innocuous and completely inoffensive. In any event, he disputed the Government's assessment of contemporary religious sensitivities in Ireland.

72.   The Court agrees that the concepts of pluralism, tolerance and broadmindedness on which any democratic society is based . . . mean that Article 10 does not, as such, envisage that an individual is to be protected from exposure to a religious view simply because it is not his or her own. However, the Court observes that it is not to be excluded that an expression, which is not on its face offensive, could have an offensive impact in certain circumstances. The question before the Court is therefore whether a prohibition of a certain type (advertising) of expression (religious) through a particular means (the broadcast media) can be justifiably prohibited in the particular circumstances of the case.

73.   Turning therefore to the country-specific religious sensitivities relied on by the Government, the Court has noted that . . . during the debate on the introduction of [the challenged regulation] . . . the Minister emphasized at some length the extreme sensitivity of the question of broadcasting of religious advertising in Ireland. . . .

Moreover, the domestic courts found that the Government were [sic] entitled to be prudent in this context. In particular, the High Court considered relevant the fact that religion had been a divisive issue in Northern Ireland. It further considered that Irish people with religious beliefs tended to belong to a particular church so that religious advertising from a different church might be considered offensive and open to the interpretation of proselytism.... The Supreme Court ... agreed that the Government had been entitled to take the view that Irish citizens would resent having advertisements touching on these topics broadcast into their homes and that such advertisements could lead to unrest.

74. The Court has also observed that the impugned provision was designed to correspond, and was indeed limited, to these particular concerns and that the bounds of the prohibition are an important consideration in the assessment of its proportionality.

The prohibition concerned only the audio-visual media. The State was, in the Court's view, entitled to be particularly wary of the potential for offence in the broadcasting context, such media being accepted by this Court ... as having a more immediate, invasive and powerful impact ... on the passive recipient. [The applicant was] free to advertise the same matter in any of the print media (including local and national newspapers) and during public meetings and other assemblies.

Moreover, the prohibition related only to advertising. This Court considers that this limitation reflects a reasonable distinction made by the State between, on the one hand, purchasing broadcasting time to advertise and, on the other, coverage of religious matters through programming (including documentaries, debates, films, discussions and live coverage of religious events and occasions). Programming is not broadcast because a party has purchased airtime and, as outlined by the Government, must be impartial, neutral and balanced, the objective value of which obligation the parties did not dispute.... Advertising, however, tends to have a distinctly partial objective: it cannot be, and is not, therefore subject to the above-outlined principle of impartiality and the fact that advertising time is purchased would lean in favor of unbalanced usage by religious groups with larger resources and advertising.

Consequently, other than advertisements in the broadcast media, the applicant's religious expression was not otherwise restricted.

75. Such considerations provide, in the Court's view, highly "relevant reasons" justifying the Irish State's prohibition of the broadcasting of religious advertisements.

76. The applicant, however, also maintained that these reasons were not "sufficient" and, in particular, that the State could have achieved its aims by a more limited prohibition.... However, the Court considers persuasive the Government's argument that a complete or partial relaxation of the impugned prohibition would

sit uneasily with the nature and level of the religious sensitivities outlined above and with the principle of neutrality in the broadcast media.

77.   In the first place, the Court would accept that a provision allowing one religion, and not another, to advertise would be difficult to justify and that a provision which allowed the filtering by the State or any organ designated by it, on a case by case basis, of unacceptable or excessive religious advertising would be difficult to apply fairly, objectively and coherently. . . . There is, in this context, some force in the Government's argument that the exclusion of all religious groupings from broadcasting advertisements generates less discomfort than any filtering of the amount and content of such expression by such groupings.

. . .

78.   Secondly, the Court considers it reasonable for the State to consider it likely that even a limited freedom to advertise would benefit a dominant religion more than those religions with significantly less adherents and resources. Such a result would jar with the objective of promoting neutrality in broadcasting and, in particular, of ensuring a "level playing field" for all religions in the medium considered to have the most powerful impact.

79.   Thirdly, the applicant did not dispute the Government's concern that allowing limited religious advertising would result in unequal consequences for the national and independent broadcasters.

. . .

81.   Finally . . . the Court observes that there appears to be no clear consensus between the Contracting States as to the manner in which to legislate for the broadcasting of religious advertisements. Certain States have similar prohibitions (for example, Greece, Switzerland and Portugal), certain [States] prohibit religious advertisements considered offensive (for example, Spain . . .) and certain [States] have no legislative restriction (the Netherlands). There appears to be no "uniform conception of the requirements of the protection of the rights of others" in the context of the legislative regulation of the broadcasting of religious advertising.

82.   In the circumstances, and given the margin of appreciation accorded to the State in such matters, the Court considers that the State has demonstrated that there were "relevant and sufficient" reasons justifying the interference with the applicant's freedom of expression within the meaning of Article 10 of the Convention.

In consequence, it concludes that there has been no violation of the Convention.

* * *

KOKKINAKIS v. GREECE

260 Eur. Ct. H.R. (1993)
European Court of Human Rights

48.   [A] distinction has to be made between bearing Christian witness and improper proselytism. The former corresponds to true evangelism, which a report drawn up in 1956 under the auspices of the World Council of Churches describes as an essential mission and a responsibility of every Christian and every Church. The latter represents a corruption or deformation of it. It may, according to the same report, take the form of activities offering material or social advantages with a view to gaining new members for a Church or exerting improper pressure on people in distress or in need; it may even entail the use of violence or brainwashing; more generally, it is not compatible with respect for the freedom of thought, conscience and religion of others.

2. *Protecting Proselytism*

KOKKINAKIS v. GREECE

260 Eur. Ct. H.R. (1993)
European Court of Human Rights

PROCEEDINGS BEFORE THE COMMISSION

56.   The Commission observes that the applicant was convicted for manifesting his religion, by propagating his religious beliefs in a particular way which was punishable under national law. The Commission considers that the measure in question constituted interference with the exercise of the applicant's right under Article 9(1) of the Convention to manifest his religion. Moreover, this point has not been contested by the Government.

57.   Consequently, the Commission must examine whether this interference was justified under Article 9(2). In this connection, the Commission must state its opinion as to whether the measure concerned was 'prescribed by law' and whether it was 'necessary in a democratic society' in pursuit of one of the legitimate aims listed in Article 9(2) of the Convention.

. . .

71.   The Commission observes that, according to the judgment of the Crete Court of Appeal, the conduct held against the applicant consisted in talking his way into the house of Mr. and Mrs. N,

beginning a discussion about [a particular politician] and pacifism, reading passages from a book containing professions of faith by Jehovah's Witnesses, analyzing certain passages in Holy Scripture and offering similar books to N with [the] intent to undermine her religious beliefs.

72.   The reasons put forward by the national courts to justify the applicant's conviction, and consequently for the infringement of his freedom to manifest his religion, cannot be deemed sufficient in themselves. It is hard to see how the words and opinions attributed to the applicant, whose inoffensive nature seems obvious, could have encroached on Mrs. N's freedom of conscience in religious matters.

73.   In particular, the Commission does not see on what evidence the national courts could have based their finding that the applicant had taken advantage of the 'inexperienced,' 'feebleness of mind' and 'ingenuousness' of Mrs. N, none of which, in any event, have been established.

74.   Even taking into account the margin of appreciation enjoyed by Contracting States with regard to the protection of the population's religious sensibilities, the Commission cannot accept that, having regard to the circumstances of this case, the applicant's conviction was justified by a pressing social need. One particular fact appeared decisive to the Commission, namely the lack of proportion between the conduct held against the applicant and the criminal penalty for that conduct, which seriously infringes the applicant's fundamental freedom to manifest his religion. In addition, that penalty is incompatible with the spirit of tolerance and broadmindedness which should obtain in contemporary democratic society.

III.   EVALUATING THE RELATIONSHIP BETWEEN RELIGION AND SPEECH

Peter G. Danchin
of Prophets and Proselytes: Freedom of Religion and the Conflict of Rights in International Law

49 Harv. Int. L. J. 249, 251–52, 265, 268–74, 288–89, 293–95 (2008)

International and regional human rights instruments recognize at least four rights directly related to religion and belief: the right to freedom of thought, conscience, and religion; the right to equal protection of the law, including the prohibition of discrimination on the basis of religion; the right of persons belonging to religious minorities to profess and practice their religion; and the right to protection from incitement to discrimination, hostility, or violence. In addition to these four rights, a number of other rights and freedoms bear a close relationship to religion and belief. These include most directly, as noted above, the rights to freedom of opinion and expression, freedom of assembly, and freedom of association.

. . .

[It can be argued that restrictions on proselytizing involve competing claims grounded on religious liberty.] On the one hand, a proselytizer may argue that the law coercively impairs her freedom to follow the central tenets of her most deeply held religious beliefs. On the other hand, a person subject to proselytism—assuming that she is an unwilling listener whose consent to the conversation is, in some respect, compromised . . . may argue that without the protection of such a law she is subject to a form of coercion and harm that interferes with the peaceful enjoyment of her freedom of religion (which may include religious or non-religious beliefs such as atheism or agnosticism). In other words, both the proselytizer and the target of proselytism can advance rights claims based on freedom of religion or beliefs that are in conflict with each other. The consequence is that [whatever the state's decision may be regarding the regulation of proselytizing, it] . . . will restrict the freedom of religion of either the proselytizer or the target of proselytism. While [a law restricting proselytizing] . . . will burden the free exercise of religion of proselytizing faiths, its absence may in certain circumstances burden the peaceful enjoyment of religious or fundamental beliefs of non-proselytizing faiths or groups—assuming, of course, that proselytizing groups are present and active in the state.

. . .

[Restrictions on proselytizing also implicate both religious freedom and free speech principles.]

A.   THE RIGHTS OF THE PROSELYTIZER

[T]he proselytizer's strongest claim is one of free exercise—the freedom to manifest her religion or belief under [international law.] She also has a claim, however, to freedom of expression under [international law]. Approached in this way, some different considerations and results may be reached, especially where claims to manifest religion are conjoined with claims to freedom of speech. . . .

. . .

. . . [W]hile human rights law regards the holding of religious beliefs to be a matter of inviolable individual freedom, the attempt to persuade others of those beliefs is subject to certain (as yet unspecified) restrictions. We should note, however, that it would be preposterous to invoke a similar notion in relation to political speech: for example, to say that while you can hold political views, any attempt to persuade others of such views is subject to certain limitations. The logic of free speech is that "debate on public issues should be uninhibited, robust and wide-open," and this idea makes little sense unless individuals can aggressively present their views to others–even to those for whom they are unwelcome or upsetting. This idea was powerfully expressed during the Danish cartoons affair, especially in the United States where, as Robert Post has noted, the First Amendment has been held to protect all religious polemic from legal sanction–even expression that aims "deliberately and provocatively to assault the religious sensibilities of the pious". [Robert Post, *Religion and Freedom of Speech: Portraits of Muhammad*, 14 CONSTELLATIONS 72, 73 (2007)]

The invocation by proselytizers of the right to freedom of expression creates tremendous pressure on the targets of proselytism to explain why religious speech should be treated differently from political speech....

. . .

B.   THE RIGHTS OF THE TARGET OF PROSELYTISM

. . .

1.   The Freedom to Change Religion or Belief

Similar to the question of whether the freedom to manifest religion or belief includes the freedom to proselytize, the question of whether freedom of religion encompasses the freedom to *change* religion has been a controversial question in international law. Even today there remain marked points of disagreement among states as a matter of practice. While the freedom to change one's religion or belief is entrenched in positive human rights standards, its acceptance by many states remains controversial. In many Muslim states, for example, it is considered a central tenet of Islam that there may be no coercion in matters of religion. Certain contemporary interpretations of Islam, however, do not accept the right of a person to abandon their religion or to convert to another, and it is a capital offence (apostasy) under Islamic law in some countries for a Muslim to repudiate his or her faith in Islam. Accordingly, many Islamic states do not formally accept the Human Rights Committee's interpretation of the right to "have or adopt" a religion [recognized in Article 18 the International Covenant on Civil and Political Rights] as meaning the right to replace one's current religion or to adopt atheistic views....

. . .

2. The Freedom to Have or Maintain a Religion

Exerting pressure in the opposite direction are the freedoms of the target of proselytism to "have or adopt" a religion and to be free from "injury to religious feelings." We must consider each claim in turn. In relation to the first—the freedom to "have" a religion—the question here is the extent to which this includes a right to the peaceful enjoyment of that freedom (i.e., either to maintain one's religion or to change one's religion without being subject to proselytism) such that the state must act to limit the freedom of others to proselytize. This was the question that confronted the European Court of Human Rights in the seminal case of *Kokkinakis v. Greece.*

. . .

. . . [I]f we proceed on the assumption that the target of proselytism is *unwilling* in some specified sense, then the Court is faced with a genuine conflict of rights. If, for example, the Court were to uphold the law on the basis that the state has a legitimate interest in protecting the rights of individuals to the peaceful enjoyment of their fundamental beliefs (whether religious or non-religious), this would require privileging the rights claims of the targets of proselytism over those of proselytizers. Conversely, if the Court were to find that the law infringed article 9 by unjustifiably restricting the freedom to manifest religion or belief, this would require privileging the rights claims of proselytizers over those of targets of proselytism.

3. Freedom from Injury to Religious Feelings

There is . . . a final bundle of claims by the target of proselytism that we must consider–the right to be free from injury to religious feelings.

There is no explicit provision in the international instruments stating that individuals or groups have a right to be "free from injury to religious feelings." However, article 20(2) of the ICCPR provides that "[a]ny advocacy of national, racial or religious hatred that constitutes incitement to discrimination, hostility or violence shall be prohibited by law." Furthermore, article 19(3) qualifies the right to freedom of expression by stating that the exercise of this right carries with it special duties and responsibilities . . . [and] may therefore be subject to certain restrictions . . . provided by law and . . . necessary:

a.   For respect of the rights or reputations of others;

b.   For the protection of national security or of public order (*ordre public*), or of public health or morals.

The specific words "injury to religious feelings" are also found in the jurisprudence of the European Court and former Commission. The Commission stated in *Wingrove v. United Kingdom* that while religious believers could not expect to be exempt from all criticism and must tolerate the denial by others of their beliefs, the state has a responsibility to ensure the peaceful enjoyment of believers' rights under article 9 and the English law of blasphemy was "intended to suppress behavior likely to cause justified indignation among believing Christians." As a consequence, it was "intended to protect the right of citizens not to be insulted in their religious feelings.

We are thus confronted here with a conflict between the freedom of the proselytizer (or, for present purposes, the blasphemer, whether religious or irreligious) either to manifest her religion or belief or to exercise her right to freedom of expression (or both), and the freedom of the target of proselytism to be free from injury to her religious feelings in those circumstances, as yet undefined, which are legitimately protected by the offense of blasphemy.

The answer [to this conflict], I believe, lies in Post's rejection of the second possible state interest in suppression–the protection of religious groups. Post criticizes the logic of the European Court's statement in *Otto Preminger Institute v. Austria* that "persons have a right not to be insulted in their religious beliefs because offense of this kind inhibits the right to practice a religion." Such a rationale excludes from public discourse those whose convictions are offensive to religious groups. The difficulty for Post is the notion of toleration that lies at the heart of the Court's attempt to balance the competing interests. In response to the Court's assertion that a "spirit of tolerance must be a feature of democratic society," Post replies that "democracy does not require toleration in the sense that persons abandon their *independent evaluation of the beliefs and ideas of others*"; otherwise, "[t]o the extent that democracy suppresses my expressions of disapproval or condemnation for the actions of groups that I dislike, it excludes me from the formation of public opinion.

While defensible in a particular constitutional or philosophical tradition, this proposition rests on an underlying bias that cannot simply be assumed as a matter of international law. Individual freedom of thought, conscience, and expression, justified on Enlightenment rationalist and secular modernist grounds, is the dominant value in Post's normative scheme. Freedom of religion, however, is compatible with this view primarily to the extent it is understood to encompass an inviolable private or inner realm of "belief"—the so-called *forum internum* [that is] separate from manifestations of that belief. On this view you may believe in any prophet or religion you wish, provided you do not manifest your beliefs in such a way as to restrict the rights of others to believe (or not to believe) or express (or not to express) themselves as they choose. The difficulty with this argument is that it relies on a prior contingent assumption equating religion with belief. This may be less problematic in a strongly immigrant and Christian society such as the United States (although even here the assumption is inherently problematic). But in contexts where religion and state have different historical configurations and where ... religious identities define the differences between majority and minority national groups, this simply will not work.

Once the right to freedom of religion is understood to include the communal, public, and sensitive aspects of religions such as Islam, Post's argument collapses and the need arises to engage with a genuine conflict of interests *internal* to the right itself. Why, for example, should Post's assumption not now be reversed, as many representatives of Islamic states have urged, and the right peacefully to manifest one's religion be regarded as the dominant value? On this view, freedom of thought and opinion remains absolutely protected, but *manifestations* of that opinion are now open to limitation to the extent they incite discrimination, hostility, or violence toward religion. The fraught task of calibrating the respective rights and interests now resumes, for example, in undertaking to draw the line between speech that is "gratuitously offensive" and speech that, though offensive, contributes to "any form of public debate capable of furthering progress in human affairs." But while the heremeneutic [sic] difficulties remain, the method and mode of reasoning has shifted. It is now respect for the intrinsic value of religious belief and practice that provides the unspoken background and tacit starting point for the ensuing rights discourse.

Notes and Questions

1. Blasphemy is an extremely serious offense in some countries. Pakistan's criminal law provides that "whoever by words, either spoken or written, or by visible representation, or by any imputation, innuendo, or insinuation, directly or indirectly, defiles the sacred name of the Holy Prophet Mohammed (peace be upon him) shall be punished with death, or imprisonment for life, and shall also be liable to fine." (Penal Code, Ch. XV–295–C (1986)).

2. The restrictions on speech upheld in *Otto-Preminger–Institut v. Austria*, *Wingrove v. UK*, and *Murphy v. Ireland* would all be struck down under the free speech clause of the First Amendment in U.S. courts. Do you understand why the European Court takes a different position in these cases? Read the excerpt from Peter Danchin's article carefully. Do you think he is right that these issues are two-sided and

hard to resolve or are you persuaded by Robert Post's criticisms of these kinds of restrictions on speech?

3.   Do you think that you can distinguish between speech that permissibly criticizes or repudiates particular religious beliefs and speech that crosses the line and causes unjustified offense to adherents of the disparaged faith? Consider the following statement expressed by a Protestant clergyman in Sydney, Australia who was commenting on Hindus, Moslems, and Jews who lived in his community. "[These] different religions cannot all be right. Some, or all of them are wrong, and if wrong, [they] are the monstrous lies and deceits of Satan–devised to destroy the life of the believers." Quoted in Alan E. Brownstein, *Justifying Free Exercise Rights*, 1 Univ. of St. Thomas L. J. 504, 524 (2003). Would it be permissible to suppress this speech under the ECHR standards?

Index

References are to Pages

279

†